# MARKS & SPENCER

*Anatomy of Britain's*
*Most Efficiently Managed Company*

by

## Dr K. K. TSE

The Shui On Group, Hong Kong

## PERGAMON PRESS

OXFORD · NEW YORK · TORONTO · SYDNEY · PARIS · FRANKFURT

| U.K. | Pergamon Press Ltd., Headington Hill Hall, Oxford OX3 0BW, England |
|---|---|
| U.S.A | Pergamon Press Inc., Maxwell House, Fairview Park, Elmsford, New York 10523, U.S.A. |
| CANADA | Pergamon Press Canada Ltd., Suite 104, 150 Consumers Road, Willowdale, Ontario M2J 1P9, Canada |
| AUSTRALIA | Pergamon Press (Aust.) Pty. Ltd., P.O. Box 544, Potts Point, N.S.W. 2011, Australia |
| FRANCE | Pergamon Press SARL, 24 rue des Ecoles, 75240 Paris, Cedex 05, France |
| FEDERAL REPUBLIC OF GERMANY | Pergamon Press GmbH, Hammerweg 6, D-6242 Kronberg-Taunus, Federal Republic of Germany |

Copyright © 1985 Dr K. K. Tse

First edition 1985

**Library of Congress Cataloging in Publication Data**
Tse, K. K.
Marks & Spencer: anatomy of Britain's most
efficiently managed company.
(Pergamon international library of science, technology,
engineering, and social studies)
Includes bibliographical references.
1. Marks & Spencer ltd.    I. Title.    II. Title:
Marks & Spencer.    III. Series.
HF5465.G74M377    1984        381'.45'000941    84-11147


**British Library Cataloguing in Publication Data**
Tse, K. K.
Marks & Spencer.
1. Marks & Spencer (*Firm*)
I. Title
381'.12'0941        HF5465.G74M3

ISBN 0-08-030211-4 (Hardcover)
ISBN 0-08-030212-2 (Flexicover)

*Printed in Great Britain by A. Wheaton & Co. Ltd., Exeter*

# Acknowledgements

I am grateful to Lord Sieff and Lord Rayner for their assistance in the course of my research on Marks & Spencer. I owe a special debt to my colleagues in the Shui On Group for their comments and suggestions. They help ensure that the book is as readable and relevant as possible to the practising manager. Finally, I must thank my wife, Ngai Lung, a critical admirer of Marks & Spencer, without whose support and encouragement this work would never have been completed.

# CONTENTS

# Introduction: What Does Marks & Spencer Stand For?

## The Gospel According to St Michael

To most people in Britain the household name of Marks & Spencer is almost synonymous with St Michael—the brand name which is available only at Marks & Spencer stores, which in turn sell nothing but St Michael merchandise. But in recent years a growing number of perceptive observers have begun to notice two brand images at Marks & Spencer. On the one hand there is the visible St Michael merchandise. On the other, there is the intangible but nevertheless conspicuous brand image found in the stores and in the head office—the Marks & Spencer brand of management.

The company, founded in 1884, has long been regarded as one of the most spectacular corporate successes in the U.K. It has also been widely recognized as one of the best-managed companies in Europe. Indeed, as far as management excellence of the firm is concerned, the consensus is almost total in the trade, as well as in government and specialist circles.

Back in 1966, the Editor of *Management Today*, Robert Heller, wrote:

> No business has ever won more respect from customers, suppliers and competitors alike than Marks & Spencer. . . . The St Michael label has become gilt-edged household currency in a way that no house brand, here or in America, has ever matched.[1]*

Roberta Cohen, writing in *Marketing Week*, claims that

> M&S has become the most potent force in the high street today. Its success is shown by the numbers of rivals attempting to imitate its marketing methods and in its St Michael brand name, which has become a byword for quality and innovation.[2]

J. H. Davidson, in his best-selling book *Offensive Marketing: Or How to Make Your Competitors Followers*, considers Marks & Spencer as the classic case of 'offensive marketing in action'. He maintains that

> Few firms exemplify the operation of the offensive marketing approach better than Marks & Spencer. Throughout its history it has innovated new forms of retailing and

---

*Superscript references are to Notes at ends of chapters.

1

## Marks & Spencer in a Nutshell

*Size*
- M&S is Britain's largest retailer. Over 14 million customers shop at M&S stores every week.
- It has 260 stores in the U.K., totalling 600,000 m$^2$ of selling space.
- It is the fourth largest U.K. company by market capitalization with some 250,000 shareholders.

*Brand*
- M&S stores sell only one brand—St Michael—widely recognized as a symbol of quality and value.
- St Michael merchandise includes: clothing, food and wine, footwear and accessories, home furnishings, household goods, toiletries, books and houseplants.
- Over 90% of St Michael merchandise is British-made.

*Market share*
- M&S has 15% of the national clothing market. It buys approximately one-fifth of the clothing production of the U.K.
- Of the total U.K. market M&S accounts for one-quarter of the sales of socks and trousers, one-third of the sales of underwear, pyjamas, bras and nightdresses, and one-half of the sales of ladies' slips.
- St Michael foods is a leading brand in the U.K. It represents 37% of the company's total U.K. sales. It is Britain's largest fishmonger. It also sells one million chickens every week.

*Suppliers*
- Over 800 companies supply St Michael merchandise to M&S's exclusive specification.
- Nearly 150 suppliers have been manufacturing St Michael goods for over 25 years. Fifty of these companies have been associated with M&S for over 40 years.
- M&S does not have any financial stake in the manufacturers.

*Employment*
- M&S employs over 46,000 staff in the U.K. 20,000 have worked for the company for more than 5 years; 10,000 for more than 10 years. Close to half of the total employees own M&S shares.
- Some 200,000 people are engaged in the production, distribution and sale of St Michael goods.

*Overseas*
- There are seven M&S stores in France, Belgium and the Irish Republic.
- The company also has a controlling interest in over 200 stores in Canada.
- St Michael goods are sold in 30 other countries, including such major customers as Japan and Hong Kong.
- M&S exports more than any other British retailer. It is also the U.K.'s largest exporter of clothing. In 1977 it won the Queen's Award for Exports.

*Record*
- The M&S store at Marble Arch, London, features annually in the *Guinness Book of Records* for taking more money per square foot than any other retailer in the world.

followed its own distinctive course. . . . M&S must surely be one of the best-run businesses in the world, and certainly among the most marketing oriented.[3]

In international circles British firms are by no means renowned for their management achievement. Marks & Spencer has been the notable exception. It is significant that most commentators not only consider Marks & Spencer as 'the best of British' but rank it among the best-run companies in the world. Indeed, its reputation reaches as far afield as Australia and Japan, Hong Kong and Singapore, Canada and the United States.

In an in-depth study of Marks & Spencer, the Australian trade journal *Clothes* began a 20-page survey of the company with the following words: 'In the mother country the queen reigns, parliament rules, and Marks & Spencer takes over in the retail industry.' It went on to say:

> The genius of Marks & Spencer is that for the major part of its 93-year history it has carefully cultivated its reputation that nowhere else could Britons find a better value for the money. . . . Nowhere else in this still class-ridden society could working and middle-class [mothers] not only rub shoulders with the British establishment, they could afford to buy the same reasonably priced, high quality merchandise.[4]

An American writer, Marshall Dimock, in his book *Administrative Vitality*,[5] singled out Marks & Spencer as a model of efficient management and compared it favourably with the largest American corporations. He devoted a whole chapter in the book to dissecting the company's unconventional approach to administrative efficiency. In 1975 a case study on Marks & Spencer was produced by Harvard Business School focusing on its unique approach to store development. Since then this has become a 'best-selling' case in American business schools. The international reputation of the company was further enhanced when it received the International Retailer of the Year Award from the National Retailer Merchants Association (NRMA) in the U.S.A. in 1983.

No less an authority than Peter Drucker has hailed Marks & Spencer as a managerial giant in the Western world. He was particularly impressed by its 'singularly high productivity of capital':

> the productivity of the Marks & Spencer retail store exceeds, to my knowledge, anything to be found any place else, including even Sears, Roebuck or Kresge, the acknowledged store management virtuosi of the American retail scene.[6]

According to Drucker, Marks & Spencer have pioneered and excelled themselves in a whole range of 'modern' management methods, notably strategic marketing, consumer research, product innovation and development, personnel management, staff training and management development, quality assurance and technological-oriented purchasing. Above all, the Marks & Spencer experience demonstrates forcefully the 'power and purpose of [corporate] objectives'. Drucker has written:

The Marks & Spencer story reaffirms the central importance of thinking through 'what our business *is* and what it *should* be'. But it also shows that this, by itself, is not enough. The basic definition of the business and of its purposes and mission have to be translated into objectives. Otherwise they remain insight, good intentions, and brilliant epigrams which never become achievement. . . . Marks & Spencer from the start converted objectives into work assignments. It thought through what results and contributions were needed in each objective area. It assigned responsibility for these results to someone and held him accountable. And it measured performance and contribution against the objectives.[7]

Although there is no dearth of insightful commentary on the Marks & Spencer operation, there is as yet no systematic and comprehensive study of the company's unique management philosophy and practice. The present volume attempts to fill this gap by offering an anatomy of some major areas of this much-acclaimed enterprise.

## Topping the League

Marks & Spencer is not a retailer in the conventional sense. It is sometimes referred to as a 'manufacturer without factories'. As will be demonstrated in subsequent chapters, there is a substantial element of truth in this description. For the moment, however, let us briefly review how Marks & Spencer compares with other retail chains in the U.K. scene.

The figures that follow place Marks & Spencer among the ten major retail chains in Britain. Figure 1 indicates that Marks & Spencer is by far the greatest profit-earner among the national retailers. Its profit occupies the 13th position in *The Times 1000*, although it ranks only 22nd in terms of turnover and 16th in terms of capital employed.

Figure 2 shows annual turnover and profit margin in 1981. Marks & Spencer is a leader in terms of turnover but, more importantly, its profit margin is significantly higher than its major competitors. Only British Homes Stores, which is trying very hard to imitate Marks & Spencer, compares closely with the latter; but in terms of turnover, British Homes Stores' sales are still only about a fifth of Marks & Spencer's.

Figure 3 provides a comparison in the amount of capital employed and the profitability levels of the ten retailers. Again, Marks & Spencer leads the way. Profitability for Marks & Spencer in the period is 32.4%, which is very high indeed by British and even international standards. Once again, it is only the much smaller competitors who come close to Marks & Spencer in terms of profitability.

In Figure 4, the *productivity* of the ten companies is highlighted. It shows the relative figures for sales per employee and profit per employee. On both counts Marks & Spencer is well above the others, especially so in profit per employee.

These figures are representative of the pattern in the past decade[8] and square

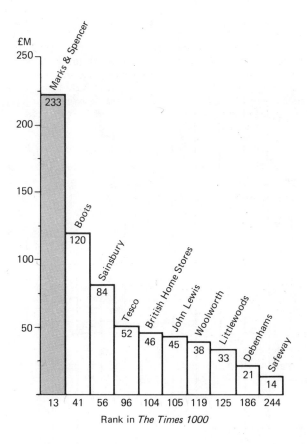

Figure 1    Net profit, 1981 (Source: *The Times 1000*, 1982 edition, published by Times Books)

nicely with Peter Drucker's observation on the company's high productivity of capital.

The impressive performance of the firm is readily recognized in the trade and not the least by the stock market, in which Marks & Spencer is one of the bluest of the blue chips.

## The Open Secrets of Success

If there are any secrets in Marks & Spencer's corporate achievement, they are by and large *open* secrets of success. The company is most ready to discuss with the outsider the formulae underlying its success. Indeed, by British as well as international standards the company is a very open corporation, and it is no

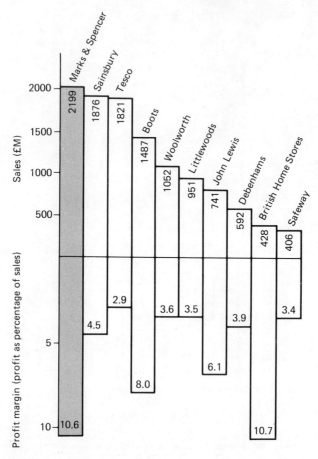

Figure 2   Sales and profit margin, 1981 (Source: *The Times 1000*, 1982 edition, published by Times Books)

coincidence that there are far more in-depth analyses on various aspects of its management in the national media than any other British companies.

In essence, the company's outstanding achievement has much to do with three obsessive concerns:

quality/value for money/human relations

### Quality

By refusing to compromise on the quality of its wide range of products the company has built a reputation for reliability which is a major factor in its continuing success. Consistently high quality is not easy to achieve. The

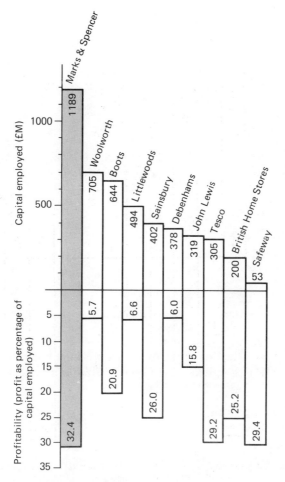

Figure 3   Capital employed and profitability, 1981 (Source: *The Times 1000*, 1982 edition, published by Times Books)

company's technical staff—350-strong in 1982—is responsible for laying down exacting specifications at each stage of the production process, starting with the selection of raw materials. It pioneered in the pre-war years what today would be called total quality control.

**Value for Money**

This is not to be confused with cheap prices. The stringent quality standards are extremely demanding on time and effort, both from the company and the suppliers, and have to be paid for. St Michael prices are not low but relative to

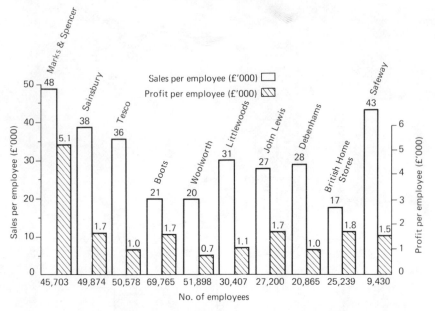

Figure 4    Sales and profit per employee, 1981 (Source: *The Times 1000*, 1982 edition, published by Times Books)

the quality offered they represent exceptionally good value for money. The company has also managed to keep prices controlled in a number of ways, such as:

(1) Offering suppliers large orders because of its policy of concentrating on products with a wide appeal. This reduces the production cost of each item considerably.
(2) The commitment, in conjunction with the suppliers, to the development of new raw materials and production and packaging methods, which often lead to a lowering of costs.
(3) The incessant quest for administrative efficiency which brings the running costs of the business to an impressively low level. The successive waves of 'anti-bureaucracy' campaigns begun in the fifties have kept the organization singularly lean and effective.

## Human Relations

The company is committed to fostering 'good human relations' with all those who come into contact with it: staff, suppliers, customers, and the community at large. It offers excellent salaries and a comprehensive benefits package to its staff, which are well above the norm in the industry. More significantly it has excelled itself in providing career-long training and development for its staff, to allow success and growth with the company, to enable all members of staff to contribute to the full extent of their ability. It has maintained a very special relationship with the suppliers who are regarded as partners in a 'joint effort for a common purpose'; indeed, this relationship is often quoted as an exemplary collaborative relationship in Parliament and the press. As far as the customers are concerned, Marks & Sparks, as it is affectionately known, enjoys perhaps far more goodwill in the eyes of the shopper than any other high street chain. The company is also a leading charity donor and an active supporter of community causes.

## The Basic Principles

Despite the idealistic overtones of some of the company's objectives, Marks & Spencer is a very practical and down-to-earth organization. It has persistently pursued certain key strategies over the past decades, but it did not start with any master blueprint or a comprehensive corporate plan. There was, and still is, a strong sense of direction in the minds of the management of the company, but it does not feel the need to draw up a statement of business mission as such. What it has laid down, however, is a set of fundamental principles which are to be the bases of all business activities. These principles are:

(1) to offer our customers *a selective range of high-quality, well-designed and attractive merchandise* at reasonable prices under the brand name St Michael;
(2) to encourage suppliers to use the *most modern and efficient production techniques*;
(3) to work with suppliers to ensure *highest standards of quality control*;
(4) to provide *friendly, helpful service and greater shopping comfort and convenience to our customers*;
(5) to improve the efficiency of the business, by *simplifying operating procedures*; and
(6) to foster *good human relations with customers, suppliers and staff and in the communities in which we trade.*

These are simple and straightforward ideas. The secret of Marks & Spencer's success resides primarily in the total embracement of these principles by all levels of staff and their single-mindedness in focusing everyone's effort on those activities guided by these principles.

The rest of this book is divided into four major parts, corresponding roughly to the company's relationship with the customers, suppliers, staff and the community at large. Part I deals with the marketing—in the broadest sense—aspect of the firm. Part II analyses the company's unique relationship with the suppliers and its exceptional quality control effort. Part III argues against the popular paternalistic label of the company and attempts to put its good human relations with its staff in perspective. This is followed by Part IV, in which the company's community involvement in various facets will be discussed, including a chapter on the work of Vice-chairman Lord Rayner in his capacity as Mrs Thatcher's adviser on streamlining the Civil Service.

## Notes

1. Robert Heller, 'The inimitable magic of Marks', *Management Today*, September 1966.
2. 'What 1982 holds in store for Marks & Spencer', *Marketing Week*, 4 December 1981.
3. *Offensive Marketing: Or How to Make Your Competitors Followers* (Harmondsworth: Penguin Books, 1979), p. 10.
4. *Clothes*, January 1978.
5. London: Routledge & Kegan Paul, 1960.
6. Peter Drucker, *Management: Tasks, Responsibilities, Practice* (London: Heinemann, 1974), p. 98.
7. *Ibid.*, p. 99.
8. For detailed comparisons, see the annual editions of *The Times 1000* and *Business Ratio Report—High Street Trading* (London: Inter-company Comparisons Ltd, 1980).

# PART I

# WHAT DOES THE CUSTOMER REALLY WANT ?

## THE MAKING OF A MARKETING PHILOSOPHY

# CHAPTER 1

# From Penny Bazaar to Superstore

Michael Marks, the founder of the firm which was to become Marks & Spencer, was born in 1863 at Bialystok, a Jewish village in what was then Russian Poland. Little was known of his childhood, except that he and his family shared the poverty and hardship suffered at that time by the great majority of Jews in Poland and Russia. The persecution of the Jews was greatly intensified following the assassination of Tsar Alexander II in 1881, and the Jews responded by a great wave of emigration, mostly to North America and in part to Britain.

Michael Marks arrived in England in 1882 when he was 19 years old. He was penniless, he had not been trained to any trade, he had no relations or acquaintances in the country, and, above all, he spoke no English and could neither read nor write. It was not unlike many a Chinese immigrant in the last century who at the end of a tortuous journey landed on a new continent far away from their poverty-stricken native villages.

London was Michael Marks' first stop, but he did not settle there. He soon moved on to Leeds, and from then onwards the North of England was to be the centre of his activities. The major reason he chose Leeds might have been that the city at that time had already a Jewish community of over 6000 people, mostly employed in the rapidly developing clothing trade. It was an occupation which did not require much skill or training, and among his people in Leeds Michael Marks was fairly certain of finding the work and help which they were accustomed to give to all those who came from a land of persecution.

Leeds was in many respects a typical product of the industrial revolution which was transforming Britain from an agricultural country into a manufacturing nation. Its predominantly working-class population was enjoying a rise in real income which enabled it to exercise an effective and increasing demand for articles of domestic consumption which had hitherto been beyond its reach. Between 1870 and 1880 real incomes per head in the U.K. rose by about 10%; between 1880 and 1890 they rose by some 40% and between 1890 and 1900 by a further 12%. Thus the first two decades of Michael Marks' business life corresponded with a period in which real income rose considerably, and to this may be attributed a large part of the success which he achieved.

Michael Marks started his career in retailing at a time when the trade was undergoing profound changes, in ways comparable to those which had already taken place in industry. The traditional retailing outlets, such as pedlars, fairs, markets, and the like, were increasingly giving way to the fixed shop. The craftsman-producer who retailed his own products was gradually disappearing from the scene. The last two decades of the nineteenth century witnessed the gradual and dramatic growth of the department store and multiple shop. These changes were a response, on the one hand, to the appearance of a large and homogeneous working-class market as a result of industrialization and urbanization, and, on the other, as in the department stores, to a large middle-class demand, particularly for goods other than food. At the same time, these changes were also a response to the large-scale production of consumer goods, appearing for the first time in history in large volume, which required new forms of outlets and agencies for their efficient distribution.

In Michael Marks' short working life—he died at the age of 44—he reproduced almost every stage of the transformation which was taking place in retailing, graduating from the most primitive stage of the pedlar to the stage where he created an original and unique type of chain store.

The young Marks began his business as a pedlar; the modesty of his resources hardly allowed him any alternative. Carrying his merchandise in his pack, he traded along the dales of the West Riding and the agricultural and mining villages around Leeds. His stock was necessarily small, being limited to what he could carry on his back, and consisted of buttons, mending wools, pins, needles, tapes, woollen socks and stockings. On his marriage certificate he described himself as a 'licensed hawker'.

One of his first suppliers was the firm I. J. Dewhirst Ltd., then a wholesaler selling primarily to pedlars. Today they still remain suppliers to Marks & Spencer. Mr. Alastair Dewhirst, the present chairman of the firm, has described how his grandfather, Isaac Dewhirst, first met Michael Marks[1]:

> One day my grandfather was walking down Kirkgate when he was addressed by a stranger with the single word 'Barons'. My grandfather spoke to the man and quickly realized that he did not speak or understand English. With my grandfather, however, was his manager, who spoke a little Yiddish, and was able to talk to the man in that language. He discovered that he was a Polish refugee, who had come to Leeds looking for the firm of Barran Clothiers, whose generosity in giving work to refugees was known as far afield as Poland.
>
> My grandfather was fascinated by the stranger. He took him back to his warehouse, where he learned that he was looking for work and had no money. He offered to lend him £5, and Michael Marks asked if he might use it to buy goods from the warehouse. My grandfather agreed, and as Michael Marks paid off the debt in instalments, he was allowed to make further purchases to the same amount. This was my grandfather's first contact with Michael Marks.

The life of a travelling pedlar in the Yorkshire countryside and climate was a harsh one. It was particularly hard for someone of Michael Marks' frail physique. He did not remain a pedlar for long. In 1884 he opened a stall in the open market in Leeds. The stall consisted of a trestle table 4 ft. by 6 ft., displaying the same kind of merchandise he had previously carried on his back; it was open for business on market days, which were Tuesday and Saturday.

## The Birth of the Penny Bazaar

From the open market in the city, Michael Marks subsequently moved to its covered market hall, which had the advantage of giving protection against the weather and of being open for trading throughout the week. Here he soon introduced an innovation which was to be of fundamental importance to the development of his business. He divided his stall into two sections, and placed all those items costing a penny in one section and all those costing more in the other, where the prices were individually marked. Above the penny section hung a board with the slogan: 'Don't Ask the Price, It's a Penny'.

This proved to be, as Goronwy Rees observed, one of the most successful advertising slogans ever invented. 'It was not only that it was striking and simple and easily understood; it corresponds to a genuine popular need. Michael Marks was catering for working-class customers, then largely illiterate . . . who were keen to satisfy their domestic needs at a low price; the combination of open display, easy inspection, and at a fixed price made shopping easy and convenient for them. 'Don't Ask the Price, It's a Penny' quickly proved so popular that Michael Marks adopted the principle of the fixed price on all his stalls and henceforward sold nothing that cost more than a penny.'[2]

The success of this novel way of selling had certain important bearings on the subsequent development of the business. It proved not only to be convenient to the customer—whose preference was strikingly manifested in increased turnover—it was also extremely convenient to the stall owner. Michael Marks never kept any accounts, and conducted his business operation by mental arithmetic; adopting a single fixed price of a penny greatly simplified all his calculations. This element of operational simplicity was to become a central feature of the business and was an important factor in the relative ease and success of the subsequent multiplication of stalls and shops throughout the country.

The revolutionary nature of this innovation could not be overstated. Michael Marks had discovered and put into practice two simple ideas—self-selection and self-service—which were to become cardinal principles in retailing in the second half of the twentieth century. As Israel Sieff has written in his Memoirs[3]:

In shops at this time, which more often than not were small and dark, it was still customary to keep goods in drawers under the counter or on shelves behind it. You had to ask for everything before you even saw if it was there. It was, and remains, a feature of people who acquire a purchasing power to which they are not used to be shy sometimes of going into shops and discussing purchasing: sometimes they avoid it, in case they show their ignorance, or for fear that sophisticated shopkeepers, or shop assistants, might look down on them or exploit them. This did not happen when people came to shop with Michael Marks. They could walk around Michael's penny bazaar, thirty to seventy feet in length, six to thirteen feet in width, without being pestered to buy. They were at ease. Out of the psychology of this approach to selling goods were to emerge two of the most important principles of mid-twentieth century retail distribution: self-selection and self-service for the customer, and the organization of the emporium to that purpose.

The adoption of a fixed price policy had also another far-reaching effect. It meant that Michael Marks had to search incessantly for as wide a variety of goods as possible, and of as high a quality as possible, that could be sold for a penny; as a result he had to accept very low margins of profit, and make up for this by achieving as large a turnover as possible. This pricing policy was the forerunner of a dual pre-occupation of the firm in subsequent years: achieving an ever-increasing high volume of turnover at relatively low margins on the one hand, and sourcing and creating products of high quality to be sold at a relatively low price on the other.

## The Partnership

By 1890 the young immigrant was operating five Penny Bazaars, at Leeds, Castleford, Wakefield, Warrington and Birkenhead, all selling under the same slogan of 'Don't Ask the Price, It's a Penny'. He undertook all the work of general management supervision, buying and distribution, as well as travelling to prospective new openings. Assistants were appointed to take charge of each stall, run on simple procedures and strict economy. In 1892 a warehouse was established in Wigan as a centre of distribution and by 1894 two more Bazaars and one shop were opened. The business was becoming too large for one man to manage, and Michael Marks looked around for a partner to share the responsibilities. He approached Isaac Dewhirst, his first business contact, with a view to forming a partnership. But Dewhirst's own business was already very prosperous, and he did not feel able to accept the proposal. He recommended, however, Tom Spencer, his cashier, who he thought could offer the kind of help Michael Marks was looking for. A friendship had already developed between the two men, though their characters and temperaments were worlds apart. Spencer, an excellent book-keeper, was sharp and authoritative in manner, but he could also be kind and considerate. He had little imagination or enterprise, but was something of an organizer, with an eye to small economies. His experience in Dewhirst could enable him to put Michael Marks in direct touch with other manufacturers. Most important of all, perhaps, the two men liked and trusted each other.

On the 28th of September 1894 the firm of Marks & Spencer was formed. For his half share in the partnership Spencer paid £300. The two men were from first to last equal partners in the business. Michael Marks was then thirty-one. It was ten years since he had, as a poor immigrant, last wandered about in the Yorkshire countryside with a pedlar's pack. Now he had built up a modest but flourishing business—a considerable achievement for a penniless young immigrant.

A substantial part of Michael Marks' success must be attributed to his personal qualities. He was thrifty, extremely conscientious and hardworking, and in his business dealings appreciated the virtues of simplicity, honesty, and directness. But he had some other qualities which are rarer to encounter. He had a gift of sympathy and imagination which enabled him to appreciate the needs and wants of his working-class customers; it is the kind of gift, as Goronwy Rees pointed out, which can give retailing something of the quality of a social service. He had known suffering and want himself and they aroused his sympathy when he encountered them in others. 'He inspired', as noted by Harry Sacher, a distinguished historian and son-in-law of Michael Marks, 'confidence and affection in even casual acquaintances; he never quarrelled; and he never lost a friend. Withal, he had an unlimited capacity for work and no nonsense or vanity as to the kind of work as long as it was honest and useful.'[4]

The first decade of the newly formed company witnessed spectacular growth both in sales volume and the number of bazaars. By the end of 1900 there were thirty-six branches, of which twenty-four were in market halls and twelve were shops. The majority of these were still concentrated in North England although there were at this time already six branches in the South, including three shops in London. In 1897 the headquarters of the firm were transferred from Wigan to Manchester. In 1903, when the number of branches reached 40, three regional supervisors, or 'stocktakers' as they were called, were appointed. They were based at the head office in Manchester and their duties were to visit the bazaars, take stock and regulate deficiencies, and supervise staff, expenditure and layout of the bazaars.

1903 was a critical year for the company. Business had progressed so far that it was felt that the time had come to transform it into a limited company. In that year the firm of Marks & Spencer Limited was registered. In the same year Thomas Spencer retired; he died 2 years later, at the age of 53. The most immediate effect of Spencer's departure from the business was the immediately increased burden of work upon Michael Marks. It was all the more formidable because of the very rapid expansion of the business. Between 1903 and 1907 another 24 branches were opened. In total, there were more than 60 branches throughout the country by the end of 1907.

It is perhaps not surprising that the burden of managing the rapidly growing business, without the support of his former partner, should within a few years have proved too heavy for Michael Marks. Two years after Thomas Spencer he died, in December 1907, leaving a widow, and one son and four daughters.

The sudden and unexpected departure of the two partners left the striving business in disarray. Simon Marks, Michael Marks' only son, was only 19 years old at the time of his father's death. He had only just joined the company, and was still too young and inexperienced to take over. In the decade that followed, the control and management of the company fell into the hands of members outside the families of the founding partners. There were sharp disagreements among the remaining members of the board over the direction in which the business should develop. A deadlock was created and was sustained for years before it was finally resolved through legal action by the Marks family. The long struggle for the control of the company was ended only in 1917, with a new board being constituted. The young Simon Marks, at 28, became chairman of the board.

## Changing Character of the Stores

The turn of the century had seen a gradual yet profound transformation in the character of the business. Apart from the dramatic increase in the number of branches and the changing pattern of their geographical distribution, the nature of the stores themselves was also undergoing fundamental changes. By 1907 only a third of Marks & Spencer branches were in market halls or arcades—which belonged to a declining phase in retailing. It was apparent that future development would lie mainly in shop development. Between 1907 and 1914 the number of branches had more than doubled to 140; less than 10% were in market halls and arcades. The overwhelming majority of the shops were located in prime high street sites and in the new shopping centres.

The success of Marks & Spencer, and their fixed price policy, had provoked widespread imitation in the trade, so much that M&S had to distinguish themselves from the competition by the claim: 'The Original Penny Bazaar'. One major competitor had been the London Penny Bazaar Co., which operated 30 bazaars, most of which were in the London area. Ever since the death of Michael Marks there had been persistent attempts by the board to acquire the whole company. In 1914, for the sum of £15,000 in cash, Marks & Spencer bought the London Penny Bazaar Co. outright, taking over all its stores in London. This acquisition established Marks & Spencer in the London area. Before that it had been primarily a provincial operation, with its heart in Manchester. At around the same time there emerged a new and even more formidable competition in Woolworth's, which had already 600 branches in the U.S.A. when it opened its first British store in Liverpool in 1909.

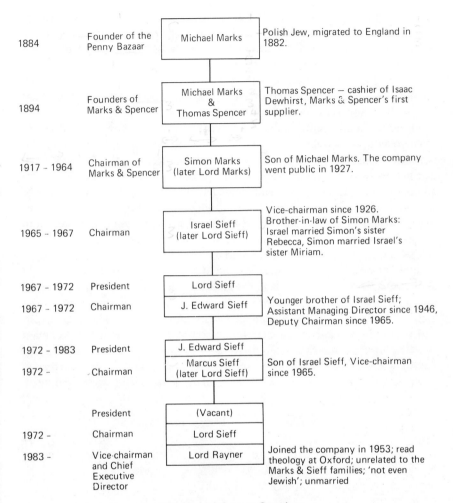

| 1884 | Founder of the Penny Bazaar | Michael Marks | Polish Jew, migrated to England in 1882. |
| 1894 | Founders of Marks & Spencer | Michael Marks & Thomas Spencer | Thomas Spencer — cashier of Isaac Dewhirst, Marks & Spencer's first supplier. |
| 1917 - 1964 | Chairman of Marks & Spencer | Simon Marks (later Lord Marks) | Son of Michael Marks. The company went public in 1927. |
| 1965 - 1967 | Chairman | Israel Sieff (later Lord Sieff) | Vice-chairman since 1926. Brother-in-law of Simon Marks: Israel married Simon's sister Rebecca, Simon married Israel's sister Miriam. |
| 1967 - 1972 | President | Lord Sieff | |
| 1967 - 1972 | Chairman | J. Edward Sieff | Younger brother of Israel Sieff; Assistant Managing Director since 1946, Deputy Chairman since 1965. |
| 1972 - 1983 | President | J. Edward Sieff | |
| 1972 - | Chairman | Marcus Sieff (later Lord Sieff) | Son of Israel Sieff, Vice-chairman since 1965. |
| | President | (Vacant) | |
| 1972 - | Chairman | Lord Sieff | |
| 1983 - | Vice-chairman and Chief Executive Director | Lord Rayner | Joined the company in 1953; read theology at Oxford; unrelated to the Marks & Sieff families; 'not even Jewish'; unmarried |

The Marks & Spencer Genealogy

By the time Simon Marks became chairman of the board Marks & Spencer could be regarded as having completed a new phase of development. It was now a fully-fledged variety chain store, organized on a national basis.

The decades between the two world wars were, for Britain, years of rapid social and economic change. The Victorian era of imperial and industrial supremacy had already brought into being a prosperous middle class by the turn of the century and, between the wars, it gave birth to a growing and maturing working-class market. At the same time scientific invention and technical innovations were making their impact on the needs, tastes and habits of the population. The revolution in transport, improvements in communications, the growth of the popular press and of advertising, all directly affected people's lives and attitudes in ways which were profoundly important to the large-scale retailer. Thus, for instance, the growth in the mass media made people of all classes, especially women, increasingly aware of fashion and style, and created a growing homogeneity and uniformity of taste throughout the country. All these accelerated the trend towards large-scale retailing which had already been apparent before 1914.

The growth of the multiple chain stores in size and number was accompanied by increased competition between them in the quality and variety of the services and the amenities which they offered their customers. This was partly due to the practice of resale price maintenance, which restricted retailers from competing in price and thus encouraged them to engage in other forms of competition. As a result, the stores not only became brighter, cleaner, and more convenient to shop in, they also offered better customer service, more attractive merchandise display, and a greater variety of goods.

The new business environment posed serious challenge and opportunities to retailers such as Marks & Spencer. Simon Marks, on assuming responsibilities as chairman of the company, had little idea how and where the firm should best develop. Woolworth had by then become a formidable and threatening competitor. It enjoyed the advantage of large financial resources, American experience, American management know-how and American methods of mass retailing. Indeed, the threat represented by Woolworth was one of the main factors which forced Marks & Spencer to find ways and means by which it could create for itself a specialized position in the field of chain-store retailing.

### Simon Marks' Pilgrimage to America

One of the most decisive influences on the post-World War I development of Marks & Spencer was Simon Marks' visit to America in 1924. In an unpublished autobiography,[5] Simon Marks recalled,

> Having assumed control of the Company, I was free to face up to its problems. Woolworth's had been making extraordinary progress and were rapidly developing throughout the country. They had become a household word, a great commercial institution. We had marked time, and could report no change since the days of my father, other than a few more branches. I was conscious of my own shortcomings and ignorance. I had never worked in a shop. I had no training in the business. . . . I felt that somehow I had to expand my experience, learn from other people how to face up to the competition from this commercial giant. . . .
>
> I did not realize how open, helpful and generous American businessmen were in showing strangers how they operated. . . . It was there that I learned many new things. It was about my first serious lesson in the chain store art. I learned the value of more imposing, commodious premises, modern methods of administration and the statistical control of stocks in relation to sales. I learned that new accounting machines could help to reduce the time to give the necessary information to hours

instead of weeks. . . . I learned the value of counter footage, that is, that each counter foot of space had to pay wages, rent, overhead expenses, and earn a profit. There could be no blind spots on the counters in so far as goods are concerned. This meant a much more exhaustive study of the goods we were selling and the needs of the public. It meant that the staff who were operating with me had to be re-educated and retrained. It meant new people, new forces.

The American visit was an eye-opener for the new chairman; he returned to England with the clear conviction and determination to transforming his own business into a chain of what he was later to call 'super stores'.

The visit was decisive in shaping three major, interrelated areas of the company's development: store development strategy, customer intelligence system and pricing policy.

The concept of a 'super store' based on the American model implied a large and continuous flow of merchandise over the counters, and this in turn implied the central organization of a chain of such stores which can command a huge volume of business on the one hand and can appreciate and assess the changing needs and tastes of the customers on the other. The chairman's American tour convinced him that a large retailer, being in daily contact with thousands and even millions of customers, could be a most sensitive barometer of what the public wants at any particular moment. But up to that time Marks & Spencer, like other retailers, still obtained the great bulk of their supplies from the wholesaler, who acted as a middle-man between them and the manufacturers, while the ultimate decision of what should be produced for the market lay in the hands of the manufacturer, who was far too removed from the point of sale to the customer to be a quick and accurate interpreter of his demands. The new concept of retailing in the mind of Simon Marks was something very different. He firmly believed that the large-scale retailer should be an *interpreter to industry* in terms of the needs and tastes of the public and that, under the chain-store system of organization, the scale of the retailer's operations could be such that the orders it placed with the manufacturer would justify long continuous runs of production and so secure the benefits of the consequent economies in costs.

But in a business as volatile as retailing, an interpreter's role cannot be properly performed unless there is an effective system whereby the knowledge gained as a result of millions of individual sales over the counter can be quickly and accurately collated and analysed. What was called for was an intelligence system which could ensure easy and rapid information exchange between the head office and the sales counter. At the time of the chairman's visit to America there was no effective system of this kind; it might take a couple of months before reports from stores reached the head office, and when they reached there they were difficult to handle and to monitor.

The chairman learned from the American chain store a rapid method of channelling information from the sales counter to the centre—a device known as a checking list which reported the weekly sales of every class of merchandise in the catalogue. This handy system provided the chain store with a kind of central nervous system which made it swiftly responsive to the demands of the customer. It was so simple and efficient that it is still being used today in the stores almost 60 years after its introduction in the mid-1920s.

A third area on which the chairman's American visit had a direct impact was pricing policy. Most of the American chain stores had at the time a price limit of five or ten cents, corresponding roughly to the penny price limit of the pre-war bazaars, but some had a price range of up to a dollar. In 1924 Marks & Spencer had still not found a way out of the difficulties entailed by inflation and the abandonment of the penny price policy during the war. In line with the new strategy for store development the chairman was anxious to adopt a simple price structure similar to that of the penny price limit. He was particularly attracted by the idea of a five shilling (5 s.) price limit, because of the wide variety of goods which the American chain stores were able to sell over their counters at the maximum price of a dollar.

The new price limit of 5 s. might appear an arbitrary choice. But its significance was far more than simply providing a simple price structure. In a way analogous to the original penny policy the company had henceforth to secure adequate supplies of good-quality merchandise which could be sold within the maximum price of 5 s., and where this merchandise did not exist it was necessary to create it. The implication was that, once the 5 s. limit was adopted, it was no longer possible for Marks & Spencer to be merely a passive recipient of what the wholesalers or manufacturers had to offer. They had to adopt the active—or in the eyes of many at the time, aggressive and offensive—role of trying to persuade the manufacturer to produce the goods which their customers demanded at prices which were within their income. This initiated a dual preoccupation which was, and still is, fundamental to the company's merchandising policy. On the one hand, where merchandise was available at prices which the customer could meet, consistent attempts were made to improve the quality in order to satisfy public standards of taste, which were becoming increasingly more discriminating. On the other, where merchandise of good quality existed which was outside the price range, they tried, in co-operation with their suppliers, to find ways of reducing costs of production without loss of quality. This meant that in their merchandising policy the emphasis came to lie with increasing weight on the problem of reducing the costs of production in order to be able to provide their customers with goods of high quality and at a price within their reach.

## A New Relationship with the Manufacturer

Such a merchandising policy was not only imaginative and unconventional, it was in fact singularly at odds with the prevailing retail trade practice at the time. It implied above all an altogether different relationship between the retailer and the manufacturer; it meant, on the one hand, developing mutual trust, confidence and long-term relationship between the two parties, and on the other, overcoming elements of prejudice, mistrust, and old-fashioned clinging to established customs and practices. 'In our early days', recalled Lord Marks, 'there were manufacturers who would only enter our premises by the back door in case it should become known that they were dealing with us.'

The first step in implementing such a policy involved a radical move: eliminating the wholesaler. But this was not something which could be put into effect either quickly or easily. Not unexpectedly, it met with strong opposition from both the wholesaler and the manufacturer, who in many cases had not much confidence in doing business with a company which was still associated with the days of the Penny Bazaar. There was also the very real influence exercised by the wholesalers' organizations, such as the Wholesale Textile Association, which attempted to prevent direct trading between retailers and manufacturers.

The first firm with which Marks & Spencer were able to establish a direct relationship was the hosiery firm of Messrs Corah of Leicester, which produced under the brand name 'St Margaret'. In 1928, when Marks & Spencer registered their own brand name for goods manufactured to their orders, a number of saints' names were considered to go along with 'St Margaret'. Simon Marks finally chose 'St Michael', partly because his father's first name was Michael and partly because the archangel Michael was the guardian angel and patron of the Jewish people.

The dramatic origins of the business relationship between Corah and Marks & Spencer were revealing. Israel Sieff, who joined the company as vice-chairman in 1926, made three visits to the hosiery manufacturer without even being allowed to enter Corah's premises. On the fourth he was given the privilege of speaking to the chairman of the company, but was unable to persuade him to accept a direct order from Marks & Spencer. It happened, however, that the factory manager was also at the meeting. He was attracted by the large orders which Marks & Spencer were in a position to place and was fascinated by the possibility that such orders might create for planning production ahead, and the long continuous runs which would reduce production costs. When Israel Sieff left the chairman's office, once again disappointed, the manager approached him and the two came to an agreement by which Marks & Spencer would place their orders with the manager personally, on a secret order number whose identity was concealed from other members of the firm.

The secret, as could be expected, was not kept for long. Israel Sieff was soon summoned to a dreadful interview with the chairman of Corah, at which the manager was present, and was informed that their arrangement had been discovered and that as a result the manager was dismissed. Once again, Israel Sieff had to apply all his powers of persuasion to convincing the chairman that the deal was in fact to the mutual benefit of both. Fortunately he was successful and the manager was reinstated. Corah has remained a supplier to Marks & Spencer to this date.

This first association with Corah provided the pattern for the relationship which was later established with other suppliers. But the story conveys the feeling that there was something almost unethical in a direct relationship between the retailer and the manufacturer. By breaking through custom and tradition, Marks & Spencer had pioneered a new type of relationship between the retailer and the manufacturer, which became the cornerstone of a new business strategy consciously adopted by the company.

## A Decisive Break from Conventional Retailing

The primary objective of the new merchandising policy was to secure adequate supplies of good quality products which could be sold within the 5 s. price limit; in the chairman's words: 'to discover, and where necessary create, a range and variety of goods which had not been previously available at this price'. It was also imperative for the success of the 'super store' that the goods thus obtained should be kept moving swiftly and continuously across the counters of the stores. As a result the emphasis rested increasingly on the production and sale of those ranges of goods which sold most easily and quickly, and the elimination of those which failed to find as assured a market. Between various ranges of merchandise an intense competition developed for space on the counters, and those which lagged behind were ruthlessly eliminated.

This had a most far-reaching effect on the character of the store. It meant, in sharp contrast to other chain stores, a progressive *reduction* of the range and variety of the merchandise offered for sale. From this point onwards it became increasingly difficult to fit the company into any of the normal categories of large-scale retail organization. They were distinguished from the department stores because of their chain store method of organization, because of their largely working-class customers, and because they did not attempt to satisfy all their wants under one roof. They were unlike the multiples because they were not restricted to one particular range of product. They differed also from other variety chain stores because they concentrated increasingly on those lines which could be most efficiently produced within the 5 s. limit.

The reduction in range and variety of products for sale followed directly from the conviction that the large-scale retailer could be the interpreter to industry and the associated policy of obtaining large-volume and high-quality goods directly from the manufacturer. The catalogue must necessarily be highly selective. The criteria for selection were relatively simple; the focus should be on those lines in which continuous improvements in quality and reduction in cost could be achieved. This applied especially to textiles, with the effect that by 1932 over 70% of the items listed in the 1926 prospectus had disappeared from the stores. Between 1928 and 1932 seventeen departments had been entirely eliminated, and their disappearance showed that Marks & Spencer no longer aimed to cover all a household's needs. Hardware, china and earthenware had gone, and so had cutlery, stationery, and boot and shoe accessories. Fancy goods were restricted to clocks, watches and travel goods; the range of toys had been greatly reduced.

But while entire departments were eliminated, turnover rose dramatically, as counter space was freed for those lines of merchandise which sold most easily and rapidly. The reduced range of merchandise meant increased specialization, quicker response to public demand, more refined specifications of products. The increased turnover, on the other hand, enabled larger orders to be placed with the manufacturer who benefited from a more stable and secure volume as well as the long-term continuous run which in turn made possible the costs of production to be progressively reduced.

The relentless pursuit of this policy gave the Marks & Spencer stores a very special position in the retail sector. What was remarkable about this development was that it occurred not by chance or by pressure of economic forces, but by a deliberate policy, with clearly formulated objectives in view, which in many ways contradicted those of other forms of chain-store organization. So successful was this policy that by the mid-1930s the company had become the largest retailer of textile products in Britain and in Europe. Throughout the 1930s, sales of textiles continued to grow; turnover multiplied more than three times between 1933 and 1939 and by the latter date represented two-thirds of the company's total sales.

By the time of World War II, Marks & Spencer had become a strange animal in terms of retail trade classification, but the chairman's grand design of the 'super store' was already materializing to a substantial degree. Simon Marks has referred to the interwar years as the 'formative period' of Marks & Spencer; indeed they were, insofar as a well-conceived business strategy and corresponding policies were explicitly formulated and forcefully executed. The war once again interrupted the development of the company, but the basic strategic orientation of the business had by then been firmly established. The post-war years witnessed an even more comprehensive and rigorous implementation of these policies, which was a primary factor underlying the company's much-envied success.

**Simon Marks in Perspective**

Simon died on 8 December 1964. He had been chairman of the company for nearly 50 years. He has been dead long enough for me to see him in a perspective I never saw him in when he was alive. While he was alive he dominated me. I always deferred to him; it never occurred to me to do anything else; I grew up in the assumption of his superiority, as a brain, a business leader, and as a human being. Since he died I have in one sense felt a freer person: my decisions and judgements are not related to those of anybody else as they were to Simon's. I am perfectly ready to revise my estimate of his worth, but in fact, as every year of his absence from my life goes by, I miss him more, and understand better what I owe to his creative genius.

I certainly see him more clearly now, five years after his death, than I did before. I see, for example, that his whole life was bound up with the business in a way mine never has been. It was not that he could not relax or give himself to other interests, but that he saw Marks and Spencer as an integration of human life. What I mean is well conveyed in a remark he made after listening to a concert given by Moiseiwitsch: 'You know, his playing made me wonder why we couldn't do better in the business.' He had a sense of harmony and essential human experience which he groped for in his daily work, sensing when enjoying the perfection of philosophy and art how far his work was falling short of his ideal. His failings, and they were slight, were impatience and high-handedness, never displayed to the salesgirl and the salesman on the shop floor—to them no man could be more considerate—but to those around him. He was aggressive in argument, authoritative in manner, and ambitious in outlook; but only his equals or his rivals got the brunt of this. Simple as my nature was compared with his more complex ego, mine was aged and sophisticated in general attitude to life. He could never believe in his own achievements. He spoke of them sometimes like a child at a birthday party wondering if it is really happening after all, and if it is, whether it will go on.

(From Israel Sieff, *Memoirs*, p. 188.)

# Notes

1. Quoted in Goronwy Rees, *St. Michael: A History of Marks & Spencer* (London: Weidenfeld and Nicolson, 1969), p. 5.
2. *Ibid.*, p. 7.
3. Israel Sieff, *Memoirs* (London: Weidenfeld and Nicolson, 1973), p. 57.
4. Unpublished manuscript, quoted in Rees, *op. cit.*, pp. 10–11.
5. Quoted in Rees, pp. 74–5.

CHAPTER 2

# St Michael: A Merchandising Revolution

Simon Marks and Israel Sieff, co-architects and a perfect team, reshaped Marks & Spencer during the interwar years. Shortly after World War II the company emerged as one of the most successful businesses in the Western world—unique and inimitable. The uniqueness had many dimensions and in this chapter we shall confine ourselves to those features associated with the company's brand name St Michael, the creation and development of which constituted no less than a merchandising revolution.

All of the 260 Marks & Spencer stores in the U.K. carry only one brand of merchandise—St Michael, a sharp and striking contrast to most other retail chains. All of the products are either designed by the company or jointly designed with the manufacturer; the company does not buy any ready-made line from the suppliers as do most other retailers. The products thus designed are manufactured by the suppliers (none of them owned to any degree by Marks & Spencer) against precise and exacting specifications furnished by the company to ensure high and consistent quality. To this end, the company employs over 350 technical personnel in the head office who work closely with the manufacturer advising on and monitoring such matters as choice of raw materials, choice of production processes and techniques, quality control, production engineering and the like. Given the intense care and attention to each single product line, the range of merchandise sold in the stores is significantly narrower than those of other chain stores. But the quality of all the products sold is fully guaranteed by the company; indeed the brand name has become a byword of quality in the British scene. Moreover, it has the undisputed reputation of providing the highest 'value for money' in the high street. The brand name has become the most popular household brand in the U.K. but, significantly, with virtually no advertising whatsoever. To crown all this, over 90% of its merchandise is British-made, despite the fact that most of

27

its competitors are importing heavily in comparable lines. These are some of
the unique features. Let us now elaborate and attempt to make sense of such
unconventional practices.

## What is Marks & Spencer selling?

Only one brand of products is available at Marks & Spencer stores. It is,
however, not for the sake of convenience or uniformity or trying to be
unconventional that this policy is adopted. The decision has much to do with a
fundamental aspect of the entire business: what the company is selling.

To most retailers, what a retail store sells is the *service* of making available a
good range of merchandise to the customer. They compete with one another on
the quality of service offered, such as imaginative display, shopping convenience, range of product lines and brand names, attractive atmosphere and other
customer services. This has been, and still is, the mainstream conception of
retailing.

Marks & Spencer, in contrast, had explicitly rejected this conception more
than half a century ago. Not that it ignored the 'service' elements in the
trade—indeed the company has excelled itself in many of these areas—but the
primary focus as far as the nature of the business is concerned has been very
different. The company seriously and rightly approached the question from
the other end: what does the customer really want? The company came to the
conclusion—reached in the 1930s and still firmly held today—that what the
customer really wants is not 'service' as such but a range of products of high
and dependable quality and yet within their consumption power. It thus
defined its business as *supplying to the target customers a range of products that are
of good quality and yet priced at a level they can afford.* This is of course more
easily stated than achieved. The most intriguing question at the time when this
was formulated was simply that this range of products hardly existed. 'It had
to be discovered and where necessary created.'

Take, for example, women's clothing. Until World War I the women of the
working class were still confined to the nineteenth-century costume of a serge
or tweed skirt, a blouse of sateen or velvet, flannel petticoats and woollen or
cotton stockings. Women's heavy-clothing industry, producing coats and
skirts, had been organized on a factory basis in the second half of the nineteenth
century, but in the light-clothing industry no factory organization existed
before World War I. Women of the working class continued to buy lengths of
dress material which they either made up themselves or had them made up by
a dressmaker, or patronized second-hand shops dealing in women's cast-off
clothing. But after the war an increasingly large number of the working-class
women and girls were employed in workshops and factories and there they
discovered that their clothes were totally unsuited for work. They were heavy,

unhealthy and inconvenient, they constricted movement, and under factory conditions could be hazardous and dangerous. At the same time, with their new-found independence, they began to feel it a mark of inferiority to wear the soiled and cast-off clothes of other women, while factory employment did not give them either the time or the inclination to make clothes for themselves. The rising wave of emancipation of women was marked by a growing demand for clothes which were inexpensive, light, comfortable and attractive, as befitted woman's new status in society.

This demand had remained unsatisfied for quite some time simply because the light-clothing industry had not got off the ground. To Marks & Spencer the manufacturers were far too removed from the needs and desires of the customer, especially the *potential* customer. They become convinced that to satisfy the customer, the retailer must assume the role of *interpreter* to industry of the demands and tastes of the market.

In this respect Marks & Spencer has played a highly significant part. The company was largely responsible for accelerating the development process of light-clothing industry for women. An entirely new range of products were 'created' to satisfy the new mass market for cheap, well-made and pretty clothes for working-class women and girls at a price within the reach of their household income.

Ever since the 1930s the company has pursued this new approach to retailing consistently. As a retailer it has an impressive record of product innovation. But whether it is a new product or simply a product already available in the market, they tend to offer some extra benefits to the customer. Initially, the St Michael brand name was attached only to selected lines of textile products but gradually, as they possessed the necessary resources to apply the same principle to other lines of products, all of the company's goods began to come under the same brand name.

## One Brand vs. Many Brands

Another major contrast between Marks & Spencer and most other retail chains as far as branded products are concerned is related to the question of consumer choice. In a sense the conventional retailer offers more choice to the customer in terms of brand names; there is usually a range of brands for a single (almost identical) product. Shoppers at Marks & Spencer do not have this freedom; they either take the St Michael brand or leave it. In the eyes of Marks & Spencer this reduces to some extent its attractiveness as a retail store insofar as the customer cannot readily compare the company's product with those of other brands. But the company feels that the benefits arising from this arrangement more than outweigh its shortcomings. In the first place, it rightly believes it is sometimes very difficult, if not impossible, for a customer to make an *informed* choice in face of a number of competing brands, especially when the latter carry different prices, which is usually the case. The customer may have to rely on his past experience with the competing products or information obtained from advertising and other sources, all of which may not be reliable and comprehensive enough. At times the customer may well be confused rather than aided by the range of choices available. What St Michael offers, in contrast, is the guarantee that the product in question is of high and reliable quality and, if there are different price points for the same type of products, it can be confidently assumed that the one with a higher price possesses some extra benefits or refinements. To Marks & Spencer the issue is not so much a question of choice as such, but rather whether or not the product in question can really satisfy the customers' needs. To take a somewhat extreme but nonetheless realistic example furnished by a Marks & Spencer executive, it does not seem to matter much not to have half a dozen brands of fresh chickens for the customer to choose from, as long as there is one brand about which the customer is absolutely sure of its quality and value for money. (The St Michael fresh chicken, 'created' on the same principles as other lines of products, is a spectacular success story.)

In the second place, as far as long-term production economy is concerned, the one-brand strategy appears to make more sense for the retailer and the manufacturer as well as the customer. Given the fact that most competing brands are offering only marginally different products, it is economically more efficient to produce only one standard brand. In fact this is one important source of the superiority of Marks & Spencer over many other maufacturers insofar as production is concerned. The company can place a very sizeable order for a single make, which in turn enables the supplier to achieve not only better economies of scale, but also technical innovation to bring down the cost.

Finally, the one-brand policy as adopted by Marks & Spencer which guarantees quality and value for money renders advertising and other forms of expensive promotional efforts superfluous. In contrast, many branded products have to spend heavily on advertising, with the effect that either profit margins are squeezed or the price paid by the customer is raised, neither of which is beneficial to the customer in the long or short run. What is more, in those cases where combative advertising by competing brands is epidemic, it represents a gross wastage of the society's resources with minimal social benefits. St Michael spends amazingly little on advertising; it builds up its reputation by its proven ability to identify and meet the customers' needs.

### Creating Rather than Buying Products

Given the overriding principle of offering the customer what he really wants, not what manufacturers or wholesalers decide to supply, the first task of developing any line of product is to create the product itself. Unlike other retailers, Marks & Spencer takes upon itself the decision of *what to manufacture*, not simply what to buy from the manufacturer. It has its own team of designers working closely with the supplier to design or redesign the product. It is important to note that the *design* of a product is not simply a question of taste and fashion or technical feasibility and details, it is also a commercial decision involving judgements pertaining to market trends, hidden and potential needs, cost and price elasticities of demand, impact on existing lines, etc. Moreover, it is also very much a question of having the ability and vision to capitalize on the most recent scientific advances and technological breakthroughs which may have a bearing on the final production of the product.

For instance, in the 1930s and 1940s new raw materials for textile products were emerging. The company's product 'design' was very much influenced by these changes. As Lord Marks had put it in his annual speech in 1945:

> Science is producing new raw materials and new processes as well as improving existing materials. In our own field new synthetic fibres and plastic substances are being created which will generate additional demands and wants by the public. Some of these inventions are not mere substitutes but original products which open up new fields of application and manufacture. A distributive organization like ours, in direct contact with the large public and in close association with manufacturing industry, can help to expedite the development of such new materials. Our experience enables us to translate consumer demand into production of the kind of goods our customers would desire to buy at a reasonable price, and in this way reduce the delays between the discovery and the production of the article for the consumer. We are closely watching the development of such research in order to widen the range and improve the quality of the goods we sell.[1]

To translate consumer demand into production is by no means an easy task. It underlines the complex and painstaking process the company undertook in designing and creating a product. The potential customer is not interested in man-made fibres as such, however new and marvellous their properties might be. They are interested in the garments in which the fibres are embodied, whose qualities, aesthetic and utilitarian, are not determined exclusively by the properties of their raw material. They are equally determined by the processes of spinning, knitting, weaving, dyeing, finishing and garment-making. It was necessary that the raw material, the fibre, should be adaptable to such processes, and should preserve its properties when subjected to them, so that it should finally emerge in the form of a finished garment which would be readily saleable. It was also necessary that the intermediate manufacturers should understand the nature of the new fibres, and be prepared, if necessary, to modify their manufacturing processes in such a way as to preserve and, if possible, enhance its properties. Through its textile technologists and its merchandising departments Marks & Spencer undertook to ensure that at every stage of production, back to the primary producer of the raw fibre, the needs of the consumer were represented and at each stage of production its specialists and technologists collaborated with the firms responsible. Initially the fibres were themselves expensive and they required new machinery, new processes and techniques if they were to satisfy the consumer. Both through its textile technologists and, at the garment-making stage, through its Production Engineering Department, Marks & Spencer was able to offer advice and guidance on the production problems involved; and because of the large market it offered it was able to create conditions under which plants could be operated continuously and at full capacity, and to give manufacturers the confidence to invest in the new machinery and new processes demanded for efficient production.

In undertaking all these, Marks & Spencer performed a function which was of vital importance to the growth of the man-made fibre industry in the U.K. By 1965 the company used man-made fibres for over half of their textile products. It did not buy from the manufacturers ready-made merchandise; it played a primary role in creating them in the first place.

### Specification Buying

Not all products were created in as dramatic a way as the ones from man-made fibre, although the latter is by no means untypical. But all products bearing the St Michael label do have one important thing in common, and that is, they are all manufactured against the very detailed specifications of the company.

The specifications are notoriously exacting and demanding. They provide the primary basis for ensuring high and consistently high quality. The company specifies not only the sizes and dimensions of the product, but, more significantly, the materials employed as well as the processes applied to them. For each and every item of raw materials used there is an approved list of suppliers from which the manufacturer is obliged to obtain the material. These materials are being tested on a regular basis by the technologists at the head offices to monitor quality standards. The company also specifies the method of production or processes to be used by the manufacturer, many of which are designed and set up jointly by the technologists and the technical personnel of the manufacturer concerned. As Lord Marks has said, 'It is easy enough to test goods when they are made. What is more important is to be sure they will be well made from the start. What we want to have is process control and testing at the point of production.'

In Marks & Spencer, therefore, the function of buying became something essentially different from what it is in the normal retail organization. The art of buying normally consists in the skills with which the buyer, out of his experience, knowledge and flair, chooses among the various lines which are offered to him by a variety of competing suppliers. At Marks & Spencer, specification buying entails the working out of standards which lay down in exact detail the requirements to which the manufacturers must conform.

This practice is most unique among mass retailers to the extent that the company is being drawn into many activities which may seem more closely related to the function of production than of distribution. In this important work the technologists played a vital role. Marks & Spencer as a retailer employs by far the greatest number of technically trained personnel in the U.K. and probably in the rest of the world.

## A Symbol of Quality

We have seen in the preceding discussion what exactly Marks & Spencer attempts to offer to the customer; it is not so much the conventional service offered by most retailers, but the supply of a range of products of high quality and reasonable prices. To this end, tremendous efforts and substantial resources are being expended to create and develop product lines that can meet this requirement. Given the intensive attention required by each line, it is natural that the range of products offered is necessarily more selective and much narrower than that of most other retail chains. It is perhaps a vindication of the foresight of Simon Marks that this policy was first formulated and implemented in the 1930s. It went against the main current of the time when almost every retail chain was attempting to satisfy as far as possible all the household's needs under one roof.

### The Japanese Connection

Japan has in recent years emerged as a manufacturing giant; in sector after sector her industry has surpassed the West in both quality and productivity. Retail distribution, however, remains one of the weakest links in the Japanese economy; relative to manufacturing, it is notoriously backward and inefficient.

About two decades ago a Japanese retail chain, barely 5 years old, set out to learn from the West the most advanced form of retailing, and it was no accident that they looked upon Marks & Spencer as their model. Today, Daiei, which calls itself the Conglomerchant, has become the largest and most diversified retailer in Japan; and in 1983, shortly after celebrating its 25th anniversary, it overtook Marks & Spencer in terms of turnover which the latter has taken almost 100 years to build.

These two most successful retailers in their respective lands have a lot in common, not the least because Daiei happens to be the franchised dealer of St Michael merchandise in Japan. Both of them are unconventional and anti-tradition in their own ways. But perhaps the most paradoxical similarity is the fact that while Marks & Spencer is sometimes likened to the Japanese company, Daiei has been considered to be un-Japanese and too Western.

Daiei has often been accused of being 'unfamiliar with Japanese business practice'. But Isao Nakanchi, founder and president of the company, thinks otherwise: 'Our way of thinking might be a step or two ahead of the era . . . as time goes by, the others' way of thinking will change.' Nevertheless the president is known to be 'very aggressive and a person thinking of the destruction of a traditional order', according to Professor Yoshihiro Tajima, an expert on retailing.

Many Japanese companies export heavily. Daiei imports heavily. This is close to a mortal sin, in a land where generations of businessmen are weaned on the credo that Japan, to survive, must produce and export only. It is still widely held that service-oriented industries such as chain stores are not good for Japan. Indeed, 'there still seems to be a feeling that to produce something is good for the country but to consume it is immoral'. Daiei dismisses this as 'prewar thinking' and asserts that 'service-oriented industries would be the locomotive of the Japanese economy in the future'.

Like Marks & Spencer, Daiei was convinced that the wholesaler and the traditional manufacturer has not always had the interest of consumers at heart. Daiei has been one of the few who have challenged the power of the manufacturers and tried to counterbalance it. As the president put it in the 1982 annual report, 'We have proven over the years that, with pressure on manufacturers, consumers can obtain better merchandise at lower prices. . . . I think our position in the market indicates the degree of consumer appreciation of our efforts. . . . We have no vested interest in selling a particular line of products. If we identify a consumer need which no

product in the world meets, then we have the capabilities to design this product and have it produced. In that sense you might say that we are a manufacturer without a factory [sic!].'

Unlike Marks & Spencer, the company used to have an explicit policy of 'buying from the best sources of the world'. But over the past few years it has progressively adopted a policy of supplying private-label merchandise, the bulk of which is produced domestically according to the company's specifications. The private-label goods fit into three categories: 'quality', with over 10,000 items priced 10–20% below national brands; 'price', represented by the 'savings' line of 145 items 15% cheaper than the quality brands— these are specifically designed by Daiei to cut excess features and bring savings to consumers; and over 40 generic items, i.e. no brand goods, which are roughly 30% below competing national brands. The private-label lines account for close to two-fifths of total turnover and take up a high proportion of sales of clothing, processed foods and daily necessities.

The distribution sector in Japan is entering a period of restructuring in which there is serious debate about how the value-added component from production to marketing should be divided among various parties. Manufacturers, wholesalers and retailers are all being forced to re-examine their strengths and leverage points. Whether or not Daiei would succeed in providing the revolutionary link between mass production and mass distribution—in ways analogous to what Marks & Spencer have achieved in Britain— remains to be seen.

Even today, Marks & Spencer has only a range of about 5000–6000 items, compared to the typical national retail chain of 20,000–30,000 items. This major gap in the range of products offered also underlines the fundamental difference in the ways Marks & Spencer and other retail chains define their respective businesses.

It is also because of this relatively narrow range of product that Marks & Spencer has been able to turn the company's brand name, St Michael, into a certificate of good quality and good value. It would be extremely difficult, if not outright impossible, for the brand to achieve such a high reputation had the company been attempting to offer a more comprehensive range.

The St Michael brand name carried with it the assurance that articles sold under this name were produced to the company's specifications and conform to the high standards it prescribed in regard both to materials and to manufacturing methods. The manufacturers who supplied St Michael merchandise to Marks & Spencer were in many cases among the best-known firms in the country, with a very high reputation for craftsmanship and efficiency and their products, distributed through other channels, came into the class of luxury goods rather than of utility.

St Michael merchandise, though of high quality, by no means comprises the best-quality products around. But relative to the price at which they are sold the products represent perhaps the best value for money available in the high street stores. In this respect no other brand names pose a serious challenge to its position. 'The St Michael label', in the words of Robert Heller, 'has become gilt-edged household currency in a way that no house brand, here or in America, has ever matched.'[2]

Despite the high quality of St Michael merchandise, the company still adopts a 'No questions asked' refund policy. Products bearing the St Michael brand name can be returned or refunded for cash for defects or any other reasons. The Marks & Spencer stores do not have changing rooms; customers are assured that the size will fit, as long as they know their correct sizes, and are encouraged to try the garment at home and return or exchange it if they are not satisfied for whatever reasons.

Such a policy has two major implications. First of all, the fact that the company accepts change of merchandise or refund for defective items implies the recognition that the quality of the products is not 100% perfect. This is understandable as the cost of perfection is prohibitive. Figure 5 may serve to put the issue in perspective. It is apparent that the perfection of quality is subject to escalating costs and diminishing returns. It is socially unfair and commercially unwise to ask consumers to pay for a fruitless search for absolute perfection. The St Michael merchandise is already produced at a cost far above those of other brand names, if only because of the technologists' involvement in the procurement and manufacturing processes and the high standard of

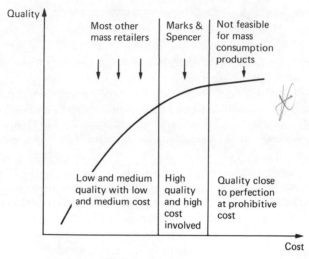

Figure 5

quality control. The liberal refund policy ensures that the customer will not be penalized in any way by a defect in the product undetected by the system.

In the second place the refund policy is also indicative of the kind of relationship the company tries to establish with the customer. It is not so much a public relations exercise that the customer is allowed to exchange goods and obtain refund so easily. It has more to do with the company's conviction that the merchandise is there to satisfy the customer's needs, and if the latter is not satisfied, for whatever reason, the transaction is not complete. The company seems to be practising exactly what Peter Drucker has long preached: 'the product offered culminates in the actual consumption of it, not just when it leaves the seller's premises'. What the company attempts to foster is a long-term relationship with the customer who can feel that the products purchased from the stores are dependable, and has no doubt that he obtains the benefits he pays for.

### A Price Within Reach

The pricing problem has not been a major headache for the Marks & Spencer managers, at least until recently when St Michael merchandise began to go progressively up-market. From the days of the Penny Bazaar the operating principle as far as pricing was concerned was relatively simple: fix a price limit for all the merchandise sold in the stores within the reach of the working-class customers and then search for the range of products that could be sold with a profit at that price. This was what the Penny Bazaar was built upon, and similarly what Simon Marks had established at the 5 s. ceiling following his visit to America. Even after World War II, when the fixed price limit began to give way to a more flexible price structure, the basic principle of providing the mass of the population with the necessities of life at the lowest prices compatible with good quality has remained intact.

In a significant sense, what Marks & Spencer has pursued in terms of pricing policy is analogous to what Henry Ford has done in pricing his automobiles. As Theodore Levitt has reminded us, most people have admired Henry Ford for the wrong reason, his production genius.

> His real genius [Levitt maintains] was marketing. We think he was able to cut his selling price and therefore sell millions of $500 cars because his invention of the assembly line had reduced the costs. Actually he invented the assembly line because he had concluded that at $500 he could sell millions of cars. Mass production was the *result* not the cause of his low prices.[3]

Ford has himself expressed his operating philosophy succinctly:

> Our policy is to reduce the price, extend the operations, and improve the article. You will notice that the reduction of price comes first. We have never considered any cost as fixed. Therefore we first reduce the price to the point where we believe more sales will result. Then we go ahead and try to make the prices. We do not bother about the costs. The new price forces the costs down. The more usual way is to take the costs and then determine the price, and although that method may be scientific in the narrow sense, it is not scientific in the broad sense, because what earthly use is it to know the cost if it tells you that you cannot manufacture at a price at which the article can be sold? But more to the point is the fact that, although one may calculate what a cost is, and of course all of our costs are carefully calculated, no one knows what a cost ought to be. One of the ways of discovering . . . is to name a price so low as to force everybody in the place to the highest point of efficiency. The low price makes everybody dig for profits.[4]

This mirrors almost exactly what Marks & Spencer has done for over half a century. In conceiving a product, whatever its current costs and selling price in the market, the initial step has always been to think of a price that is within reach of the mass of the population (such as the working class before World War II and the middle class in recent years). Only then does the company try to discover and create those conditions whereby the products can be produced profitably at this price. Simple as this may appear to be, it is not something which is easily adopted by most retailers. It is only the very special relationship Marks & Spencer has had with the supplier and its intimate involvement in the manufacturing process that make possible the pursuit of such a pricing policy.

### An Advertising Non-advertiser

By almost any standard, 'St Michael' must rank among the most well-known and reputable brand names in the U.K. Yet it has achieved this status with

**Answering the People's Prayers**

Why did we continue, not exactly to flourish, but certainly to grow, when all around us our competitors found themselves in difficulties? Because we answered the people's prayer. Their prayer for goods at prices which even in their days of impoverishment they could just about afford to buy.

I remember the day when a letter arrived at our head office written by the Minister of the Baptist Church in Mountain Ash, Glamorgan, South Wales. I have said that at this time there were three million men unemployed. That, however, is a figure for the country as a whole: in some parts of the country, the north-east coast of Scotland, around Whitehaven, for example, in Glasgow, in Northern Ireland, or in Lancashire, the proportion was much higher: one man in three was out of work. That was the situation around Mountain Ash. And worse. There were four thousand people living in that town, and, the Baptist Minister said, there was hardly a man who had a clean shirt, or a clean shirt that wasn't ragged. It wasn't enough, he said, for men to have a clean shirt if that shirt was ragged. He had some money at his disposal, and he had worked out what the men of Mountain Ash could afford to pay: they wanted no charity, all they wanted was a chance to pay for a clean unragged shirt. Could we do anything about this? He had read something about our general approach to business, and he wondered whether we might.

It was not a very difficult decision. I gave instructions at once that five hundred dozen shirts should be sent free to Mountain Ash immediately. A curious story. By mistake, the consignment was invoiced to him, as though they were buying them—quite a natural error—at the cost price which was two and elevenpence. Simon and I knew nothing about this until a few days later we received a letter from the Baptist Minister. He said that he would never have believed a shirt could be bought for two and elevenpence, a price which he thought was within the purchasing power of even the completely unemployed man in Mountain Ash, and he thanked God for it. And he went on, 'thank God for men who understand what self-respect means to an out-of-work miner.'

We were extremely embarrassed to find he had sent us a cheque for the shirts. We sent it back, apologised for our mistake, and made it clear that we had intended to send the shirts to help, free. Later in life Max Nicholson said to me, 'You know, Israel, you've done something of tremendous importance. You've taken away envy out of the poorer classes. They can buy an article from you which looks like what a duchess can buy, and it makes them feel as good as she is. That is the real revolution.'

(Source: Israel Sieff, *Memoirs*, pp. 154–5.)

surprisingly little advertising. To say that it is a paradox in the history of advertising is to understate it. As Rodney Millard, chairman of Saward Baker Advertising who had handled Marks & Spencer's modest account for over 20 years, puts it, 'It is a well-known name, but a non-event from an advertising point of view. They go around making speeches about being non-advertisers.'

In a sense, the company had been a pioneer in advertising. 'Don't Ask the Price, It's a Penny' had been one of the best of all advertising slogans. But throughout its 100 years of existence the company's use of paid advertising has been minimal, and has been largely confined to informative advertising of store extensions and the launching of new products. This is supported by occasional prestige advertising in cinemas, on television and through fashion shows in which Marks & Spencer's sales assistants play a part.

Why can Marks & Spencer afford to spend so little on advertising? We may approach this question from its competitors' point of view. The company faces two types of competitors: other retail chains on the one hand and manufacturers turning out competing lines on the other.

As far as retail competition is concerned, the company's steadfast resistance to heavy consumer advertising is all the more remarkable in view of the recent boom in retail advertising. Between 1970 and 1976 retail advertising increased from £56 million a year to £206 million, a rise from 10.1% of total advertising expenditure to 17.3%. In 1981 the ten leading retailers' advertising expenditures are as shown in Table 1.[5]

TABLE 1

|  | £ |  |
|---|---|---|
| Woolworth | 9,600,000 | |
| Boots | 9,364,000 | |
| Co-op Local | 7,195,000 | |
| Tesco | 7,087,000 | |
| Debenhams | 5,959,000 | |
| Co-op National | 4,998,000 | |
| Sainsbury | 4,038,000 | |
| Safeway | 329,000 | |
| Littlewood | 259,000 | |
| British Home Stores | N.A. | (insignificant) |
| Marks & Spencer | 74,000 | |

Writing in the pages of the advertising trade magazine *Campaign*, John Koski has attempted to answer the question 'Why should Marks be able to operate so successfully without spending millions on advertising?' with the following.[6] Firstly,

the company has a name which money can't buy, built up over nearly 100 years into a byword for quality at reasonable prices. . . . Of course, many other retailers—Boots and Sainsbury are two examples—also have very good names. The major difference, however, is that most retailers are selling the same branded goods and have to fight for customers to buy from them what they could just as easily buy elsewhere. Hence the need for heavy advertising. Marks & Spencer, on the other hand, only sells own-brand merchandise, under the St Michael lable, which can't be bought elsewhere. Secondly, the company considers its stores as its best advertisement and word of mouth as its best medium. Only when it is thought that word of mouth will not operate quickly enough to communicate what is happening in its stores—as in the case of say, a store expansion—will the company use advertising. Or as Gerry

Griffiths, Marks & Spencer's executive for Publicity and Economic Affairs has put it, 'If you enjoy many millions of people going through your stores the most potent form of advertising is word of mouth.'

Interestingly and significantly enough, Marks & Spencer does not see its principal competitors in the other retail chains. This has of course much to do with the way it defines its business; it is not selling the kind of service that most retailers are offering. And this has an important bearing on how it approaches the question of advertising and sales promotion. The major competitors, from the company's point of view, are the manufacturers of competing lines. To confront these competitors Marks & Spencer has the distinct advantage of being in direct contact with the consumer, and the focus of competition, as the company sees it, lies in *production* rather than sales promotion. Israel Sieff has written:

> Since the Second World War we have advertised comparatively little. It is not so much because we feel our goods sell themselves, or that we can rely on word-of-mouth publicity, or that the less we spend on advertising the lower our costs and therefore the lower our prices. The fact is that our problem has never been one of selling. We had only stocked what we know would sell because we knew the public *wanted* it. The problem has been one of getting the stuff to sell at the right quality and the right price; the problem was of production, not of sales.[7]

Goronwy Rees has emphasized the same point:

> Given the object at which Marks & Spencer aimed, which was to provide the best possible article at the lowest possible price, Marks & Spencer's problem was less that of increasing sales [through advertising] than of obtaining merchandise of the required quality, and in sufficient quantity, at prices which were within the reach of all classes of the population. *It was a technical problem, and a problem of production, rather than of sales*. Their prices after the war were not cheap. But given the quality which their merchandise embodied, it offered better value for money than anything else on the market. To sell such goods was a comparatively easy matter, and the public responded eagerly to the values which Marks & Spencer offered them; the difficulty was to create them. Marks & Spencer's main problem was not one of persuasion, hidden or otherwise; it was the technical problem of creating the merchandise and bringing it to the market. . . . The Company's attitude to advertising throws into sharp relief the principles underlying its merchandising policy, and it also reveals how much they differed from those of the typical large-scale modern business concern.[8] (Emphases added)

It is fair to add, as Rees maintains, that savings made in the cost of advertising should be set against the company's large investment in technological services and personnel, which other firms might well regard as being outside the business of a retailer. It is apparent, however, that the two forms of investment, on advertising and on technical services, had different objectives in view. The primary purpose of the former would be to increase sales, though no doubt with the intention that increased turnover would lead to economies in the cost of production. The object of the latter was to improve quality and reduce costs,

Fig. 1. The founders: Michael Marks (left) and Thomas Spencer.

Fig. 2. Simon Marks (left) and Israel Sieff in the thirties.

FIG. 3. Lord Israel Sieff, Vice-Chairman 1926–65
Chairman 1965–67.

FIG. 4. J. Edward Sieff, Chairman 1967–72.

FIG. 5. Lord Marcus Sieff, Chairman 1972–84.

FIG. 6. Lord Derek Rayner, Chairman since July 1984.

FIG. 7. Artist's impression of the original penny bazaar set up in Leeds market place in 1884 by Michael Marks.

FIG. 8. Grainger Market Hall Bazaar, Newcastle, still exists in its original form.

though no doubt with the intention that this would lead to increased sales. 'The difference between the two attitudes in fact reflects a difference between two entirely opposed philosophies of business.'[8]

In the age when the hidden persuaders of every kind were triumphant, the Marks & Spencer approach is both courageous and admirable. It takes an organization of exceptional foresight and profound faith in its beliefs and principles to sustain a policy that goes so much against the current around it.

## St Michael Patriotic?

Marks & Spencer is perhaps the only national retail chain which has an explicit and well-publicized policy of buying primarily from British sources. (Despite its name, British Home Stores import far more heavily than Marks & Spencer.) This is an intriguing phenomenon and certainly a difficult policy to sustain, if only because the bulk of what Marks & Spencer sells has been light manufacturing products, for which the international centre of production has been shifted progressively to the developing world, notably the Far East. For Britain it is particularly these areas of production that are most exposed to the threat of foreign competition.

Does it make sense to say that it is patriotism that drives the company to insist on buying British? The company's publicists would be the first to deny it, although we are told that 'Simon [Marks] was intensely patriotic. He loved his country. He had a special sense of obligation to the people of Lancashire and Yorkshire. He felt it was a moral duty to provide as much employment as possible for the men and women who bought in our stores.'[9] However intense his patriotism may be, it certainly has not been the major underlying reason for the very systematic bias toward sourcing from local manufacturers.

It has in fact far more to do with the special relationship the company has entered into with the manufacturers, and which has become the cornerstone for the company's unique merchandising policy. When Marks & Spencer first established direct contact with the manufacturers in the 1930s, it had literally to *educate* the latter to accept its way of doing things.

As early as 1931 Israel Sieff, then vice-chairman, had remarked:

> We are . . . paying increasing attention to the quality and finish of our goods, and if necessary we help our manufacturer to select, and to purchase under the most favourable conditions, his raw materials. We see no reason why an article, because it is low priced, should not have most of the refinements and neatness of a higher-priced article, . . . I think that we have done a great deal of educational work in this respect with British manufacturers. By our encouragement we have helped our own suppliers to work out a progressive policy, to create a more efficient manufacturing organization, and to appreciate how important it is that they should be in intimate and regular contact with a large distributing organization such as ours.[10]

Given the intimate relationship the company has had with the manufacturers and the technical involvement on the part of the technologists in almost every single process of manufacturing, it is difficult to envisage that this relationship can be effectively maintained over a long distance. In a sense the company is buying *production* from the factories, not products. What is more, it sees their relationship with the suppliers as a partnership lasting for a long time rather than the normal buyer–seller relationship. Under these circumstances the bias towards local, i.e. national, suppliers is logical as well as necessary.

By 1934 over 94% of the merchandise sold in Marks & Spencer stores was of British manufacture. Today the stores are still claiming that over 90% of the products are locally made. The company does have some import lines but they are mostly confined to those items of merchandise which are not available in the British Isles, such as certain foodstuffs and handicrafts items. As for the small number of lines which could be manufactured in the U.K. but nonetheless have been obtained from abroad, the company as a rule favours sources from high-income countries, such as the EEC and Israel, rather than those from the low-income ones. In any case, wherever the supplier may be, the company attempts to build up the same kind of collaborative effort as with local manufacturers and its technologists follow the suppliers throughout the world.

The company's buy-British policy has a progressive impact on the national economy. Not only has it meant employment for tens of thousands of workers; it has also helped transform and streamline a significant number of industrial sectors, notably the garment and processed-food industries. Moreover, even though this may not be a comforting thought to the Britons, St Michael has proved to the world that high-quality products are *still* available from this once-renowned 'workshop of the world'. Indeed, St Michael has been spreading its gospel overseas; Marks & Spencer has now become a leading exporter in the country and received the Queen's Award for Export in 1978.

## More than a Brand Name

From the foregoing discussion, it can be seen that St Michael is really more than a brand name; it epitomizes a distinct and radically progressive business philosophy that is almost unique in the retail world. It has, as many observers have pointed out, given an entirely new meaning to the word 'retailing'.

Praise and envy aside, the revolutionary impact of the triumph of St Michael is often poorly understood. Its ultimate significance has been the bridging of two major revolutions in the economic sphere that have occurred in the past 150 years; namely, mass production of consumption goods started in the latter half of the nineteenth century on the one hand, and mass distribution in the form of retail chains which began to mature in the first half of the twentieth century on the other. No company in the world has had a better appreciation than Marks & Spencer of the potential social benefits that can accrue in organically relating these two revolutions, and certainly hardly any company has succeeded in providing the crucial link to these two revolutions as imaginatively and effectively than the creator of St Michael. To consider St Michael as simply an ordinary brand name, albeit a highly successful one, would be to miss the epoch-making significance of one of the most important revolutions of our time.

## Notes

1. Quoted in Rees, *op. cit.*, pp. 188–9.
2. 'The inimitable magic of Marks', *Management Today*, September 1966
3. 'Marketing myopia', *Harvard Business Review*, vol. 38, no. 4, July–August 1960.
4. Henry Ford, *My Life and Work* (New York: Doubleday, 1923), pp. 146–7, quoted in Levitt, *ibid.*
5. *MEAL Report* (London: Media Expenditure Analysis Ltd., 1982).
6. 'The stubborn giant: can M&S afford to stay aloof from the high street war', *Campaign*, 15 September 1978.
7. *Memoirs*, p. 182.
8. Rees, *op. cit.*, p. 211.
9. Israel Sieff, *Memoirs*, p. 156.
10. Quoted in Rees, *op. cit.*, p. 129.

# CHAPTER 3

# 'Value for Money' and the Incessant Quest for Efficiency

There is no such thing as marketing skill by itself. For a company to be good at marketing, it must be good at everything else, from R&D to manufacturing, from quality control to financial control.

Howard Morgans, Chairman of Procter & Gamble

Marketing cannot begin to be effective within a company unless it has the full support of general management and penetrates every nook and cranny of an organization. . . . Marketing is the function of every employee. The marketing approach challenges every member of a company, whatever his specialist function, to relate his work to the needs of the market place and to balance it against the firm's own profit needs.

Hugh Davidson, in *Offensive Marketing*

Marks & Spencer is renowned for its imaginative marketing—above all, its insight into 'What the customer really wants'. The last chapter examined the distinctive ways the company tries to satisfy these needs effectively. This chapter looks at the issue from yet another angle: how its obsessive concern about administrative efficiency contributes to the marketing effort.

To most people the relationship between administrative efficiency and marketing may seem remote. But not so to the Marks & Spencer management; they are thoroughly convinced that efficiency in every aspect of its operations has a direct bearing on the company's ability to meet the customers' needs, particularly the ability to offer customers the best value for money they can obtain.

Administrative costs, which include the maintenance of elaborate systems and procedures and the associated staff requirements, constitute a significant slice of the company's operating costs. Instead of treating them as 'overheads' pure and simple, Marks & Spencer has been noted for its persistent attack on the Parkinsonian tendency of swelling bureaucracy throughout the organization. For a long time the company was not immune from the malaise of paper bureaucracy; and with the dramatic growth of the organization in recent decades the problem assumed larger and larger proportions with every year that passed. As the company is more than a retailer in the conventional sense but is involved in a whole range of activities that most retailers would not have undertaken, the overall operation became all the more complex. As Goronwy Rees has pointed out,

> In Marks & Spencer, as elsewhere, size brought its own penalties, in the shape of mechanical and bureaucratic procedures, of increasing specialization of functions, of an increase in paperwork, of a tendency to aim at efficient administration for its own sake, without considering the purpose which was to be achieved; all being reflected in a steadily mounting burden of overhead administrative costs.[1]

Or as an American observer, Marshall Dimock, author of the book *Administrative Vitality*, in which Marks & Spencer is quoted as a model of efficient management and favourably compared with the largest American corporations, has put it:

> In spite of its general progressiveness and flexibility, however, and even in spite of the dynamic leadership provided from the top, Marks and Spencer is no more immune than other institutions from bureaucratic influences that threaten to cramp these flexibilities. The firm's experience proves again that size, organization and careful attention to method are always accompanied by the dangers of overorganization and especially overregulation through internal forms and procedures.[2]

Shortly after World War II it became obvious to the top management team that a radical review must be taken to streamline the whole operation and that a permanent war must be declared on the stifling restraints of bureaucracy which had been multiplying. The chairman was painfully aware of the fact that

> growth was not confined to sales and profits alone. Overheads were growing even faster, so that profits before tax expressed as a percentage of turnover were being steadily eroded from 10.5% in 1945–6 to 8.5% in 1955–6.[3]

The company was

> determined not to join in the annual lament of company chairmen about the rising operating and overhead costs. Instead, we resolved to take positive, even drastic, action to arrest and reverse the trend as far as our own company was concerned.[4]

Lord Marks, who was the driving force behind the initiative, had an instinctive mistrust of bureaucracy in all forms, and he was aided in recognizing the symptoms of this disease by the close personal contact which he maintained with the company's stores. It was his life-long custom to make frequent personal visits to the stores; on such visits he observed the operations of the store with a minuteness which extended to every detail.

> On one such visit, in 1956, he noticed the lights burning in a store well after closing time and found two girls bringing stock cards up to date. On another he asked a manager for some simple information; the manager opened a file, out of which fell a

## The War on Paper Bureaucracy

Top managers must accept a revision of the administrator's task because for too long top management has expected from administrators cast iron guarantees that the systems and methods used in their business are fool-proof. In pursuit of satisfying this expectation, countless instructions and regulations have been developed and every mistake made has given rise to a further output of rules and regulations, apparently written largely on the assumption that all employees fall into two categories, stupid or crooked.

Every system should be regularly examined by top management with the objective of simplifying, or better still eliminating it. Unless your organizations are different from those of which I have had experience, once a system is set up it will rarely eliminate itself when the reason for existence is over. The result is that in every large organization—unless steps are taken to the contrary—there can only develop more and more splendid systems which will keep many people occupied.

Wherever there is a continual pressure for more staff, especially those in the clerical and junior grades, you can be certain that bureaucracy is rife. . . . Do not imagine that an organization will of itself reduce numbers, or invent ways of managing with fewer people. While every ambitious manager will for himself accept a greater work load, test his reaction to a similar suggestion in respect of his staff. In seeking staff savings you will almost certainly be told that the most important work in your business will suffer, or not be done.

Do not believe this for one moment, but instead go and examine for yourself which tasks occupy the time; I shall be surprised if you cannot discover how substantial savings can be made without loss of efficiency. This area, above all others, is one for management by example, not by delegation to staffing experts.

For success, do not allow anyone in management to opt out of the exercise. Expect to be told, 'I have no time', or 'It does not occur in my area.' You will be in good company listening to this particular choral society. In my experience it is those areas of management where these excuses are most often heard which are in greatest need of detailed examination.

To summarize briefly how the causes of bureaucracy must be tackled we must:

Break down work into comprehensible packages.

Delegate responsibility and authority for those packages to line management.

Treat people as individuals and allow them to contribute as individuals.

If the sum of what I have said so far seems very difficult to implement, then I have made my point, because there is no simple solution.

One final point: our drive for efficiency and better use of resources in Marks & Spencer revealed that it is usually from faulty and complicated systems, and not from thoughtless people, that errors and wasteful practices arise. The real solution is the application of common sense and the development of flexibility of mind. Both are rare human qualities, and their exercise is not always encouraged by the growth in size of an organization.

(Excerpted from Sir Derek Rayner, 'The war on paper bureaucracy', Occasional Paper, Institute of Administrative Management, No. 4, 1975.)

thick batch of forms, which proved to be statistics of the previous year's sales. On another, he found a girl filling in the form which was necessary in order to renew supplies from the stockroom. The chairman had a mind which did not easily come to conclusions; but when stimulated to ask a question, he did not rest until he found an answer which satisfied him. The question he now asked was whether these forms and procedures were really necessary and what useful contribution they made to the company's main purpose of selling goods across the counter.[5]

In that year the chief accountant came to the chairman with a spending budget for administrative costs, millions in excess of the previous years. The chairman 'blew his top and began to throw out paper'. He said to the vice-chairman, 'Israel, it's not a law of business growth that administrative costs continue to increase. Anyway, if things go on like this, we shan't be able to sell women's blouses for less than ten pounds apiece.'

## Operation Simplification

The chairman began to mount a major campaign which was subsequently known as 'Operation Simplification'. The campaign was led by a group of top company executives headed by Marcus Sieff (who later succeeded his father Israel Sieff as chairman). Freed from their other duties for as long as necessary, these executives were charged with the responsibility of reviewing thoroughly all the systems and paperwork of the business. Marcus Sieff made it known to all in the company that 'those in his team were to rid the company of wasteful practices, but that there were to be no foolish savings and no lowering of standards. The campaign was not to be an economy drive, but a drive for more effective use of resources.'

The members of the team set about their work by getting out into the corners of the business to see exactly what went on. They spent full weeks in individual stores; they worked in clerical departments and all administrative offices; they thoroughly investigated the system and the functions of specialists from accountants to technical laboratory assistants. When they believed that they had found something absurd or unnecessarily time-consuming, immediate action was taken to stop the existing system. When in doubt they suspended the system until they could institute something better.

As a result of the campaign, the annual use of 26 million forms was stopped, the number of filing cabinets was dramatically reduced, and staff numbers run down from a peak of 27,000 to 20,000. Most important of all, people were freed from the demands of paper to deal with the demands of the business. In the 12 years that followed, the company was able to increase its sales from £120 million in 1955–6 to over £282 million while actually employing 2000 less people than in 1956, counting 40 hours' part-time work as the equivalent of one full-time staff. Allowing for the effect of inflation, productivity per staff in the 12-year period mentioned more than doubled, enabling the company, while increasing its rates of pay substantially, to lower or maintain many prices in the face of generally rising national costs. Profits before tax had risen from £10 million in 1956 to £34 million in the period, but, what is even more significant, profits as a percentage of turnover had risen from 8.5% to 12%.[6]

The Operation Simplification campaign was a watershed in the company's development. The significance of the campaign lies not only in the impressive results achieved but more importantly in the discovery and formulation of a number of core principles which were to be the primary weapons for fighting the permanent war on the paper bureaucracy. These principles were:

(1) Sensible approximation—the price of perfection is prohibitive. Where it is costly to account precisely, an approximation is likely to do just as well, with considerable economies.
(2) Most people can be trusted—once this is recognized a whole host of checks and cross-checks can be eliminated.
(3) Decategorization of staff—that is, ensuring the largest possible number of staff to be removed from watertight compartments and placed in general categories.
(4) Never legislate for exceptions—that is, never attempt to legislate for every contingency and every eventuality; that would only swell the numbers of manuals.
(5) There is no substitute for personal probing—do not be afraid of only a simple first-hand investigation; most statistics and reports conceal a multitude of inaccuracies and omissions.

## Sensible Approximation

One of the first lines of attack in the Operation Simplification campaign was the paperwork related to various kinds of information systems operating in the company. The first target was the system used to provide merchandising information from the stores on which the production of goods, and their eventual distribution, was based. The company had a very detailed system of recording sales, stocks and requirements which was theoretically sound. Unfortunately, it took many people much time to collect the information, and even far greater time to digest the information and to act upon it. They were tied to paper and could not see the merchandise for the figures. The whole system was fundamentally challenged during the review; since then very much shorter summaries were sent to head office and many simple ways had been developed for giving the stores a reasonably balanced supply of goods. The principle emerging here was that of sensible approximation. The price of detailed information is prohibitive; the actual and opportunity cost of having this information but not making use of it is even more unacceptable. As Sir Derek Rayner had written:

The price of perfection is prohibitive: sensible approximation costs less. . . . Aim towards perfection, but for goodness sake do not try to achieve it. Productivity applied to administration means one man trying to achieve 95 per cent efficiency and reaching it, rather than two men trying to achieve 100 per cent and reaching perhaps 96 per cent.[7]

## People Can be Trusted

With the acceptance of this principle a wide range of checks and monitoring can be discarded, and replaced by 'managers managing and supervisors supervising'. One small example, which met with considerable press publicity at the time, was the decision to abolish time clocks. The assumption was that if a supervisor is worth her salt she must know the people under her, their strengths and weaknesses, and she will certainly know whether they are punctual or not. As a result of this measure punctuality actually improved, and there was no doubt that it was a very popular move with the staff. From this, and many similar instances, the important general lesson emerged that if people are trusted, and so gain self-confidence, the necessary degree of management control can be achieved by means of occasional spot checks. This is far more satisfactory, and far more economical, than a whole series of permanent control systems. It also makes an invaluable contribution to morale.

## Decategorization of Staff

It was realized that the staff in the store can become too specialized, even where their tasks do not require a high degree of professional training. At the same time it was also felt that the rigid compartmentalization of different functions in the store was hampering the efficiency of the operation and particularly the rational utilization of human resources. For example, the stockroom was staffed by a team of employees distinct from the sales floor. The stockrooms and sales floor were virtually isolated from each other. Sales assistants had to fill up a form if they required stock for their counters or if they returned stock to the stockroom. This stock was sorted out by a stockroom staff and eventually delivered to the counters. This practice was abolished after the simplification campaign and the stockroom was thrown open to all, so that at quiet business hours the sales assistant could simply go and replenish her counters. This not only saved time and paper, and speeded up the flow of goods, but it also paid an unexpected dividend in that the sale staff quickly became far more interested in their jobs. (This was a revolutionary system when Marks & Spencer first introduced it almost 30 years ago and it anticipated much of what has been known in the seventies as 'job enrichment'.)

Another step was taken. Pressure of business in the retail trade is most uneven. There are times when the sales floor staff can help the stockroom or

**Who's Afraid of Operation Simplification?**

Other businesses know their own business best but what I've seen of
government operations makes me feel strongly that more trust and less
form-filling would be an experiment well worth trying.

I have discussed the matter with leading politicians and I still find them
opposed to the general approach. A very eminent political leader said to me on
one occasion: 'That kind of thing is all very well for a private concern, Lord
Sieff, but for a public enterprise it is out of the question. If a Minister loses a pair
of boots or a knife and fork in his department three or four years later he may
be called upon to give an account in Parliament of why and how the loss
occurred, on what basis the replacement was made, and how the deficiency
was financially made good; that is why I keep so many pieces of paper.'

I said to him, 'If when you were asked about those boots in Parliament you
said you were sorry but you could not give the record of that pair of boots
because you no longer had the piece of paper which referred to them, and that
because you no longer kept such bits of paper you had saved a hundred million
pounds of the nation's money, you'd be cheered to the echo.'

Ministers ought to live in fear not of what they lose from time to time but
what the people would say about paying the taxes to pay for the paper
permanently to record the loss.

(Israel Sieff, *Memoirs*, p. 161.)

the clerical office, and there are times when everybody behind the scenes is
better employed in selling goods to the public. It was found that, with a free
interchangeability of work, there was greater total productivity. More could be
done with even fewer people. At this point it was decided to reduce the number
of staff categories and to call everyone 'general staff' below the management
and supervisory grades. The idea was quickly appreciated and people were
only too ready to drop their specialized status and give help whenever it was
needed. By this means the stores were able to stop recruitment for 2 years and
allow natural wastages to bring the number of staff to the level quoted above.

The staff payroll is by far the greatest expense in any retail operation, and it
can be appreciated how this reduction in numbers made a substantial contribution to the operating costs of the company. Such savings have made it possible
to benefit the public by lowering prices, to help finance further development,
and to increase the salaries of the remaining staff.

**Never Legislate for Exceptions**

Out of the Operation Simplification campaign emerged another principle of
major importance: Never legislate for exceptions, but instead leave as much as
possible to the common sense of those who are trusted in managerial positions.
Marks & Spencer, like most large organizations, developed over the years an
extensive collection of manuals to deal with every known problem likely to be

encountered. It is very tempting to collect and amplify instructions into manual form. Once a department becomes manual-minded the manuals grow. By replacing these with a set of guiding principles and an understanding of the company's philosophy, management began to manage instead of becoming interpreters of the written word.

## No Substitute for Personal Probing

The campaign renewed and reinforced the emphasis placed by the board on the need for closer personal contact between all sections of the business. Elaborate systems were swept away. Letters and information circulars were virtually banned. Instead, conferences of managers of various quarters were held and head office staff were encouraged to be more energetic than ever before in visiting the stores and studying how they operated first-hand. From this intensive two-way traffic ideas emerged which were to lead to a much more personal and more streamlined business.

The chairman took the trouble of writing a definition of probing which read as follows:

(1) Probing is the method whereby the interested and enquiring mind of the executive and his colleagues penetrates beneath the surface of things and discovers the real facts.
(2) It discloses the trends in each group of lines, so that we can anticipate the rise and fall in the sale of articles . . . thereby minimizing the accumulation of counter-cloggers and increasing the sales of good-selling lines.
(3) Probing is, in fact, an attitude of mind to proper merchandise control in the stores. It is an effort to bring the executive and his staff closer to the operational level of the stores which are the arteries of the business.
(4) Sole dependence on statistics or electronic devices can only result in remoteness of control and lack of knowledge of what is really happening in the stores. Statistics, anyhow, are mainly post-mortem and can deal only in a mechanical fashion with what has happened. They ignore all feeling for merchandise, which is essential for upgrading. The robot-mind merely records. It has no perception, no understanding, and it cannot take initiative—vital elements in the art of probing.

## The Permanent War

The achievement and the significance of the campaign was widely recognized in the national media and elsewhere as a very distinctive contribution towards solving the problems of controlling the growth of overhead costs which presents itself to any modern large-scale business organization. The effect of the publicity which the campaign attracted was reinforced by the steps which the company itself took to draw attention to the principles which it believed were involved in its campaign. In 1956 it opened at its head office in Baker Street an exhibition centre illustrating the methods it had adopted to eliminate administrative wastefulness; in the 20 years that followed, the exhibition was visited by over 18,000 businessmen, representing some 5000 of the largest firms in Britain and overseas, who had come there in the hope of throwing some light on their own administrative problems.

Since that major drive there has been a continual awareness in Marks & Spencer of the need to challenge systems and methods. Even so, it still remains necessary from time to time to repeat the kind of exercise carried out in the mid-fifties. In 1975 another major offensive, known as the 'Good Housekeeping' campaign, was mounted under the chairmanship of Marcus Sieff. The company was in no way under the illusion that people's attitude of mind can be transformed through one great battle. Instead, persistent effort was made to keep up the spirit of simplicity and efficiency. In 1981 another campaign was initiated. The war on the paper bureaucracy continues.

Marks & Spencer's reputation in offering the customer value for money is not easily achieved. As is evident from the preceding discussion, the exceptional value originates not only from good product design and quality-conscious production but also to a large measure from the administrative efficiency that the company is able to achieve. Indeed, it is the company's objective of satisfying the needs of customers as effectively and efficiently as possible that drives it to place such emphasis on administrative efficiency. Sir Derek Rayner has put it succinctly:

> Why then the fuss? Why the priority? Have not most businesses a full time job in keeping up with events which so often seem outside their control? The reason is simple: we must recognise that we live in a world of change, yet the strongest force in a large organisation is inertia. Top management can too easily be fully employed in dealing with current problems. Unless priority is given to setting time aside to probe continuously, and question why the business is being conducted in the way that it is, bureaucracy will win. Top management must create the necessary activity and encourage others to do so at all levels in the company, otherwise the systems which have become anachronistic and irrelevant to the future of the organisation will dominate management time and may even destroy the business.[8]

## Notes

1. Rees, *St. Michael: A History of Marks & Spencer* (London: Pan Books), p. 230.
2. London: Routledge and Kegan Paul, 1960, p. 169.
3. Rees, *op. cit.*, pp. 231–2.
4. *Ibid.*, p. 232.
5. *Ibid.*, p. 232.
6. *Ibid.*, p. 237.
7. Sir Derek Rayner, 'The war on paper bureaucracy', Occasional Paper, Institute of Administrative Management, No. 4, 1975.
8. *Ibid.*

CHAPTER 4

# Strategic Marketing *par excellence*

The preceding chapters have attempted to trace the origins and development of Marks & Spencer's marketing philosophy. We have seen how its marketing strategy has been consciously formulated and executed by the company rather than simply 'evolved' in the passage of time. The St Michael revolution represents a classic case of strategic marketing. Its obsession with administrative efficiency, on the other hand, reveals its thoroughness in adopting an integrated approach to marketing: every single aspect of the operation is geared towards meeting the needs of the customer. This chapter will attempt to put its whole marketing philosophy in perspective.

## The Power of Objectives

Peter F. Drucker, in his book *Management: Tasks, Responsibilities, Practices,*[1] singles out Marks & Spencer as a company in which the power of objectives is most apparent. The business of Marks & Spencer, as Drucker sees it, was not retailing; it was social revolution.[2] In the mid-twenties

> Marks & Spencer redefined its business as the subversion of the class structure of nineteenth-century England by making available to the working and lower-middle-classes upper-class goods of better than upper-class quality, and yet at prices the working and lower-middle-class customer could well afford. . . . What made Marks & Spencer unique and successful . . . was its *conversion of the definition of 'what our business is, and should be' into clear, specific, operationally effective and multiple objectives.*[3]

The Marks & Spencer story brings out the central importance of the specifications of objectives for a business. According to Drucker the principal lessons from the Marks & Spencer experience are as follows:[4]

(1) Objectives must be derived from 'What our business is, what it will be, and what it should be'. They are not abstractions. They are the action commitments

53

through which the mission of a business is to be carried out, and the standards against which performance is to be measured. Objectives, in other words, are the *fundamental strategy of a business*.
(2)  Objectives must be *operational*. They must be capable of being converted into specific targets and specific assignments. They must be capable of becoming the basis, as well as the motivation, for work and achievement.
(3)  Objectives must make possible *concentration* of resources and efforts. They must winnow out the fundamentals among the goals of a business so that the key resources of men, money, and physical facilities can be concentrated. They must, therefore, be selective rather than encompass everything.
(4)  There must be *multiple objectives* rather than a single objective. Much of today's lively discussion of management by objectives is concerned with the search for the 'one right objective'. This search is not only likely to be unproductive . . . , it does harm and misdirects.

Finally, there is need for profit—otherwise none of the objectives can be attained. However, 'Profit goals have been anathema at Marks & Spencer. Obviously the company is highly profitable and highly profit conscious. But it sees profit not as an objective but as a requirement of the business, that is, not as a goal but a need. Profit, in the Marks & Spencer view, is the *result* of doing things right rather than the purpose of business activity. . . . Profitability is a measurement of how well the business discharges its functions in serving market and customer.

What Marks & Spencer has done and achieved in the realm of retailing may not be directly relevant for most other businesses, but the ways in which the company's objectives have shaped and penetrated the entire operation appear to have much wider implications. Like many of the more successful corporations in the West—such as IBM, Kodak, Procter & Gamble, and Hewlett-Packard—Marks & Spencer shares with them the characteristic feature of a set of corporate objectives understood and fully grasped by staff at all levels. These objectives provide the strategic orientation of all aspects of the operation.

## What the Business Should Be

Marks & Spencer was among the very few companies which began to think through the strategic issues of 'What our business is, what it will be and what it should be' at a very early stage of its corporate development. In today's terminology, what they did almost half a century ago may be called *strategic marketing*. They redefined their target market, specified what that market really wanted, and organized and created the resources required to meet its needs. In the previous chapters we have seen how the implementation of this marketing strategy had brought the company into a whole range of activities that are normally considered to be outside a retailer's domain. In order not to leave readers with the impression that Marks & Spencer is *simply* unconventional and unique, I shall now attempt to put this uniqueness in proper perspective. It will be shown that if we approach the issue from the viewpoint of 'What the business should be' as defined by the company, their 'uniqueness' is hardly unique at all.

To facilitate this analysis, I shall briefly introduce a simple concept widely used in the marketing literature: *product life cycle*. In its simplest form the concept suggests that any product (or service) moves through recognizable stages during its life and typically exhibits the generalized pattern of sales shown in Figure 6.[5]

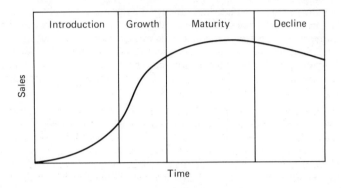

Figure 6    Stages of the life cycle

In the *introduction stage* the product is new in the market and it takes considerable time and money to get the product accepted commercially and proved technically. Sales are low and creep along slowly.

If it is successful the product then moves into its *growth stage* when demand begins to accelerate and the size of the total market expands rapidly. Repeat purchases grow, and word-of-mouth reputation develops. Often competitor organizations see a potential market, imitate the product and, by adding their weight to the promotional expenditure, accelerate further the growth of the market.

However, no market opportunity is infinite and ultimately the rate of sales slows down as the product moves into the *maturity stage* of life. At this stage there are few new sources of customer available. Repeat purchases from loyal customers, along with some customers won from competitors, are the only source of a possible increase of sales.

Eventually the product enters the *decline stage* of its life cycle where, despite often desperate actions, sales continue to decline as the product is replaced by a new generation of product innovations.

A number of questions readily comes to mind:

(1) Given a proposed new product, how and to what extent can the shape and duration of each stage be predicted?
(2) Given an existing product, how can one determine what stage it is in?
(3) Given a product in a certain stage of its life cycle, what could be done to improve its profit performance?

(4) Given the product must go through most or all stages, can the shape of the growth curve be affected through product innovation and repositioning?

The marketing literature is filled with discussions and prescriptions of possible strategies to tackle questions such as these. For our purpose here it suffices to mention a useful summary of some of the more important contributions on the issue. Figure 7 outlines the typical features of different marketing considerations at various stages of the product life cycle.[6] The figure highlights the different areas of focus required at various stages of the product life cycle.

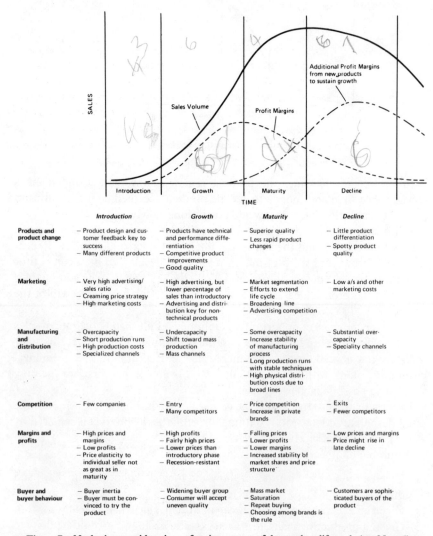

| | Introduction | Growth | Maturity | Decline |
|---|---|---|---|---|
| **Products and product change** | – Product design and customer feedback key to success<br>– Many different products | – Products have technical and performance differentiation<br>– Competitive product improvements<br>– Good quality | – Superior quality<br>– Less rapid product changes | – Little product differentiation<br>– Spotty product quality |
| **Marketing** | – Very high advertising/sales ratio<br>– Creaming price strategy<br>– High marketing costs | – High advertising, but lower percentage of sales than introductory<br>– Advertising and distribution key for non-technical products | – Market segmentation<br>– Efforts to extend life cycle<br>– Broadening line<br>– Advertising competition | – Low a/s and other marketing costs |
| **Manufacturing and distribution** | – Overcapacity<br>– Short production runs<br>– High production costs<br>– Specialized channels | – Undercapacity<br>– Shift toward mass production<br>– Mass channels | – Some overcapacity<br>– Increase stability of manufacturing process<br>– Long production runs with stable techniques<br>– High physical distribution costs due to broad lines | – Substantial overcapacity<br>– Speciality channels |
| **Competition** | – Few companies | – Entry<br>– Many competitors | – Price competition<br>– Increase in private brands | – Exits<br>– Fewer competitors |
| **Margins and profits** | – High prices and margins<br>– Low profits<br>– Price elasticity to individual seller not as great as in maturity | – High profits<br>– Fairly high prices<br>– Lower prices than introductory phase<br>– Recession-resistant | – Falling prices<br>– Lower profits<br>– Lower margins<br>– Increased stability bf market shares and price structure | – Low prices and margins<br>– Price might rise in late decline |
| **Buyer and buyer behaviour** | – Buyer inertia<br>– Buyer must be convinced to try the product | – Widening buyer group<br>– Consumer will accept uneven quality | – Mass market<br>– Saturation<br>– Repeat buying<br>– Choosing among brands is the rule | – Customers are sophisticated buyers of the product |

Figure 7   Marketing considerations of various stages of the product life cycle (see Note 6).

## A Manufacturer in Disguise

Let us now consider what the foregoing analysis has to do with Marks & Spencer's business. We have tried to introduce the concept of product life cycle here to indicate how the marketing manager (or product manager or brand manager as some of them are called) of a manufacturing concern would 'manage' the product. Meticulous attention has to be given to the various stages of the product's life cycle, which call for different emphases and effort from a number of functions: marketing, engineering, manufacturing, distribution, etc. Above all, it requires a high degree of integration and coordination if the life cycle is to be managed effectively and achieve optimal profit performance.

Manufacturers (or their marketing staff) may or may not consciously employ the concept of product life cycle in managing their products, but there is hardly any doubt that the responsibility to do so remains theirs. As far as retailers are concerned, conventional wisdom declares that it is none of their business. The typical retailer simply buys from the manufacturer and would hardly concern himself with the complex question of product life cycle. Marks & Spencer, as we pointed out above, has not defined its business in the way that most retailers have done. The mission of the former has been to create a range of products for their target customers which are of high quality and reasonable prices. The company is, in fact, a manufacturer in disguise. To say that it is a 'manufacturer without factories' is in a sense misleading, insofar as it understates the company's close resemblance to a manufacturer, and in particular, its assumption of the marketing function of the manufacturer.

## Introduction Stage

At Marks & Spencer, unlike most other retailer chains, each line of product is 'managed' by the company, in a way analogous to what a product manager does for a manufacturer. Before the introduction stage, the buying team at head office—which typically consists of a selector, a merchandiser, a technologist and a quality controller—develops the product idea based on interpretation of market needs, assesses its commercial potential, studies the materials and manufacturing processes required, and projects the sales volume likely to be attained in the initial and subsequent stages of the product's life cycle.

The introduction stage is a critical stage of the product's development. At Marks & Spencer most of the new or refined products go through a test market; that is, display and sales of the product at selected stores to test market response and obtain customer feedback. Only when the test market results are favourable will the company proceed to launch the product full-scale with possible modifications based on customer feedback.

To underline the importance of this stage of the product life cycle, Theodore Levitt has put it succinctly in a classic article:[7]

M & S-E

While it has been demonstrated time after time that properly customer-oriented new product development is one of the primary conditions of sales and profit growth, what have been demonstrated even more conclusively are the ravaging costs and frequent fatalities associated with launching new products. Nothing seems to take more time, cost more money, involve more pitfalls, cause more anguish, or break more careers than do sincere and well-conceived new product programs. The fact is, most new products don't have any sort of classical life cycle curve at all. They had instead from the outset an infinitely descending curve. The product not only doesn't get off the ground; it goes quickly under ground—six feet under.

Launching a successful new product is by no means an easy task. To become an acknowledged leader in product innovation is even far more difficult to achieve. Over the past few decades Marks & Spencer has had an enviable record in product development and this has certainly much to do with two major factors. Firstly, the company has had for each line of product a buying team who acts more or less as the product manager of the line and conducts meticulous market research and pre-launch planning for the products in question. The fact that this team is represented almost equally on the commercial and technical sides greatly enhances its effectiveness. Secondly, the company, unlike most manufacturers, has direct access to one of the most highly developed distribution channels in the country—its own stores—which immensely facilitate the planning and execution of the test market for new products. This puts it in a distinctly advantageous position over its manufacturing competitors. For example, the new products can be displayed, and related services offered to the customer, in the Marks & Spencer stores in a way that few manufacturers can persuade their retailer outlets to do without substantial outlay. At the same time, the sales floor staff at Marks & Spencer can obtain and channel customer feedback to the manfacturer through the buying team in a far more direct and effective manner than most other retail stores.

### Growth Stage

The growth stage presents an entirely different set of problems and priorities. Design must be frozen at this stage and attention is focused on ensuring that the product is available in sufficient volume to gain full market acceptance on quality, price and performance.

The characteristic feature of this stage is a steep rise in sales; but although this is to a large measure anticipated once the product survives the introductory phase, the steepness of the curve cannot always be accurately projected. For most manufacturers the problem could be one of undercapacity if sales turn out to be growing at a faster rate than expected, and vice-versa. For M&S the problems are primarily two-fold. First of all, the buying team—and here the technical personnel plays a particularly prominent role—must ensure that the proven product is being produced on a cost-effective basis which on the one hand satisfies quality specifications and on the other maximizes the economy of scale offered by the network of suppliers producing for the company.

Secondly, the buying team has to watch very closely the change in sales growth of the product, and make speedy adjustment as far as production is concerned. For instance, if sales are growing unexpectedly well, it may be necessary to expand production at very short notice, which can be accomplished either through placing a larger order with the existing supplier or bringing in additional suppliers to produce that product. Similarly, if sales have not been growing as expected, the decision may have to be made to slow down production or reduce the order drastically. Because of the very special relationship Marks & Spencer has had with the manufacturer, these kind of arrangements are accepted as a way of life—or more precisely, a way of business. As the suppliers of Marks & Spencer used to say, 'They are not buying products from us, they are buying production capacity.' This is an apt description of the basic relationship between Marks & Spencer and its suppliers; and that is why successive chairmen of the company have always insisted that to them the problem is never one of sales but *production*.

## Maturity Stage

The first sign of the advent of the maturity stage is market saturation. This means that most of the potential consumers have already become actual customers. Sales now grow about on a par with population. Price competition becomes more intense and brand loyalty is critical for holding existing customers. In this stage of the product life cycle some of the possible strategies are:

(1) promoting more frequent usage of the product among current users;
(2) developing more varied usage of the product among current users;
(3) creating new users for the product by expanding the market; and
(4) finding new uses for the basic material.[8]

The objectives of efforts such as these are to extend the life cycle of the product as illustrated by Figure 8.

At Marks & Spencer considerable attention is given to product development by the buying team. Product lines are constantly appraised, especially those at the maturity stage, to identify development possibilities. Typically, few products on the shelves of Marks & Spencer stores are not substantially modified and refined in a relatively short span of time. Given the fact that most of the St Michael range are daily necessities, the constant upgrading of the merchandise serves at least two important functions. On the one hand it contributes to maintaining brand loyalty of the existing customer. On the other, it attracts customers away from competing lines by offering them

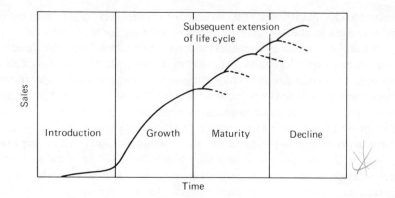

Figure 8   Extending the product life cycle

superior products and better value for money. Again, this important task is executed through the joint effort of the buying team in the head office on the one hand and the thermometer on the sales floor—the sales personnel—on the other.


## Decline Stage

Every product faces the inevitable stage of decline. In this final stage of the life cycle three major phases are sometimes recognizable. In the initial phase the company concerned may make desperate attempts to extend the life cycle by more intensive product development, heavy promotion, price variations and the like. Sometimes this may succeed, but in most cases the efforts may prove to be futile. Then the product may enter the second phase in which the company would attempt to 'milk' the product's profit by holding on to whatever number of customers remain on the one hand, and drastically cutting production costs and related overheads of the product on the other. This measure will not be far removed from the final phase which is consummated by the planning and execution of 'exit'.

Marks & Spencer is known for its ruthlessness in planning the exit of 'slow-moving' product lines. The fortnightly checking list, which provides sales information on every single product item and which is systematically used at all of the stages above, is also the principal instrument for identifying product items or lines which need to be phased out. The Marks & Spencer store operation emphasizes very much the concept of *counter footage*; that is, each counter foot of space has to pay wages, rent, overhead expenses and earn a profit. There can be no blind spots on the counters insofar as goods are concerned, which means that all the slow-moving lines are to be identified and speedy action taken to decide their fate. The buying team of respective lines is charged with the responsibility of developing the catalogue of that line, and this includes eliminating those items which are not contributing to sales.

In contrast to other retail chains, there are far fewer blind spots in the Marks & Spencer stores. The company has not only a free hand but a direct stake in planning the exit of products which have entered the decline stage. In most other retail stores the decision on product exit remains in the hands of the manufacturers, and it is not uncommon to witness products due—or long overdue—for exit still occupying valuable counter and storage space in these stores for an unduly long period of time.

As Theodore Levitt has forcefully argued, the crucial job of the product manager is to 'exploit the product life cycle', by which he means addressing the specific problems and opportunities in each stage of the life cycle and taking appropriate and effective action to capitalize on the profit potential of each stage of the cycle. We have seen that M&S, by rejecting the conventional definition of retailing, has assumed the role of the product manager. What is more, its organic relationship with the suppliers has enabled it to take an integrated and comprehensive approach to product management, which is far more effective than most manufacturers' marketing departments.

We have focused our discussion around the product life cycle concept at such length so as to demonstrate one crucial point; that is, the common reference to Marks & Spencer as unique and unconventional has obscured the fundamental character of the company. The company's basic objective has been to 'offer the customers a selective range of high-quality, well-designed and attractive merchandise at reasonable prices'—not simply the 'service' of a retail outlet— and in order to achieve this objective, what the company has set up and invested in managing the product life cycle can hardly be seen as unique. It is rather the *sine qua non* for its success.

## Competitive Strategy in Perspective

To conclude our discussion of Marks & Spencer's marketing strategy, let us attempt to draw another simple, though not always appreciated, lesson from Marks & Spencer's experience. In a seminal work, *Competitive Strategy: Techniques for Analysing Industries and Competitors*,[9] Michael Porter of Harvard Business School has suggested that the state of competition in a given industry depends primarily on five basic competitive forces, which can be depicted as shown in Figure 9. The five competitive forces—threat of entry, threat of substitution, bargaining power of buyers, bargaining power of suppliers, and rivalry among current competitors—jointly determine the intensity of industry competition *and* profitability. Under particular circumstances the strongest force or forces may be overwhelming and become crucial from the point of strategy formulation. For example, even with a very strong market position in

Marks & Spencer

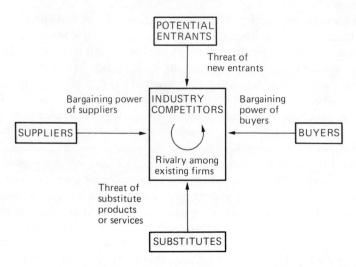

Figure 9     Forces driving industry competition

an industry where potential entrants are no threat, a firm will earn low returns if it faces a superior low-cost substitute. Even with no substitute and a high barrier to entry, intense rivalry among existing competitors will limit potential returns.

The goal of competitive strategy, according to Michael Porter,

> *is to find a position in the industry where the company can best defend itself against these competitive forces or can influence them in its favor.* Since the collective strength of the forces may well be painfully apparent to all competitors, the key for developing strategy is to delve below the surface and analyse the sources of each. Knowledge of those underlying sources of competitive pressure highlights the critical strengths and weaknesses of the company, animates its positioning in its industry, clarifies the areas where strategic changes may yield the greatest payoff, and highlights the areas where industry trends promise to hold the greatest significance as either opportunities or threats.[10]

Let us examine Marks & Spencer's position in terms of these competitive forces.

The analyses in this part may have demonstrated rather vividly that it is difficult to identify the principal competitors of Marks & Spencer. The fact that the company is attempting to manage the product life cycle of every single line being sold in the stores distinguishes it from the conventional retailers. At the same time, it is not competing with the manufacturers of branded products on the same terms, because it possesses a distribution network on a nationwide scale. It is fairer to say that other retail chains and manufacturers of competing lines are *both* Marks & Spencer's competitors, but because of its special position, it has a distinct competitive edge over both of them.

In an important sense, Marks & Spencer is providing an entirely new service to its customers, a service which is not adequately described by the term 'retailing'. To this extent the company is well protected as far as potential entrants are concerned. There are very high barriers to entry, as the supply of a 'service' comparable to that of Marks & Spencer not only requires substantial financial resources, but also a very long period of time for the potential competitor to master the skills and expertise in providing the link between mass production and mass retailing.[11] In all likelihood the potential entrant would be either a retail chain integrating backward (functionally, not necessarily financially as well) or a manufacturer integrating forward. Both are of course possible, but the capital requirement of either is prohibitively high. What is even more important, the critical issue is not simply the risks inherent in investing in a new type of business, but the adoption of a management philosophy and outlook characterized by long-term strategic thinking.

Similar points can be made as far as threat of 'substitute' is concerned. Largely as a result of the company's success in offering a very distinct and unique product to the customer, the threat of substitution is significantly reduced, though by no means eliminated. Again, because of the high costs and long gestation period required to bring out a product that can have substitute potential against the St Michael merchandise, the latter is in a relatively secure position.

The issue of bargaining power of buyers is an interesting subject. In the retailing trade there is, of course, no formal bargaining between the buyer (i.e. shoppers) and the seller as such. The bargaining process manifests itself perhaps in the interplay between the retailers' efforts to attract the customers' patronage on the one hand and the customers' indication of their preference by casting the money vote on the other. In this, Marks & Spencer has been successful to a notable degree. By consistently providing quality and value to the customer it has generated an amount of customer loyalty hardly found in other retail chains. Another major factor is, of course, the fact that the St Michael merchandise is only available in Marks & Spencer stores, whereas for most other retailers it is difficult to discourage the customers from 'shopping around', as many of them are selling similar ranges and brand names.

The bargaining power of the supplier presents another set of issues. As has been pointed out above, the company has a very special relationship with its suppliers. In a sense, once a manufacturer has passed the stringent test and becomes a Marks & Spencer supplier, its bargaining power in the conventional sense will be somewhat limited. The special skills and production facilities developed to meet the specific requirements of Marks & Spencer may not be of use to other retailers. The 'switching' costs for both the supplier and Marks & Spencer are equally high, but probably more so for the supplier. For this and similar reasons, there is sometimes the complaint that M&S is in a position to squeeze its suppliers. (This, as will be shown in Part II, is not a fair statement.

Marks & Spencer does have its own ways of controlling the suppliers, but their mutual relationship needs to be understood in its proper perspective.) Suffice it to point out that the company has been markedly successful in maintaining a long-term relationship with its suppliers, and their collaborative efforts have been a major factor in delivering the high-quality merchandise for which the company is famed.

## Creative Differentiation

Taken together, Marks & Spencer's competitive strategy resembles one of the three generic strategies that Michael Porter has identified. It is the strategy of *differentiation* on an industry-wide basis by offering uniqueness in service as perceived by the customer.[12] In Porter's words:

> Differentiation, if achieved, is a viable strategy for earning above-average returns in an industry because it creates a defensible position for coping with the five competitive forces, albeit in a different way than cost leadership. Differentiation provides insulation against competitive rivalry because of brand loyalty by customers and resulting lower sensitivity to price. It also increases margins, which avoids the need for a low-cost position. The resulting customer loyalty and the need for a competitor to overcome uniqueness provide entry barriers. Differentiation yields higher margins with which to deal with supplier power, and it mitigates buyer power, since buyers lack comparable alternatives and are thereby less price sensitive. Finally, the firm that has differentiated itself to achieve customer loyalty should be better positioned vis-à-vis substitutes than its competitors.[13]

Marks & Spencer's strategy has been a differentiation strategy *par excellence*. The nature of its differentiation must, however, be distinguished from 'artificial differentiation', referring to some manufacturers' attempts to include unnecessary or marginally necessary features in their products in order to 'artificially' distinguish them from the market. It is also to be distinguished from 'tactical differentiation' in which the manufacturers do offer some genuine refinements of the product ahead of others but with the ready anticipation that competitors will soon be able to follow suit and render the distinct elements obsolete. The secret of success of M&S's differentiation strategy lies in the fact that *it has clearly identified a genuine need on the part of the customers and has set and achieved such high standards in satisfying this need that it becomes extremely difficult for its competitors to emulate.*

## Notes

1. London: Heinemann, 1974. Chapter 8 bears the title: 'The power and purpose of objectives: the Marks & Spencer story and its lessons'.
2. *Ibid.*, p. 96.
3. *Ibid.*, p. 96.
4. *Ibid.*, pp. 99–100. Reprinted by permission of William Heinemann Limited.

5. Readers already familiar with this concept may proceed directly to p. 56.
6. This figure is adapted from Michael E. Porter, *Competitive Strategy: Techniques for Analysing Industries and Competitors* (New York: The Free Press, 1980), pp. 159–61. Porter's original, much extended, figure draws on the following literature on the subject: R. D. Buzzell, 'Competitive behavior and product life cycles', in *New Ideas for Successful Marketing*, edited by J. Wright and J. L. Goldstucker (Chicago: American Marketing Association, 1966); B. Catry and M. Chevalier, 'Market share strategy and the product life cycle', *Journal of Marketing*, October 1974; D. K. Clifford, Jr, 'Leverage in the product life cycle', *Dun's Review*, May 1965; W. E. Cox, Jr, 'Product life cycles as marketing models', *Journal of Business*, October 1967; J. Dean, 'Pricing policies for new products', *Harvard Business Review*, November 1950; T. Levitt, 'Exploit the product life cycle', *Harvard Business Review*, November 1965; A. Patton, 'Stretch your product's earning years', *Management Review*, June 1959; R. Polli and V. Cook, 'Validity of the product life cycle', *Journal of Business*, October 1969; J. E. Swallwood, 'The product life cycle: key to strategic market planning', *MSU Business Topics*, Winter 1973; L. T. Wells, Jr, *The Product Life Cycle in International Trade* (Cambridge, Mass.: Harvard Graduate School of Business Administration, 1972).
7. 'Exploit the product life cycle', *Harvard Business Review*, November 1965.
8. *Ibid.*
9. New York : Free Press, 1980.
10. *Ibid.*, p. 4.
11. A classic example is British Home Stores which is adopting similar policies as Marks & Spencer towards some of its suppliers and is to some extent posing a threat to Marks & Spencer. But in the early eighties it has less than a fifth of Marks & Spencer's turnover, and its BHS label is still a remote challenge to St Michael.
12. The other two strategies are overall cost leadership and focus on particular segment. See Porter, *op. cit.*, chapter 2, 'Generic competitive strategies'.
13. *Ibid.*, p. 38.

PART II

# WHERE DO QUALITY PRODUCTS COME FROM ?

REVOLUTIONIZING MASS PRODUCTION AND
MASS DISTRIBUTION

# CHAPTER 5

# 'A Joint Effort for a Common Purpose': Partnership with the Supplier

Where conflict exists between manufacturers and retailers it is as a direct result of their different interests. The manufacturer is aiming to promote his product and gain display in the store; the retailer wants simply to promote his store and increase customer traffic and therefore has no special interest in promoting individual brands. Manufacturers are constantly striving to gain in-store support for their promotions. Retailers want to maintain a sensible promotional balance aimed at attracting customers. Obviously the primary need for both sides is co-operation and a good rapport, but the alliance is frequently an uneasy one. Retailers feel that manufacturers suffer from a lack of understanding of their problems, and manufacturers feel that retailers fail to lend sufficient support to their promotions in store.

These are the findings of a special report, *Research into Retailers' and Manufacturers' Attitudes to Sales Promotion*, published by Harris International Sales Promotion Intelligence.[1] According to the report, although relationships between manufacturers and retailers may be superficially good, co-operation is often difficult to achieve in practice.

We have seen in the preceding chapters that Marks & Spencer is not a retailer in the conventional sense. But before we examine its special relationship with the supplier, it is instructive to review briefly the more general pattern of relationship between manufacturers and retailers.

## The 'Us' and 'Them' Syndrome

Why is co-operation so difficult to achieve between the two parties? And what impact does this have on their ability to satisfy the customer? In a follow-up survey by the trade journal *Marketing*, subsequent to the publication of the above report, Julia Piper has furnished some additional insights on the issue.[2]

One of the retailers' long-term promotional objectives is to build customer traffic through the store and thereby increase the amount of money spent there.

So one of the most important criteria for a manufacturer's brand promotion is that it must enhance the retailer's good-value-for-money image. According to Ray Tucker, Marketing Controller for Spar, products promoted in Spar stores must be known-value items which are important to the housewife because they are basic commodities.

But retailers do look for other things when a manufacturer's brand promotion is presented to them. Exclusivity to their stores is often a prime ingredient, and a promotion should fit into the retailer's own promotional programme and be compatible with his overall objectives. Keith Padder, Buying and Marketing Director of Fine Fare, explains that his company makes its own decisions about which products to promote, irrespective of the plans of manufacturers. He says that the most important factors to him are potential sales, profit and exclusivity.

It appears that the retailer calls the tune to a large extent; the increased sophistication and concentration of retailing over the past few decades has accentuated this. With fewer outlets the manufacturer has to work twice as hard to promote his goods. It is not surprising therefore that the above-mentioned report finds that one of the most frequent complaints from manufacturers is that it is difficult to obtain support from retailers.

To the manufacturer, in-store display support is vital to the success of many forms of promotion. Without that link the manufacturer cannot reach the consumer. Often, in order to get their products to the attention of consumers, manufacturers perpetuate a 'double-think' in sales promotion by creating consumer promotions designed solely to appeal to retailers and gain their in-store display support. For example, the manufacturer does not necessarily want customers to enter the competition he is using to promote his product. Its sole purpose could be to encourage the retailer to feature the associated display material prominently in his store. No wonder that many retailers find competitions to be a waste of time. One retail buying executive commented: 'A manufacturer launches a competition to get the uninitiated to build large displays hoping to increase sales. He gets them, not because of competitions, but because of the displays.'

Manufacturer respondents in the survey understandably 'seemed to be wary of promotion schemes which required much support from the retailer'. This indicates that gaining co-operation from the retailer was often found to be difficult. A spokesman for Brooke Bond Oxo felt that the simpler the promotion the better, because promotions which require a great deal of retailer support could be a problem. And Jeremy Sandys-Winsch, Group Product Manager at Kellogg, agreed that he would 'shy away from a promotion which requires a great deal of retailer support'.

On the other hand, retailers are often not satisfied with the support afforded to them by manufacturers for their own sales promotion programmes. According to the report, the main help retailers needed for their own programmes from manufacturers was financial. 'They want price reductions, advertisement allowances, help towards the cost of printing and bonusing.' Some manufacturers questioned in the survey felt that participation in the trade's schemes was worthwhile—but an equal number complained that retailers often asked too much. One such respondent, the marketing manager of a manufacturing company, remarked, 'They have us by the throat. If they ask us to co-operate it is difficult to refuse.'

The survey shows that both the manufacturer and the retailer agree that there is a need for increased co-operation and discussion of each other's problems. Nevertheless, some of the respondents who advocated closer co-operation also expressed some caution about maintaining a realistic balance of power. One marketing manager from a manufacturing firm said that his company should 'listen to the retailer but keep the reins firmly in our own hands'. Another commented that he was 'very reluctant to see the retailer with more power'. 'Yet', as Julia Piper concludes her report, 'without a continuing improvement in communication the interests of each side may be neglected by the other and ultimately it is the consumer who will suffer.'[3]

## 'A Joint Effort for a Common Purpose'

The preceding analyses pertain, of course, to the conventional manufacturer and retailer. Marks & Spencer, fortunately, does not fall into this category and is thus spared much, if not all, of these nightmares. This does not, of course, imply that the company is free from any problems with its suppliers—indeed, given its own ways of running things, the problems encountered tend to be a bit more complex and also more taxing to overcome. But it does imply that the company on the whole does not have to grapple with the perennial problems mentioned above, which appear to defy sensible solutions. And if the reader recalls the discussion of the product life cycle in the preceding chapter, which underlines the imperatives of different marketing emphases at different stages of the life cycle, the uneasy relationship between the manufacturer and the retailer is all the more disturbing: it poses serious difficulties for introducing a new product, it hinders speedy reaction in response to sales trends in the growth stage, it creates unduly large promotional costs in the mature stage, and it may not facilitate the proper planning and execution of product exit when the product has outgrown its saleability.

In a significant sense, Marks & Spencer had anticipated all of these problems half-a-century ago. By focusing attention on *what the customer really wants*, the company found that as retailer it could hardly obtain the products it knew it could sell—largely because such products did not exist. The company also felt very strongly that manufacturers were not producing quality products in sufficient quantity and at realistic prices for the mass market. It was under such conditions that it developed its primary objective: to discover, and where necessary create, such products. It became convinced that the greatest stumbling block lay in the fact that manufacturing and retailing had been operating as two distinctly separate business entities. This the company saw as the fundamental flaw. It believed that in order to serve the customer effectively and efficiently, mass manufacturing and mass retailing must somehow be organically linked together. The history of Marks & Spencer since the 1920s is best summed up as the relentless effort to achieve precisely this.

What the company used to refer to as 'partnership with its suppliers' is hardly a rhetorical expression. The suppliers' relationship with Marks & Spencer is not simply a matter of co-operation; the acid test of the worth of the relationship is the degree to which they succeed in achieving what the two parties set out to do—to satisfy the customer. In this sense, it represents 'a joint effort for a common purpose'.[4] The extent of the organic relationship achieved between the company and its suppliers is reflected in the statement by a leading industrialist describing Marks & Spencer as a 'manufacturer without factories' working with manufacturers who were 'retailers without stores'.

## How It All Began

Chapter 2 indicated the tortuous ways by which the company established direct contact with the manufacturers. Although it was apparent to Simon Marks and Israel Sieff that such a relationship would be to the mutual benefit of both parties, it required a tremendous amount of persuasion to convince the manufacturer to give it a try. The first order placed with Corah's is instructive.

Marks & Spencer had been buying women's stockings from the wholesaler at 9 s. 6 d. a dozen; Corah was able to supply them direct at 8 s. 6 d. But the sequel to the reduction in price had an even more interesting result. Marks & Spencer neither took the additional 1 s. profit themselves nor passed it direct to the customer. Instead, they discussed with Corah's how it could be applied to improving the quality of the product. The reduction in cost was thus passed to the customer in the form of higher value for money. This resulted in increased sales, and this initial transaction provided a pattern which Marks & Spencer followed consistently in later dealings, both with Corah's and with other suppliers. This constitutes, as pointed out by Lord Sieff,

> one of the most important of our operating principles. . . . The reduction in cost was passed on to the customer, but in the form of higher value for the same amount of money paid. We benefited because our reputation for quality was increased. Our suppliers benefited because they were now producing a superior article with better methods of production which they had not had to finance themselves. The customer benefited. And, last but not least, the workers benefited because fresh capital had gone into giving them better plant and improved working conditions. . . . Later, when we were strong enough, we did not hesitate to put pressure on firms to follow

in the path that this firm had blazed when it was found possible to supply goods at lower cost.[5]

Another example furnished by Lord Sieff indicates the price elasticity of the typical St Michael products. The company was buying a woman's cotton ribbed pullover to sell at 2 s. 11 d. The question arose whether, without any loss of quality, it could be made to sell at 1 s. 11 d. The company was willing to cut its profit margins by 5%. The trade union agreed to accept a reduction in its piece rate, in the hope of increased production. The manufacturer agreed to reduce his price. As a result sales increased by five times, both the manufacturer and Marks & Spencer increased their profits as a result of increased production and larger sales, and the workers benefited by increased weekly earnings and assured employment.

Examples such as this convinced Marks & Spencer that the economies of large-scale production and large-scale retailing, if genuinely devoted to offering better value to the consumer, provided an answer to many of the problems which afflicted British industry during the thirties. The company found, for instance, that lower prices could increase sales by as much as eight or ten times, that the prospect of an increasing market encouraged manufacturers to take risks which they would not otherwise have contemplated, while in fact Marks & Spencer was able to place orders on a scale which in practice eliminated all risk to the manufacturer. From the latter's point of view it meant that over a large part of his production he could plan ahead with confidence for long runs which would employ his machinery continuously and to their greatest economic advantage; it meant also that he was relieved of many of his overhead costs, in particular the costs of marketing and of advertising. From such experience emerged what Goronwy Rees has called 'a genuine philosophy of business, in which the activities of production and distribution were conceived of as a co-operative process with its own contribution to make to the social good'.[6]

It was no mere figure of speech when, each year in his address to the shareholders, the chairman emphasized the unique character of the relationship between the company and its suppliers; he was in fact pointing to an element in the business which was the product of intense effort over a long period of time, and had come to represent an asset which was to be of great value to the company. In his first annual chairman's statement in 1968, Edward Sieff paid this tribute to suppliers:[7]

We have, over the years, worked together in a spirit of mutual understanding. We have learned to appreciate each other's special problems and to deal with them in a most practical and helpful way. We give much thought to the ways in which we can achieve a steady rhythm of production and delivery. Our suppliers have invested considerable capital in order to expand still further their business with us. They have installed new machinery, increased their factory space and given special training to their staff. This is evidence of their confidence in their and our future progress.

If one looks back at the process by which this special relationship was built up, it perhaps becomes easy to see why Marks & Spencer found few imitators in its merchandising policy; one reason is certainly that the understanding and mutual trust on which the relationship was based took a lifetime to create.

**Patron Saint of Troubled Firms**

Marks and Spencer's St Michael has protected a select few of Britain's cloth and clothing firms from the slump which has left most of the British textile industry in tatters. In 1981, 26,000 jobs were lost in the industry, and a further 28 plants closed in January–June this year. In the past three years the big textile manufacturer Courtaulds has shed 40,000 workers, and half the employees of the large clothing manufacturer Tootal have lost their jobs.

A handful of companies have bucked the trend. The Leicester knitwear company Corah more than doubled its profits in the first half of this year. Its sales were up 12% to 23 m ($41.6 m). Others like I. J. Dewhirst, maker of suits, jackets and shirts, and Freddie Miller, of Glasgow, have also flourished. All three have been shielded from recession in the past because they are big suppliers to Marks & Spencer (M&S), the British clothes and food retailer, with sales of £2.2 billion ($4.2 billion) in the year to last March.

M&S takes more than 60% of Corah's production. In 1981 it took around 90% of the sales of Freddie Miller (£8.6 m) and I. J. Dewhirst (£23.2 m). M&S makes it its business to take an active (some say too active) interest in its suppliers' affairs, and can almost guarantee large orders in advance.

Margins are tight. Rigorous standards mean that a new dress or blouse is sometimes redesigned half a dozen times before it reaches the shops. Even then, it may have to be modified after a trial run at M&S stores. To ensure that standards are kept up, cash penalties are imposed when products fail to meet standards set by the supplier's own reference sample. Many suppliers welcome M&S's benevolent dictatorship. T. W. Kempton, a private Leicester knitwear company, with sales last year of £23 m (half of which went to M&S), is glad of the advice it gets from the big retailer.

M&S also encourages investment and sometimes gives financial help. Another of its suppliers, Nottingham Manufacturing, which sells 40% of its output to M&S, has completed a big investment programme that paid off with record profits last year.

Most of M&S's suppliers have sold to the chain for years. M&S likes to reward loyalty. Some, like a women's wear subsidiary of Carrington Viyella, have fallen from favour. But those that survive M&S's scrutiny are likely to survive recession, too.

(Source: *Economist*, 4 September 1982.)

## Arrogant and Humble

In order to provide the crucial link between large-scale manufacturing and large-scale retailing, Marks & Spencer has to become more than a retailer itself. The decision to recruit and maintain a team of technical personnel followed almost naturally from the new definition of its business. It is significant to note that the substantial investment in technical expertise had not been subjected to any cost–benefit analysis in the conventional sense. It is an act of faith on the part of the company's management that benefits will accrue in the long run, and the current cost of technical services should be seen as part and parcel of the operating cost of the business. From this gradually emerged what Simon Marks has referred to as the 'technological approach' to retailing. The basic principles underlying such an approach are as follows:[8]

(1) An analysis of the demands of customers, as expressed in sales across the counter, and the establishment of machinery by which its result could be rapidly and accurately transmitted to the suppliers.
(2) The provision of technical services which formed the basis for collaboration between the manufacturer and the retailer designed to achieve innovation, improvement in quality and lowering of costs.
(3) The introduction, throughout the process of production, of strict quality control. The object of such a policy was two-fold. It was designed to satisfy, and protect, the customer by creating a range of merchandise of high and standard quality which conformed to precise and detailed specifications. But the application of detailed specifications also had a second consequence. It meant that the suppliers' products could be standardized and this in turn led to a lowering of costs.
(4) Control of supplies of raw materials, whether natural or man-made, to ensure reliable, high-quality, and cost-effective supply sources. Special attention is paid to new materials and packaging technology with a view to short-circuiting the period of uncertainty for the raw materials suppliers.

Such an approach entails that the company becomes 'like a production consultant-plus', and serves as a 'funnel through which a lot of experience is poured'. Bearing in mind that Marks & Spencer has been confronted with a fragmented, inefficient industry operating in an undynamic textile market, its policy of pressurizing the manufacturers to modernize and rationalize made great strategic sense.

At any rate, Marks & Spencer has dictated a new type of relationship between the manufacturer and the retailer. Once established, it became a way of life for both parties. As Gwen Nuttall and Lucy Halford observed:

You don't have to be with a Marks & Spencer man for long before he starts to refer to 'the business'. Not 'this business', or 'Marks & Spencer's business', or even 'our business': it nearly always comes out as 'the business'. It is spoken of almost as if it had a separate existence from the people who fuel it. The supplier who said 'Marks & Spencer is a religion' was only half joking. It is a discipline that is at once both arrogant and humble: arrogant, because Marks & Spencer always knows best, humble because the whole impressive system is geared *to serve*, to provide the best service 'the business' can offer its customers.[9]

## How Close Links Pay Off

In what follows I shall briefly examine a number of cases which illustrate the pattern of relationship that Marks & Spencer has developed with its suppliers.

### Almost Like a Marriage

Peter Wolff, managing director of a dress manufacturer, was patrolling as usual round the women's counters of Marks & Spencer's Marble Arch store in the West End. It can be a hazardous job. One day a customer, suspecting his motives, turned round and slapped his face. But Mr. Wolff was not so much interested in the woman as in what she was buying because his company, S. R. Gent, of Barnsley, produces 50,000 items a day for those counters—blouses, skirts, dressing gowns and nightwear.

Marks & Spencer welcomes the attention its suppliers pay not only to their customers, but also to their customers' customers. Indeed, it would be critical of suppliers who believe that it is none of their business. The attention to detail paid by Mr Wolff, who started working life as a photo-journalist with Odhams Press, is no cosmetic operation. The stint in the store is intended to find out why customers buy or reject his clothes.

> Four years ago we introduced a nightdress that we thought would be a surefire winner [he recalled]. But watching the customers it was clear something was wrong. Visually they were attracted to it but many of them stuck their hand up the sleeve and then rejected it. It happened four times in an hour and the garments were just not moving. . . . I went up to the fifth customer and asked her what was the matter. It turned out there was a binding around the sleeve which made it look tight and uncomfortable. I raced to the manager's office, phoned the factory and got them to change the sleeve binding to a frill. We rushed the redesigned items down to London over the weekend and they sold like a riot.

Such close attention to detail has paid off. Gent was originally one of Marks & Spencer's smallest suppliers. It had a turnover of £170,000 in 1966. In 1978 annual sales were £28 million. It reached the £50 million mark in 1980 and struck £74 million in 1983, the year it went public.

Gent was formerly a bakery taken over in 1945 by Edith Wallace and her sister, Ruth Wetzel, to make blouses for Marks & Spencer. At the age of 16 Ruth's son Peter had a 2-year spell with Marks & Spencer as a trainee production engineer. By 1966 Edith had died and Ruth was very ill. She asked Marks & Spencer to send someone to help her son run the business. Peter Wolff, who was then a Marks & Spencer merchandise manager, came in as a 50–50 partner with the help of a £12,000 bank loan. Four years later he recruited another Marks & Spencer man, Leslie Booth, now joint managing director. S. R. Gent now has 20 factories in the Sheffield and Barnsley areas as well as in Australia and New Zealand.

This striking success story illustrates two points. The garment industry can be a winner—even in Britain. And much depends on management flair and dynamism.

Peter Wolff has decided views about where the future lies for his company:

> We will concentrate on fashion. It's harder for the Far East to react to short-term fashion moves. The future for the British and European garment industry is in good design based on a close knowledge of what the customer wants. Not enough is invested in the design side of our industry. I will continue to exploit the potential of computer-controlled designing and pattern making. We are now looking at how we can use the microchip.

> At the same time I spend my Saturdays in Marks & Spencer and other stores, talking to customers and finding out what they buy, and why.

As for the company's relationship with Marks & Spencer, Wolff knows in his heart that it is much more than a commercial link. It is, in his words, 'almost like a marriage'.

## The Tomato Story

Marks & Spencer has become one of the largest sellers of tomatoes in recent years; but it sells more in the winter than in the summer, which is the reverse of the pattern of sales one would expect for a country in the northern hemisphere. This is because the quality and flavour of the tomatoes they sell are much superior.

One of the U.K.'s main sources of winter supply is the Spanish Canary Islands off the west coast of Africa. Fifteen years ago their tomatoes, though good in colour, were poor in flavour and often soft. At one produce review meeting, the chairman said to Jim Lane, executive responsible for produce, 'Look here, Jim, we either have to get out of winter tomatoes or improve their quality. Why don't you make a thorough investigation in the Canaries and see what can be done?'

With a technologist specializing in tropical produce, Jim Lane made a thorough technical study of the growing, harvesting and transport of winter tomatoes in the Canary Islands. They found that tomatoes were picked green and thrown into baskets where they often remained for days to colour up, either on the quay or in the ship. In transit or in storage, eventually, they became good in colour but were poor in flavour and often bladdery.

Following the technical team's recommendation it was decided to experiment by letting the fruit ripen on the plant before it was picked and then fly it to England, a practice unknown at the time. The team managed to convince two growers to take part in the experiment. Despite a 40% increase in selling prices, caused by air freight costs, the quality of these tomatoes was so superior, both in taste and texture, that they received overwhelming acceptance resulting in a dramatic increase in sales. In the second year of the operation the company contracted 150 Boeing 707s fully laden with tomatoes— 72 hours from harvesting to the store counter. This breakthrough in quality was achieved with the co-operation of the growers as well as the wholehearted support of British Caledonian Airways who worked out special methods of loading and unloading quickly planes full of tomatoes.

## Buying Abroad When It Suits

Less than 10% of St Michael clothing is bought from abroad, primarily from high-income countries in Western Europe and Scandinavia, and the U.S.A. and Israel. It is bought from abroad when the company cannot obtain the merchandise in the U.K. in the quality and quantity it needs; but the company also actively encourages U.K. suppliers to develop similar lines to replace the imports in due course.

This, however, has not always been easy. For example, 'Italian shoes have an individual flair which is all their own. So do tailored fashions from West Germany. And the Finns have a way with anoraks.'

Nevertheless, the company firmly believes that there are areas where British manufacturers can explore and learn and match the standards of the best from the world. Buying abroad is sometimes seen as a stimulus to consider new ideas. It shows there is a market and gives an opportunity to move into it.

In 1971 Marks & Spencer decided to test men's suits. It could not find a suitable British manufacturer to supply the merchandise. So it went to Sweden, Italy and Finland in which the suit manufacturers were technically advanced, could produce the large quantities that it wanted and, above all, had the design flair, the 'knack', that cannot be learned overnight.

The test was a success, but in view of the company's policy of buying British wherever possible it tried to persuade some local manufacturers to make suits to the same technology. One of the first companies it approached was Isaac Dewhirst, who had been supplying Marks & Spencer since 1884. But at that time Dewhirst had never made a suit before; they were mainly shirt manufacturers.

We were then making men's and boys' shirts and ladies' blouses [recalled Sandy Dewhirst, chairman of the company]; we realized it was a risk and a lot of our competitors felt we would fall flat on our faces. But Marks said it was aiming to sell 20 million suits a year within 3–4 years and it seemed too good an opportunity to miss. About a fifth of our turnover now comes from suits.

Dewhirst sent a team of technical personnel to Sweden together with a Marks & Spencer technologist and, through the services of a consultant, studied the suit-making technology there. They discovered that although the basic skills and technology—spot-on accuracy in cutting and the fusing of interlinings— were the same for suits and shirts, there was a lot to be learnt in the design of the garment as well as the manufacturing processes required to produce it.

### How They Sold Their Soul to St. Michael

If they perform, the inmates of what has been described as 'pleasant imprisonment' find their production lines humming for years on end. Marks & Spencer helps them develop new products and advises them on sources of raw materials. If necessary it will sort out any major problems. And it will almost certainly ensure that the staff canteen and the lavatories are brought to St Michael's own immaculate standards.

All this is part of belonging to the Marks & Spencer family. It confers an aura which opens many other doors, not least that of the bank manager. Above all, Marks pays promptly. But the cachet of being a Marks supplier is earned by jumping to the Marks & Spencer tune, constantly calling at the Marks head office in London, giving a free run of the factory to St Michael inspectors and switching production runs at a moment's notice if a line is not selling fast enough.

In the end, St Michael agrees a detailed written specification with the garment manufacturer for each garment, right down to the number of stitches to the inch, and precise width of cuff, belt or hem. When production begins, two perfect specimens are removed and sealed in bags. One stays with the maker. The other goes to Marks & Spencer. The slightest deviation from these perfect examples is rated a reject by Marks & Spencer—whose inspectors tour the suppliers' production lines several times a week.

Even Marks & Spencer appreciates the need for a safety valve in the system. For instance, it does not actually insist that rejects have to be burnt—so a thriving trade has developed in goods that Marks & Spencer does not want. It is a market Marks & Spencer does not actively encourage, but is powerless to prevent. At the very least it is prepared to turn a blind eye. (One reject company, the Devon-based Seconds Out, runs 14 shops itself and wholesales to another 45. Its turnover was close to £6 million in 1983, 75% diverted from Marks & Spencer. And it looks it, despite the lack of a St Michael label.)

(Source: William Kay, 'How they sold their soul to St Michael', *Sunday Times*, 19 June 1983.)

On their return the technical personnel of both companies jointly designed and built a brand new factory in the north-east of England, using the most up-to-date machinery, and created jobs in an area of high unemployment. The technology was new to everyone in Britain, and manufacturing was carefully planned to enable both the Dewhirst and Marks & Spencer personnel to get used to its capability and requirements. The Marks & Spencer buying team was insistent that production began with lower price ranges. Very soon, however, they gained confidence and the ranges were moved upwards. Now suits made at Dewhirst match the standards of the best from abroad.

By 1981, scarcely 10 years from the launch of the suits, over 60% of them were British-made—and the proportion was growing.

## Dependence: Myth or Reality

One of the most frequently heard criticisms of Marks & Spencer is that its close collaboration with its suppliers renders the latter dependent on it for survival. It is also sometimes alleged that because of its powerful position in the trade the company is able to squeeze the profit margin of the manufacturer to its own advantage. Yet another complaint claims that because of the company's close involvement in the manufacturing process, it poses a permanent threat of vertical integration to the suppliers.

These are legitimate suspicions, and they may sound logical enough from the outside. Let us take a closer look at them in turn.

To say that the supplier is dependent on Marks & Spencer is only a half-truth; Marks & Spencer is equally dependent on the suppliers. It is a matter of mutual dependence, or interdependence, rather than a one-way dependence. Marks & Spencer has over 800 suppliers. On average it takes about 30% of the supplier's output. There are quite a few who are supplying Marks & Spencer close to 100% of their production. For instance, in the early eighties Dewhirst sold about 90% of its output to Marks & Spencer; Corah, about 75%; Sussman, close to 80%; Gent, over 95%. But the majority of the rest is supplying Marks & Spencer with roughly 30–50% of their production. To these manufacturers, Marks & Spencer is unquestionably their major buyer.

Except for the largest suppliers (such as Nottingham Manufacturing which is a major one, but Marks & Spencer only accounts for some 40% of its production) and some localized food manufacturers, generally speaking the higher percentage going to Marks & Spencer indicates higher reliability in quality and workmanship. These constitute the 'A-list' of Marks & Spencer suppliers and they are accorded some special privileges. For example, the company would attempt to ensure that the production capacity allocated to it is fully utilized. Marks & Spencer is as much concerned about reducing the overhead costs of these manufacturers as they would be their own; after all, the company's technical personnel is as intimately involved in controlling the costs of production as the manufacturers themselves; and once a manufacturer has proven its worth, it would become a Marks & Spencer pet source of supply and the two parties would try to maintain and develop the relationship for as long as possible.

Although Marks & Spencer does not have any financial stake in the manufacturers, it does invest very substantially in them in terms of technical support, management advice, and, above all, a thorough educational process to bring the manufacturer's outlook and operating philosophy close to that of Marks & Spencer. All of these, it must be emphasized, are a very long-term investment and only a long-term relationship, or partnership, as Marks & Spencer would call it, would guarantee a satisfactory return. To Marks & Spencer, the switching costs as far as suppliers are concerned are exceptionally high relative to other retailers—and to this extent Marks & Spencer is in fact more dependent on its suppliers than most retailers. The relationship between Marks & Spencer and the supplier is not simply 'almost like a marriage'. Depending on which culture one is referring to, it could be a lot more than a marriage.

To put the dependence issue in perspective, it can be said that both the supplier and Marks & Spencer are dependent on each other, and it is fruitless to identify who is the more dependent. The important thing is that this dependence, or interdependence, cannot be understood in the conventional sense; it must be located within the larger context of collaborative relationship in which the two parties are involved. From Marks & Spencer's perspective the suppliers—along with the raw materials suppliers, the head office staff, and the stores staff—constitute but one of the important links in a single process of satisfying the ultimate customer. All of these are interdependent on one another; they are all part of a 'joint effort' for a common purpose.

### Feeling the Squeeze?

Another oft-heard allegation is that Marks & Spencer, because of its dominant position, is able to control and squeeze the profit margin of the suppliers. Again, although there is no question that Marks & Spencer has much leverage on the profit margin of the suppliers, such an influence has had to be seen in perspective.

There is absolutely no doubt that Marks & Spencer is extremely demanding on its suppliers. It exerts a tremendous pressure on the suppliers to make them as efficient as possible. In particular it never allows any compromise on quality and, even in difficult times, it never tolerates the lowering of quality in order to

produce to a price. At the same time, it wants to be sure that suppliers do make
a profit, if only because this is the primary condition for sustaining a healthy
and progressive operation. What is more, the suppliers need the profit to
enable them continuously to upgrade the production facilities and to finance
technical innovation and business expansion. As Director John Salisse has put
it:[10]

> Our suppliers have a responsibility towards us to produce high-quality merchandise
> which will sell freely because of its good value. But we have an equal responsibility to
> our suppliers. Our responsibility is to ensure that, if a manufacturer or producer is
> efficient, then he also makes a profit. It is essential that our manufacturers make
> profits which they can plough back into their businesses, to buy the latest machinery,
> pay proper wages, implement decent staff amenities, introduce the newest technical
> aids and expand their plants to meet our increasing requirements and pay their
> shareholders.

A Marks & Spencer contract, to be sure, guarantees nothing except continuity
of production and sales. It is up to the supplier to exploit the opportunity. Over
the years many of them have grown into substantial and highly profitable
businesses. Judging from the very long-term association between the company
and its suppliers, it is hard to believe that the latter are poorly treated by Marks
& Spencer. Dewhirst, which was the very first supplier to Marks & Spencer,
has been around for 100 years. There are over 60 suppliers who have supplied
Marks & Spencer for over 50 years, and more than 100 for over 30 years. These
100-plus account for over half of the textile turnover, and among them are
acknowledged leaders in their field.

Association with the St Michael label carries with it an unusual distinction.
'When you tell someone that you supply Marks & Spencer, they look at you
with new respect because they know you have to be good', claims David
Sinigaglia, managing director of Airfix Industries. It is hardly an exaggeration
to say that being a Marks & Spencer supplier is no less than having received a
charter in professional excellence. Indeed, as early as the late sixties, phrases
like 'recommended by Marks & Spencer', 'Marks & Spencer quality', 'on the
Marks & Spencer list' became generally accepted as guarantees of high quality
throughout the industry.

Finally, as far as the threat of vertical integration is concerned, this is easily
dismissed as a groundless speculation. Unlike some major retail chains,
especially those in the U.S.A. who own a high proportion of the suppliers,
Marks & Spencer has made it very clear in words and in deeds that it has no
intention whatsoever to have a financial stake in their suppliers. As one senior
executive has put it, 'We believe in sticking to our list. We are retailers. This is
a big enough job. Our observation is that the man who mixes his business
cannot do as good a job as one who sticks to one business. Besides', he adds,
'the public wouldn't like it if we became too large and too powerful!'

## Notes

1. London, 1976.
2. The discussion that follows is adapted from her article, 'Manufacturer/retailer conflict', in *Marketing*, August 1976.
3. 'Manufacturer/retailer conflict', *ibid.*, p. 9.
4. Cf. Lord Sieff, 'How Marks & Spencer co-operates with its suppliers: a joint effort for a common purpose'. Address delivered to the Australian Retailers' Association, 25 September 1978.
5. Israel Sieff, *Memoirs*, p. 151.
6. *St. Michael: A History of Marks & Spencer, op. cit.*, p. 131.
7. *Ibid.*, p. 219.
8. *Ibid.*, p. 195.
9. 'How Marks & Spencer brings its shoppers the best', *Design*, December 1979.
10. John Salisse, 'Bonds stronger than contracts', *Chelwood Review*, January 1981.

CHAPTER 6

# More Than a Retailer—
# 'A Manufacturer Without Factories'

At the present moment, there is probably general agreement between most organized bodies of opinion that British industry and the British economy as a whole are in drastic and urgent need of reorganization and modernization; there is probably also general agreement that the most important factor in modernization is a *speedier and larger application to industry of the results of scientific and technological advance.*

Such agreement is no doubt admirable; and so are the energies devoted to persuading both management and labour to recognize the pressing need of modernization. But the application of technology to industry is not merely a matter of persuasion or of changing people's minds; *it is a matter of detailed and concrete knowledge, of practical judgement based on measurable scientific data, of the ability to assign to the specialist and the technologist an effective part in the process of production and of creating the conditions in which it is possible for them to do so.*

It is not unreasonable to say that in the post-war years it was precisely this which Marks & Spencer achieved and that this made of it a business whose methods are deserving of detailed study by the whole of British industry.

Goronwy Rees

## The Technological Approach to Retailing

I have made constant reference in previous chapters to the so-called 'technological' approach to retailing characteristic of the Marks & Spencer operation. I have also underlined the fact that the Marks & Spencer approach entails a revolutionary link between mass manufacturing and mass retailing. Traditionally, retailing has been considered as a low-technology industry, and indeed this has remained so for most retailers. But with Marks & Spencer, because of its obsessive concern about quality from the raw material stage right down to the sales counter, it becomes a highly technology-intensive operation. Thus, unlike most other retailers whose business is primary to 'trade', Marks &

Spencer has to demand from itself the ability to master sufficient scientific and technical knowledge so as to ensure 'a speedier and larger application to industry of the results of scientific and technological advance'.

In fact, the history of Marks & Spencer since the thirties is closely bound up with the history of scientific–technological development bearing on the production of mass-consumption merchandise. The co-architects, Simon Marks and Israel Sieff, were imbued with the conviction that the application of modern technology could confer great benefits on manufacturers and retailers alike, and that these benefits could be translated into reduction in price and improvements in quality. It was their vision that science and technology could play a significant part in improving the material conditions of human life, and that the joint efforts of the manufacturer and the retailer could speed up the otherwise prolonged process between a fundamental discovery and the moment when the results of its practical application become available to the consumer.

Such a vision may be regarded as a product of the peculiar brand of practical idealism that inspired the two young men in their business activities. But it is doubtful, as Goronwy Rees observes, that they would have been able to arrive at so clear and confident a view if it had not been for the influence of Chaim Weizmann, the eminent scientist and statesman, whom they had first befriended in Manchester and with whom they remained in the closest association. Chaim Weizmann, a distinguished scientist of international fame, who later became the first President of the State of Israel, had made a vital contribution to the field of chemistry during the British war effort in 1914–18. There could have been no one better qualified to teach his two disciples the revolutionary possibilities involved for industry in the scientific discoveries which were being made in their own time. One of these, which subsequently was to revolutionize their own business, was made immediately after World War I when in 1920 pure fundamental research arrived, as a result of X-ray analysis, at the concept of the chain molecular nature of fibre structure and thus demonstrated in principle that it was possible to create entirely synthetic fibres. Israel Sieff has recalled in his memoirs:

The twenties [saw] a rapid development in the application of technology to the production of goods, especially of textiles. The war gave this a great impetus. New techniques much increased the productivity of labour, and scientific discoveries made possible the creation of new types and ranges of cheap manufactured goods on a scale never known before.

The combination of these factors would obviously have suited Marks & Spencer in any event but we were very much guided and inspired to take advantage of them by the influence which Dr. Weizmann exercised upon us. It was not only that his highly specialized knowledge as an industrial chemist enabled him to advise us about new developments—he was, for instance, instructing us in the possibilities of synthetic fibres long before they were an actuality—but that he schooled us in general terms in the habit of *applying a scientific attitude of mind to the problems of industrial production.*

**The Scientist and the Executive**

A significant influence on the development of the textile laboratories and of the Merchandise Development Department was Mr. Eric Kann, who in 1935 was appointed head of the textile laboratory and later of the Merchandise Development Department. Mr. Kann, a refugee from Nazi Germany, had what was then a rare combination of scientific training and practical business experience, and before leaving Germany had been employed in the German chain-store firm of Samuel Schocken.

When Mr. Kann arrived in England, with an introduction from Schocken, as a refugee in transit to the United States, [Lord Marks] took him on a conducted tour of one of the company's stores. In the course he asked Mr. Kann's opinion of the merchandise displayed on the counters. Mr. Kann replied, in an expressive German phrase, that he did not think much of it. 'So why don't you stay and help us to improve it?' said the chairman.

The story is revealing because it indicates how eagerly, in the thirties, Marks & Spencer enlisted the help of men and of methods which they thought might assist them in improving the quality of their merchandise.

It is, today, a commonplace that industry needs to call in the skills of the scientist and the technician if it is to be successful under modern conditions; moreover, that those who possess these skills must have the opportunity of exercising a direct influence on business decisions.

Even today, however, it is a commonplace to which many firms find it difficult, or are unwilling, to give practical application, for the problem of integrating the scientist or technician with the business executive, so that the varied skills of each can be most effectively employed, is in itself a difficult one. One of the most remarkable features of the development of Marks & Spencer during the thirties was the effort they devoted to trying to solve this problem and the measure of success they achieved at a time when many firms, particularly in the retail trade, were not even aware that it existed . . .

They set about solving it in a highly effective and empirical way . . . and they were helped in finding a solution by the extremely flexible nature of their head office organization, which depended essentially on the working of loosely constituted teams and groups in which the free exchange of ideas and information was encouraged. In such an organization the scientist or technician, however different his outlook from that of an executive, could find his way more easily than in one constituted on more strictly hierarchical lines. In trying tentatively at first to enlist the aid of science and technology in their business, Marks & Spencer during the thirties learned ways of employing the specialist to the best advantage and acquired a fund of experience which was to be of immense importance to the future of the firm.

(Extracted from Goronwy Rees, *St. Michael: A History of Marks & Spencer*, *op. cit.*, pp. 146–7.)

Under his influence we did not see ourselves as mere shopkeepers. We came to regard ourselves as a kind of technical laboratory. We felt it was one of our functions to provide our suppliers with expert technical information about the new materials and processes which the advance of technology was making available. We saw ourselves as, in our limited way, production engineers, industrial chemists, laboratory technicians. We learned to exercise an active influence on production generally, and on the textile industry in particular.[1]

Since those days Marks & Spencer has gradually built up a team of qualified scientists and technologists and extended and modernized laboratories in which new materials, processes and finishes could be developed. Apart from its own team of technical personnel, the company also actively sought the service of outside research institutes and began to establish an advisory panel of distinguished scientists of international reputation, among them Nobel Prize winners.

## The Man of Science According to St Michael

The scientific and technical team at Marks & Spencer do not carry out any form of pure research as such; they are kept abreast of its results through the extensive contact they maintain with research institutes and the research departments of the industries which supply its basic raw materials. In its technical services, the company aims at:

avoiding the distinction which is often made between the academic and the industrial research worker, the former working for the sake of knowledge only, the latter for such knowledge as may be commercially applied. We need a third type, a scientist who has preferably carried out research work himself, knows the methods and understands its place and function in development and production, but who feels the urge to apply the results of research in industry, and who possesses the technical and commercial training to do so in collaboration with our suppliers. More than scientific and technical competence is therefore required; the human qualities which inspires confidence, collaboration and acceptance of our guidance, and the discriminating judgement as to whether the scientific approach is likely to solve or complicate problems.[2]

In Marks & Spencer the scientists and technologists are not advisers or consultants, 'back-room boys' who operate in mysterious isolation. They are in no way performing a staff function as most people from the outside would expect. Instead they are fully integrated into the commercial organization of the business, and are active and indispensable members of the buying departments.

The technical personnel in Marks & Spencer constitute an integral part of the buying team. Unlike the 'buyer' in most other retail stores, the Marks & Spencer buying team has a strong technical component. Indeed, given the composition and the nature of work of this team, it is hardly appropriate to consider it as performing the 'buying' function in the conventional sense.

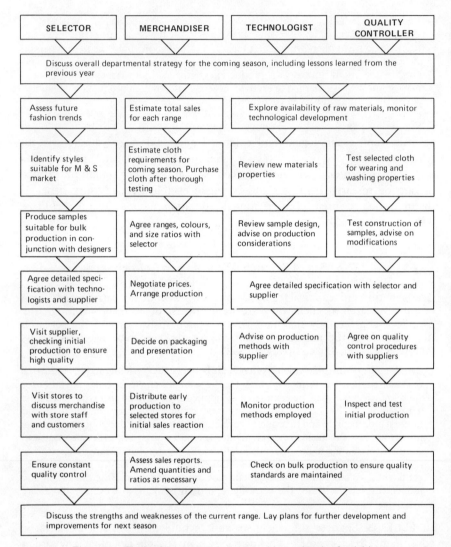

Figure 10    The buying team: typical composition and cycle of activities

Figure 10 gives a breakdown of the team's structure. Here we see the crucial part played by the technical personnel in the procurement process. Although it is apparent that there is clear division of labour among the members of the team, it should however be stressed that the technical members were trained and encouraged to become 'merchandise-conscious' themselves; that is to say, to have continually in mind the needs and tastes of the customer.

This is in fact a primary condition for the effective contribution of their technical knowledge to the business. In an in-house study of the function of the technologist in the production of fashion goods, it was reported thus:

A creative development begins with a vague idea of what is wanted and a clear idea of what is not. The vague idea is crystallized in a series of failures until the object is achieved. To make a significant contribution to a development the technologist must have in mind the same vague idea as the commercial executive and as vague ideas are difficult to communicate, he should acquire for himself the same background of ideas and experience. Such an identity of experience *cannot* be formed by periodical meetings and the technologist should immerse himself in the life of the departments in the office and in the stores. He should share the experiences which form the ideas and possibly may help to provoke them.

When he sees what is needed, he can use his knowledge of manufacturing techniques to formulate a development programme in which he works with the manufacturer from his integrated position within the business. There can be no watertight compartments at any stage. The technical problems involved may be trivial or difficult; the technologist's contribution is the same in either event because it is measured in relation to the business rather than to his own expertise.[3]

---

**A Nation of Manufacturers?**

In 1947, at a time when British industry had not yet recovered from the effects of war, my firm found it necessary to establish a production engineering department. The department was designed to assist our manufacturers in the progressive modernization of their plant, and to adapt themselves to the latest technical advances.

Production engineering may seem a surprising activity for a retailer, but we found it absolutely essential to create a department capable of advising our manufacturers on factory administration, lay-out and production problems. This approach is an important aspect of our campaign to achieve better and better values.

The truth is that, whereas once Napoleon may have been right in his jibe that we were a nation of shopkeepers, today we need to be a nation of manufacturers.

(Lord Marks, excerpts from his Address in the House of Lords Debate on the National Productivity Year, July 1962.)

---

## Specification Buying

Marks & Spencer is known for its very special way of buying, which is sometimes referred to as 'specification buying'. Largely as a result of the technologist in the buying team, it becomes possible for the company to insist that manufacturers should work to standards which can be narrowly defined, and this entails the drawing up of specifications which lay down in exact detail the requirements to which manufacturers must conform both in respect of the materials employed and of the processes applied to them.

# Marks & Spencer

Figure 11  Sample technical specifications form.

---

**MARKS AND SPENCER LIMITED**

TECHNICAL SPECIFICATION FOR FULLY FASHIONED KNITWEAR

---

FINAL GARMENT COMPOSITION: _____

SPEC. NO.: _____

---

YARN (Type, Dye Route, Fibre Denier)     :
*(Where applicable)*

    SUPPLIER     :

YARN SPECIFICATION NO.     :

---

MACHINE (Gauge and Type)     :

    BODIES & SLEEVES     :

    TRIMS     :

---

BASIC FABRIC QUALITY NO.

| KNITTING DETAILS: | RIB SET-OUT | STITCH LENGTH (TOLERANCE ÷ 2½%) | TOTAL COURSES | DOUBLING FREQUENCY | |
|---|---|---|---|---|---|
| Body & Sleeve Panel | — | | — | | |
| Waist Rib | | | | Every | Stitch |
| | | | | ( | Needle) |
| Cuff Rib | | | | Every | Stitch |
| | | | | ( | Needle) |

Trimming and Accessories

*Excluding set-up, welt and slack course.

---

FINISHED FABRIC QUALITY

| | | | |
|---|---|---|---|
| Body & Sleeve Panel | : | C.P. 3 cm/10 cm | W.P. 3 cm/10 cm |
| Waist Ribs | : | C.P. 3 cm/10 cm | W.P. 3 cm/10 cm |
| Cuff Rib | : | C.P. 3 cm/10 cm | W.P. 3 cm/10 cm |
| Trims | : | | |

---

GARMENT MAKE-UP DETAILS

SEWING SPECIFICATION NO.:

| | | |
|---|---|---|
| Seaming method | : | Threads |
| First linking | : Single/Twin Needle | M/C Gauge |
| Collar/Neck Trim attaching method | : | M/C Gauge (if linked) |
| Neck Neaten method – Back Neck | : | Vee Mitre |
| Polo/Cuff Closure method | : | Threads |
| Buttonholes – Lockstitch/Chainstitch | : Gimp and Threads | |
| Stole application method | : | End Finish |
| Pocket application method | : | Reinforcement |
| Belt/Loops – End Finish | : | Loop Inspection method |

HO 188 - 7/78

MINIMUM NUMBER OF RIBS/
NEEDLES PER KNITTED PANEL         :

                    SIZES        :

BODY

Waist Ribs                        :
Needles at Commencement           :
Needles at Waist                  :

SLEEVES

Cuff Ribs                         :
Needles at Commencement           :
Needles at Widest                 :

TRIMMINGS & ACCESSORIES           :

---

FINISHING        FINISHER         :

                 PROCESS          :

PRESSING
                 1st PRESS   Yes/No          Framed  Yes/No

                 FINAL PRESS      :

                 Type of Press    :
                 Framed Yes/No    :

---

PERFORMANCE STANDARDS             :     As the Marks and Spencer Standards and Test Methods Book

Colour Fastness                   :     Code No. C.F.

Physical performance              :     Code No. K

---

Weight per dozen                  :     Kilogrammes

---

SIGNED    Manufacturer _____ Date _____

          Technologist _____ Date _____

As an illustration, the blank form in Figure 11 indicates some of the technical specifications that would be agreed upon by the manufacturer and the technologist. The document is usually supplemented by a series of pre-established standards/test methods of specific items of raw materials and/or production processes. To be sure, most retailers above a certain size also furnish detailed specifications to the manufacturers for the merchandise ordered. But perhaps what distinguishes Marks & Spencer from most other retailers is their thoroughness in the preparation of these specifications and the comprehensive effort to ensure strict adherence to the agreed standards.

In order to carry out his task, the technologist is seldom found in the office. Apart from visting the stores, he spends a tremendous amount of his time at the suppliers' plants. He works closely with the manufacturer's technical personnel and is readily available for consultation and advice. To Marks & Spencer, a manufacturer supplying merchandise to the company is regarded almost as part of the operation. The technologist, who speaks the same languages as the technical personnel of the manufacturer, provides the crucial link between the latter and the company.

The importance of this last point cannot be overstated. As a retailer, Marks & Spencer is unique in having a team of over 350 technologists at its service. It is in the light of this that Goronwy Rees proclaimed that

> the application of technology to industry is not merely a matter of persuasion or of changing people's minds; it is a matter of detailed and concrete knowledge, of practical judgement based on measurable scientific data, of the ability to assign to the specialist and the technologist an effective part in the process of production and of creating the conditions in which it is possible for them to do so.

### The Basic Principles

The 'technological' approach to merchandising was first adopted for textile products, which had constituted the bulk of stores' turnover before World War II. Gradually the same underlying principles were extended to the procurement of all other product lines. In the early fifties, when the Food Development Department was being established in anticipation of great expansion of the food business, it was decided that the new department should perform the same role that the Merchandise Development Department had performed for textiles after its establishment in 1936. In particular, it was called upon to ensure that the company's food products conformed, both as to their materials and as to the methods by which they were produced, packed, and distributed, to the most up-to-date principles of food science and technology.

It was at this moment that the company undertook to spell out the basic principles according to which the department should function. These principles epitomize the company's fundamental approach to merchandising:

(1) The merchandising of a limited range of products in the early stages of development to ensure that both the merchandising departments and the food technologists concentrated their efforts on raising and establishing the standards of a number of basic products before advancing further.

(2) Close co-operation at all levels between the merchandisers and the technologists, and equally between them and the company's food suppliers.

(3) Development of close, personal and friendly relations with suppliers, so that they would welcome the company's technologists working with them on the factory floor on the basis of complete frankness and pooling of 'know-how' and information.

(4) The use of specified, mutually agreed, raw materials and packaging materials.

(5) Co-operation with selected manufacturers of raw materials to develop new materials and to improve the quality of existing ones.

(6) Production of goods of agreed standards of quality to agreed specifications by agreed production methods.

(7) Production from clean factories under clean conditions.

(8) Safeguarding the freshness of food products by allocating to each line a maximum life from production to 'sell-out'.

(9) Safeguarding the safety of the more perishable foods by the use of specific raw materials and reliable processing techniques.

(10) Encouragement of suppliers to co-operate with the company's technologist on the development of new lines, on methods of production, and on quality and hygienic standards.

(11) A spirit of refusal to 'accept things as they are', of applying scientific enquiry in its daily work, of asking 'how and why' and following up the answers as quickly as possible.

(12) Working to a system of agreed priorities, without trying to do everything at once, with trials on a prototype scale preceding any attempt at large-scale production.

All these may sound straightforward enough. As applied to the food industry in the early post-war period it was something of a revolution. Suppliers were often sceptical about the commercial value of such principles, and doubtful whether so technical an approach could be applied to food products. It was only with time, persuasion and painstaking educational work that they gradually came to accept this novel relationship. With hindsight, it might be said that the above statement of principles represented the blueprint of the methods by which the company expanded and developed its food business after the war, and the much-noted success it has achieved in this area is perhaps a vindication of the soundness of its approach.

## The Ubiquitous Technologist

We have noted that Marks & Spencer is sometimes being referred to as both 'arrogant' and 'humble': humble, because its whole system is geared to serve; arrogant, because it always knows best. In its relationship with the suppliers, no areas of the latter's operation are outside the company's meticulous attention as long as they might have a bearing on the quality of the merchandise. The following excerpts from a 12-page *Checklist for the Safe and Effective Use of Cleaning Materials in Food Factories*—issued to the food suppliers—are indicative of the ubiquity of the technologist on the supplier's shop floor:

### Bulk storage

Materials should be kept in a separate supervised area of the factory store or in isolated locked storage. In all cases there should be physical separation from food packaging, raw materials or products. Different products should be separately stacked and as a principle solids should be away from liquids.

### Shelf life

Many products have a definite shelf life. This information should be obtained from the manufacturers. Liquids generally have a shorter life than solids. Unstabilized sodium hypochlorite deteriorates quickly and should not be held for more than 6 weeks. Certain detergents are denatured by freezing—heated storage may be necessary in winter. All cleaning materials should be stock rotated.

### Issue of materials

Production and technical management should specify the use and allocation of materials to each particular department. The relevant details should be held in each working area. Issues should be made on a weekly basis to the user department. If products are to be decanted/weighed into smaller lots, clearly marked containers must be used. However, care must be taken, if using several coloured products from mixed sources, to avoid confusing similar coloured products of differing properties. The risk of this confusion with different manufacturers' products is very real and management must be aware of the potential hazards and safety precautions.

### Type of materials

Only approved food factory cleaning materials should be purchased. A list of manufacturers who in our experience are able to provide a competent service is attached. Janitorial disinfectant products should not be used anywhere on site.

### Control in use

Many cleaning materials are used over-strength, or wasted by lack of proper application. Most manufacturers will provide dosing equipment, dispensing aids, scoops, measures etc., to assist in better control. Dosing equipment is strongly recommended for:

(a) equipment wash points
(b) mechanical washers (liquid peristaltic pumps are preferred)
(c) tray washers (liquid peristaltic pumps also preferred).

Test kits or indicator papers should be used to determine the safe working life of materials in use. Specific test kits are available for chlorine, quats, tego, acid and alkaline detergents.

Routine checks should be

conducted daily on sterilizer strengths associated with the production of high-risk foods e.g. delicatessen products.

Safety factors

Copies of the manufacturers' safety data should be held in the factory and available at all times. Many of the accidents with cleaning materials occur outside normal working hours.

A detailed component list for all cleaning materials should be sought from each manufacturer. This information should be held with the safety and first aid officer.

## Notes

1. *Memoirs*, pp. 146–7.
2. Quoted in Rees, *op. cit.*, pp. 198–9.
3. Quoted in Rees, *op. cit.*, p. 198.

CHAPTER 7

# Company-wide Quality Control: Surpassing the Japanese?

We thought how we could define quality. The simple definition is that if the clothes we sell aren't good enough to be worn and the food to be eaten by our directors and their families, then they're not good enough for the customers.

Lord Sieff

Quality—like liberty—not only requires eternal vigilance, but for responsible organizations it is indivisible. A belief in quality spills over into all areas of the business.

M&S director Harry Shepherd

St Michael has long established itself as a symbol of quality in the high streets. But where do quality products come from? The following may be a typical response from a Marks & Spencer executive: 'Quality is never an accident. It is always the result of intelligent effort. There must be the will to produce a superior thing.' This chapter will examine Marks & Spencer's much-acclaimed quality control effort. Again, I shall demonstrate that there is hardly anything unique or mysterious about its success; it is primarily the result of a disciplined and systematic pursuit of a set of clearly formulated quality objectives.

## Quality Control in International Perspective

Over the last decade there has been a growing interest in the issue of quality control among international management circles. A major contributing factor has been the very impressive performance of Japanese industries in this area. In their attempt to confront the Japanese challenge, enterprises in the West began to study the Japanese quality control system and at the same time reflect on their own systems. Taking into consideration the Western and Japanese experience together, it is possible to distinguish four major concepts of quality management which also broadly represent four overlapping stages of develop-

96

ment of quality control activities. They are: (1) quality control (QC), (2) quality assurance (QA), (3) total quality control (TQC), and (4) company-wide quality control (CWQC).

## Quality Control (QC)

'Quality control' is the simplest and earliest concept referring to those activities whereby the products emerging from the production line are checked or tested against prescribed specifications. Essentially, a quality control system consists of three elements: (a) establishing standards: determining performance, reliability, and cost standards, (b) appraising conformance: comparing the conformance of the manufactured product with the standards, and (c) corrective action: taking corrective action when standards are not met, such as rework, reject.

## Quality Assurance (QA)

'Quality assurance' encompasses the concept of quality control but it goes one step further. In addition to identifying the defects of the manufactured products, it also attempts to trace systematically the origins of these defects and to take appropriate action to eliminate them at their source. The emphasis is on the prevention of all possible causes of defects along the entire production process, so as to assure that the product will be made to designed standards right from the first time. Quality assurance represents a more positive approach towards quality management than 'quality control' which is primarily an attempt to control quality *after* the event.

## Total Quality Control (TQC)

All too often, quality control is regarded as the responsibility of quality control/quality assurance departments or production departments. In fact, however, quality is rarely simply a matter of the shopfloor. A host of other departments—purchasing, marketing, R&D, engineering, personnel, etc.— in the organization have a direct or indirect impact on quality performance.

'Total quality control' recognizes that sustained quality performance cannot be achieved by the work of one or two departments alone, but must involve the concerted and integrated effort of a large number of, if not all, the functions in an organization. The driving force must originate from the top which directs and coordinates the institution of a total quality system. Some of the major elements of such a system are indicated in Figure 12.

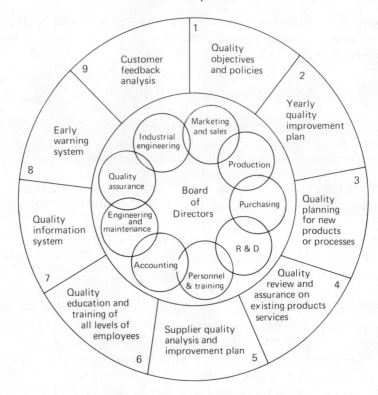

Figure 12    Total quality control (TQC)

## Company-wide Quality Control (CWQC)

TQC represents a major advance over QA and QC; 'company-wide quality control' goes yet another step further. It encompasses the TQC concept but it has one additional emphasis; namely, that quality control not only involves all the departments concerned, it also entails the commitment and active participation of all the *employees* in the departments concerned. The participation may take many forms and one of the most well-tried systems has been the now internationally renowned quality control circles (QCC), originated in the U.S.A. but most widely employed in Japan.

On the international scene, Japan has progressed the furthest in this system. It had had only primitive quality control systems in the early post-war years, but in the past few decades it has gone through the other stages in rapid succession. The West has long been leading the world in quality control and quality assurance, and it has pioneered total quality control. But most companies have marked time either at quality assurance or total quality control stages; only a tiny handful have introduced something bearing the semblance of company-wide quality control.

Let us now review where Marks & Spencer stands.

---

**Quality in the Boardroom**

The following is an excerpt from a keynote address by Marks & Spencer Director Lewis R. Goodman to an international seminar organized by the European Organization for Quality Control, London, November 1977:

I accepted the challenge to address you mainly because the title intrigued me. The theme 'Quality in the Boardroom' forced me to examine in depth and commit to paper one of Marks & Spencer's major preoccupations.

A cornerstone of our business is quality. All discussions about type and cost of merchandise inevitably involve discussions about quality. All good Marks & Spencer executives accept that repetition of fundamental principles is necessary and does not bring contempt. The quality ethos can only be sustained as an essential part of company conscience if it is constantly seen to be a total commitment of the Chairman and Chief Executive.

Throughout the 50 years of Marks & Spencer as a public company, no year has gone by when the Annual Report to Shareholders did not contain a significant paragraph or reference to this aspect of our philosophy and policy. To quote them all would take up the whole of my allotted time. For a glimpse of how the quality theme evolved it might well be interesting to hear five extracts on how succeeding Chairmen have expressed it over this half-century:

(1) In 1927, the year after we became a public company, Mr Simon Marks said, '. . . we believe we are filling a long-felt want in providing sound-quality goods'.

(2) Immediately after the war, Sir Simon Marks in 1946 said, 'We shall continue our policy of laying stress upon quality and design, and of offering our customers the best possible values [post-war] conditions permit.'

(3) Lord Marks passed away in 1964 and his brother-in-law, Lord Sieff, said in 1966, 'Quality control, which begins with the raw materials, extends right up to the counter. . . . The St Michael brand has become a hallmark of good quality, not only in this country but in countries abroad.'

(4) When his brother, Mr J. Edward, was in the chair in 1971, he declared that 'We strive for perfection in St Michael quality', and pointed out that 'Quality failures are a significant cost factor in industry.'

(5) In 1977, our present Chairman, Sir Marcus Sieff, stressed, as he has so often done before, the human element in quality achievement: 'The maintenance of high quality standards depends, first and foremost, on our most senior executives and those of our suppliers understanding the importance of proper quality control systems. It is tempting during a period of high inflation and rising costs to cut corners and reduce quality control procedures. This is a false economy and leads to increased production of poor-quality, unacceptable goods which adds to costs. High quality depends on

everyone understanding its importance right down the line.'

Although this may be regarded as constant 'nagging' it is also to be heard as the constant repetition of unvarnished truth. Implementation down the line through control systems or technology can only succeed if it is known by everyone to be a fundamental commitment at the top.

An examination of last year's Annual Reports of the top 25 British companies reveals that only one other and ourselves thought this aspect of their endeavours to be important enough for mention.

(From Lewis R. Goodman, 'Better Human Relations for Better Quality', EOQC Quality, Official publication of European Organization for Quality Control, part 3, 1978, pp. 5–6.)

## Quality Control at Marks & Spencer: The Beginnings

The first systematic attempt at quality control undertaken by Marks & Spencer began in 1935 when the company established its own textile laboratory. It was at first a small department and employed only a few qualified technicians, but it was significant as a first step towards calling in the aid of science in the company's effort to attain high standards of quality. Initially, its task was the important but limited one of testing samples of merchandise coming from different manufacturers in order to assure uniformity of quality, to detect faults and where possible trace them to their sources. This was a rudimentary form of quality control and it was felt that it could provide an important tool for ensuring that the vast volume of merchandise sold across the counters would conform to the high and uniform standards the company was committed to achieve.

Despite the impressive work carried out by the laboratory personnel, the results had not been very satisfactory. The major reason was that such an effort was basically control *after* the event which could do no more, at best, than detect and eliminate faults that had already been committed. A more active and thorough approach was felt to be in order and the search began for a form of quality control which could be exercised *before* the event, that is to say, on the factory floor itself, and to persuade the manufacturers to exercise such control for themselves.

## From Quality Control to Quality Assurance

Towards the end of the thirties the company began to experiment with drawing up precise specifications to suppliers establishing in detail not only the quantity, quality and types of material to be employed, but where necessary the method of manufacture. It was not an easy task and initially it met with strong resistance and suspicion from the manufacturers. This was the beginnings of the expanded role of the technical personnel who would act as 'a friend, consultant and adviser to the suppliers'.

In one of his annual reports to the shareholders in this period, Lord Marks remarked:

> The arguments I have brought forward for the more intimate co-operation of the [raw material] producer, manufacturer, and distributor as one of the means of increasing the country's prosperity are gathered from our own business experience. As far as practicable your directors follow closely improvements in machinery and processes. They survey all stages of production from the basic raw materials to the finished goods, and stimulate manufacturers to adopt such facilities and economies as modern techniques make available.[1]

The setting up of the Merchandise Development Department in 1936 was an important step in the direction of quality assurance. The years that followed witnessed a major expansion of the technical staff; specialist technical officers were attached to the department, which had the specific task of improving the quality of Marks & Spencer merchandise. The department was composed both of commercial executives and highly qualified technologists working in close association, and had at its disposal the results achieved in the textile laboratory. It pioneered and developed what was subsequently known as 'specification buying'; that is, it was concerned not only with testing and analysing the finished products delivered by the suppliers, but with prescribing and specifying the standards to which they should conform, both in materials and the processes employed in their production.

This quality assurance approach to quality management was most apparent with regard to textile products which constituted the bulk of the company's turnover in those days. The new department became intensively absorbed in the problems which are inherent in the production of textile merchandise by modern mass-production methods, in questions of colour fastness and shrinkage, in the investigation of basic raw materials and their availability, in the structure of textile clothes, the character of yarn and dyeing processes. The results were embodied in specifications which were in effect a series of directives to suppliers. Moreover, since manufacturing techniques affect quality, the department was interested not only in what was produced but how it was produced. It was in this sense that the chairman could say that the company 'endeavoured to survey all stages of production from the basic raw materials to the finished goods'.

Given its 'technological' approach to merchandising, the vigorous efforts that the company expanded on 'specification buying' are thus hardly surprising. It is essentially a form of 'quality assurance', albeit executed in a remarkably comprehensive and thorough fashion.

## Quality is Never an Accident

An impressive array of equipment at the Marks & Spencer head office in Baker Street provides the behind-the-scenes control which is instrumental for assuring the quality reputation of St Michael.

Laboratory work usually starts long before a garment is even designed, let alone produced in prototype. Possible fabrics—perhaps still in the earliest sample stage, not yet in manufacture—are assessed for their wear and washing qualities. Strength is important, so there is a pulling test to show tensile strength and another to indicate resistance to tearing. Shrinkage, both in washing or dry cleaning and in the steam pressing which completes the manufacturing process, is also assessed, as is crease-resistance. The latter is an awkward area, for a fabric which instantly springs out of creases caused in wear presents almost insurmountable difficulties in manufacture.

Abrasion resistance of the fabric is another concern. It is tested with a machine that rubs the fabric against itself or against another cloth. A more dramatic device is employed if the fabric is a type which might snag. Metal balls with sharp projections, looking just like medieval mace-heads, are dragged across its surface, simulating the roughest wear.

Then, following those unfortunate experiences in the past, colour-fastness testing is exhaustive. The fabric goes into hot water, cold water, is soaked, is left damp against a variety of other fabrics, is rubbed against them. Colour-fastness to light is also checked, with the highest standards expected of furnishing fabrics and those used for swimwear. But everyday garments, too, are expected to survive considerable exposure to sunlight.

One of the darkrooms in the laboratory contains an ingenious device invaluable in pre-production testing. It is a light-box which simulates the different lights—store light, daylight, domestic artificial light—in which a Marks & Spencer garment is likely to be seen. And it shows up immediately if the buttons on an olive cardigan, a perfect match in daylight, will glow a clashing emerald under a fluorescent tube.

For some tests there is simply no alternative to slow, dull human grind. Assessing the down content of a feather and down quilt, which must by law be 15% down, is one example. A 5-gram sample of filling is put into a special sealed box; the technician pushes her hands through close-fitting wristbands into it and, feather by feather, scrap of down by scrap of down, separates the two constituents into different containers. It takes hours of meticulous work, just for that tiny sample.

Quality is never an accident. The company believes that it boils down to just this: attention to the smallest detail in producing the goods and rigid and constant checking to maintain these standards. Only then are the goods awarded the St Michael label they deserve.

## How Total Can Quality Control Be?

Even with the immense effort in quality assurance, it by no means follows that the company's quality objectives can thus be confidently achieved. There are, as could be expected, quality failures at Marks & Spencer. One of the measures of this is the quantity of defective goods returned to the suppliers, who, incidentally, are fully charged for them. In the late seventies the proportion of goods returned to manufacturers was about 1 –2% of total production. In engineering terms this may well be regarded as an acceptable figure. Measured in absolute terms it accounted for lost sales of about £10 million just in textiles alone. The company deplores, as Director Lewis R. Goodman has pointed out, 'any attitude which attempts to justify doing nothing because at a "certain" minimum level it is "cost-ineffective" to do something. With that attitude of mind', he adds, 'there is only one way for failures to go—up.'[2]

Back in the sixties the company began a major effort in monitoring quality. In 1965 six of the major stores were asked to send to head office all faulty goods identified by the sales assistants or returned by customers. Mounted as an exhibition in one office, it made a horrible cemetery of errors. The defects were rigorously classified and the frequency of each was tabulated. The manufacturers were invited to see for themselves. As a shock tactic for the buying teams and the suppliers, the exercise was powerful and effective.

Since then there was a positive recognition that much could be gained by a quantitative analysis of the manufacturing source and type of faults. This has ushered in subsequent years the establishment of the so-called 'Pantheon' Quality Monitor as a management tool.

The Pantheon, as it is affectionately known, is a major Marks & Spencer store in London's West End. The 'Pantheon Quality Monitor' is based on taking all the faulty merchandise from this store into head office. Pantheon has a multi-million pound turnover, including all the new (and, therefore, likely to be troublesome) lines. It therefore reflects what is in the system as a whole.

All faulty merchandise in a particular product group is accumulated for a month and systematically categorized. Every week a different section of the business meets, and the results are discussed at a conference attended by senior executives, merchandise managers, selectors and technologists. The discussion centres around sources and correctional actions of defects, their implications for materials and production processes used, customer complaint and feedback, etc. There may be apparently trivial and unimportant issues; there may also be significant and strategic questions that surface in the discussion. But it is an opportunity for a cross-section of the company's executives to monitor closely the quality of the merchandise with a view to maintaining standards and further developing and improving on them.

This is but one example of the Marks & Spencer approach to 'total' quality control. A. V. Feigenbaum, a leading expert in the field, has defined total quality control as follows:

Total Quality Control may be defined as an effective system for integrating the quality-development, quality-maintenance, and quality-improvement effort of the various groups in an organization so as to enable production and service at the most economical levels which allow for full customer satisfaction.[3]

Underlying this definition are three principal ideas: (a) that quality needs to be systematically developed, maintained and improved upon, (b) that this multi-faceted task necessitates the concerted and integrated effort of various groups (departments) in the organization, and (c) that it must be done in the most economical manner which can at the same time allow for full customer satisfaction. In the earlier part of this chapter, I indicated that a total quality control approach usually embraces most if not all of the following features:

(1) explicit formulation of quality objectives and policies;
(2) quality improvement plans on a regular basis;
(3) quality planning and engineering for new products or processes;
(4) quality assurance and review of existing products/service;
(5) supplier quality/performance analysis and improvement plans;
(6) quality education and training of all levels of employees;
(7) quality information system;
(8) early-warning system;
(9) customer feedback analysis.

It can be said that Marks & Spencer has pioneered the total quality control approach without referring to it as such. As far as quality objectives and policies are concerned, the company has been singularly articulate and unequivocal. We have seen above that the board is obsessive about quality standards and achievement. Commenting on Lord Sieff's definition of quality 'that if the clothes we sell aren't good enough to be worn, and the food to be eaten, by our directors and their families, then they're not good enough for the customers', Robert Heller has remarked:

> the simple objection is that making goods to standards that satisfy 12 men, of whom several are highly cultivated millionaires, is a strange approach to running a mass-market retail operation. But the quality obsession, like the interlocked obsession with following goods right back down the line of production, has [been] a permanent part of the air in Baker Street.[4]

Likewise, Peter Drucker is hardly exaggerating when he asserts that Marks & Spencer's business is

> the subversion of the class structure of nineteenth-century England by making available to the working and lower-middle classes upper-class goods of better than upper-class quality.[5]

From these preoccupations evolved an organization which is structured and designed to meet stringent, almost impossible, requirements. Quality improvement plans become not only a regular but a continuous feature of the operation. Quality planning and assurance of new and existing products are looked after by the technologists in close collaboration with the commercial executives. An elaborate apparatus was created just to maintain intimate working relationships with the supppliers, as well as to monitor their quality performance. At the same time, rigorous effort was expanded in the direction

## A Fresh Approach to Food Distribution: TQC in Action

In 1980 Marks & Spencer spent well in excess of £30 million doing a job that most of its competitors leave to suppliers—delivering food to its shops. Most of the money was spent with BOC Transhield, a transport subsidiary of British Oxygen Co. (BOC), which handles about 85% of the chain's food deliveries.

'We believe that we have the most sophisticated and reliable food distribution service in the UK', says Marks & Spencer transport executive Derek Archdeacon. 'Our critics probably think that we pay too much for it. But they have no idea of the standards that we have set for the service and cost benefits we get from it.'

Marks & Spencer's success in food sales, as in other lines of its business, is geared to giving customers a plus factor. Archdeacon believes that the plus factor in food sales is guaranteed freshness. 'We believe that our food is fresher, because it is delivered more often to our stores, under more rigidly-controlled temperatures and hygiene standards than those of our competitors', he claims.

Each of Transfield's [six] purpose-built consolidation depots, strategically located around the UK, is on a direct line link to Marks & Spencer's computerized stock control centre in London. The depots really operate as transit sites. They accept food from Marks & Spencer suppliers, testing the conditions and temperature of perishables. Then they sort out the food lines into individual store shipments, which are delivered once or twice a day by Transhield's [360] refrigerated lorries.

The system has simplified the administration of the whole buying process. Buyers benefit directly from a trunking operation carried out between the depots. This enables goods from a Scottish supplier to be on store shelves in southern England within 24 hours of receipt. Buyers, therefore, can concentrate on seeking out suppliers on the basis of their quality rather than their proximity to the shops. Buyers are also able to negotiate better deals because Marks & Spencer has eliminated a lot of its supplier's distribution costs.

'We have no formal contract with each other', says Archdeacon. 'Of course, we have agreed procedures and codes of practice. We tend to work with all our suppliers on this basis, along the lines of a gentlemen's agreement.' For Transhield this means constant monitoring of every facet of its operations by Marks & Spencer officials. This includes a policy of open-book accounting which enables Marks & Spencer to know where virtually every penny is being spent. As with all its suppliers, Marks & Spencer is obsessed with the maintenance of standards at Transhield. 'Marks & Spencer stock auditors and technologists make periodic visits to all our depots to count and test merchandise', says John Cole, Transhield's Operations Director. 'We get regular visits from Marks & Spencer hygiene inspectors. Our standards must match theirs, where the back of the store is as clean as the front of the store.'

In effect, it all boils down to a new attitude towards distribution. Traditionally, management has regarded them as an add-on cost, which, in the end, increase the price of products. Marks & Spencer views its distribution cost more as a customer service which gives an added value to its merchandise.

of educating and training different levels of employees so as to ensure that 'they appreciate quality when they see it'. Finally, as described above, a variety of quality monitoring systems provide the company with systematic feedback on quality performance and reliability.

It is significant to note that total quality control, by its very nature, is never the responsibility of individual departments alone. It necessarily entails an integrated effort of all departments and all levels of the organization. Not surprisingly, Marks & Spencer has never considered quality control as a separate function; rather, it is seen as a focal point upon which the efforts of diverse functional groups in the company converge.

## Quality Circles and Company-wide Quality Control

While it appears appropriate to characterize the Marks & Spencer approach to quality management as 'total quality control', the same cannot be so easily said as far as 'company-wide quality control' is concerned. As we had defined them above, TQC and CWQC are very similar in conceptual terms, the crucial difference being that in CWQC there is the distinctive feature that not only all the departments concerned are closely bound up in the quality control effort but that *all employees* of the respective departments are actively involved as well.

The distinction is more than a matter of semantics. To have a department actively involved in the 'total quality control' effort is one thing; to have all categories of staff—including the rank-and-file—within the department taking an active part in it is quite another. This in fact points to a crucial difference between the quality control systems in the West and in Japan. Typically, though by no means universally, the average employee in Japanese enterprises takes a more active role in quality control and related activities than his counterpart in the West. The responsibilities for assuring quality and meeting company quality objectives are more generally felt throughout the organization in Japanese companies in contrast to most enterprises in the West, where the rank-and-file employees are usually uninformed of, or apathetic about, quality issues. In order to underline this very crucial point, let us briefly review a widely used Japanese system closely associated with company-wide quality control—quality control circles—or quality circles as they are more popularly known in the West.

The quality circle may be defined as a small group of rank-and-file employees doing similar work who meet voluntarily on a regularly scheduled basis, usually under the leadership of a section head or a senior worker, to identify, analyse and seek solutions to work-related problems. Its activities deal not only with problems related to product quality but also such issues as productivity, working conditions, safety, cost reduction, etc.[6]

For all its emphasis on grass-root level initiative and participation, however, the quality circle is by no means merely a shop-floor affair. A successful quality circles programme necessitates active and continuous management involvement as well as a formal structure for promotion and coordinating the circles' activities. Figure 13 depicts a typical quality circle organization.

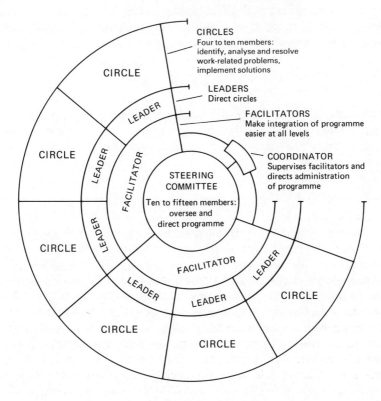

Figure 13   Quality circles organization

## Steering Committee

The steering committee, composed of 10 to 15 members, including the functional heads of such departments as production, quality assurance, industrial engineering, marketing, purchasing, personnel and sometimes the general manager or managing director, is the focal point of the organization. Under its direction the policies and procedures of the entire programme are established and implemented.

## Facilitators

Facilitators are a key element and can greatly affect the success or failure of a quality circle programme. They work in close liaison with the steering committee and circle leaders to assure the proper functioning of the circle and the continuous training of all circle members. The facilitator must be a good communicator, resourceful, and easily conversive and relaxed with all levels of the company organization.

## Leaders

Another integral part of the quality circle programme is circle leaders. Apart from providing leadership to the circle members the leader has also to perform the important role of training up the members in various methods of identifying, analysing and resolving problems. The prospective leaders must be articulate, resourceful, good at conducting meetings and command respect and trust from fellow employees.

## Circle Members

The circles form the perimeter of the organizational wheel, transforming the programme's objectives into action. The members are recruited on a voluntary basis; each circle consists of four to ten members. The circle is to identify work-related problems, and then analyse, develop and implement solutions to them. Team work is emphasized and circle activities are the joint efforts of the members concerned. Recognition of achievements is likewise directed to the group.

## The Coordinator

Assisting with all this activity is the coordinator, an important member of the quality circle management team. He is usually the steering committee chairman. He provides direction and support to the facilitators and leaders, ensures that they are properly trained to carry out their tasks, facilitates interdepartmental co-operation and co-ordination and guides the overall programme towards predetermined objectives. The co-ordinator is usually a member of the top management team.

The quality circle concept has been described at such length to underline a number of crucial points:

First, the quality circle should by no means be equated with spontaneous, unplanned, informal group activities on the shop floor. Rather, it is a conscious and systematic effort to tap the initiative, experience, creativity and collective wisdom of the rank-and-file employees with full management support and involvement.

Second, the quality circle is distinct from conventional 'meetings' of various kinds, such as department/section meetings, briefing groups, consultation meetings and the like. In the latter, the direction of information flow is primarily top-down. Quality circles' activities, on the other hand, build on a bottom-up approach and draw directly on the human resources at the shop floor.

Third—and this is a very important point—the quality circle approach, though recognizing the multi-faceted potential of the rank-and-file employees, believes that the latter need to be properly trained in order to take part effectively in quality circles' activities. Quality circles' programmes put a premium on offering systematic training to all members, primarily in problem-solving techniques. A whole series of simple yet powerful tools have evolved from the Japanese experience, such as brainstorming, the fishbone diagram, the Pareto diagram, etc. To be really effective, circle members must necessarily master these so-called quality circles techniques, which have proved easy to use and within reach of employees of even modest education.

The quality circle system is but one manifestation of the company-wide quality control phenomenon in Japan. But it is indicative of the nature of employee involvement in the quality control effort.

With such activities as quality circles in mind it is possible to distinguish two dimensions of employee involvement in company-wide quality control: breadth and depth. In some companies which have gone beyond the total quality control stage the progress towards the direction of company-wide quality control usually begins with the breadth dimension; that is, more and more levels of employees, including the junior ones, are gradually drawn into the quality control effort. It is only at a later stage that the involvement begins to 'deepen'. Successful implementation of quality circles programmes, or similar schemes, can be seen as a sign of maturity in the depth dimension.

## CWQC at Marks & Spencer

As far as the breadth dimension is concerned, Marks & Spencer may be regarded as having entered the stage of CWQC. Largely as a result of the company's preoccupation with quality from the boardroom to the sales counter, all employees are schooled in the disciplined awareness of quality and value. The sales assistants, for example, are considered to be the guardians of St Michael quality. They are trained to spot any imperfection in the merchandise and provide the last safety net on quality control in the store, as well as providing ideas of customers' future requirements. The sales assistants analyse the defects in 12 simple technical fault codes before the company returns and debits the goods to suppliers. (The major faults are fabric faults, loose dye, poor button or zip attachment, seam breakdown, dirty marks and stains, etc.)

Another notable example is in the area of food handling. The growth of Marks & Spencer's food business naturally demanded that the company should pay the strictest attention to the conditions under which food was handled and sold; in this respect the company can justifiably claim to have been pioneers in establishing higher and better standards of food handling.

The basis of the company's policy was the training of its staff in personal cleanliness and hygiene; it was an educational programme designed most of all to inculcate an attitude of mind, which it was not absurd to call, as indeed the company did, a philosophy. 'Hygiene is part of our philosophy', says the Foreword to a Marks & Spencer handbook on hygiene:

> It is based on each person recognizing his individual responsibility for carrying out the rules of clean food handling and the 'clean as you go' principle. By 'clean as you go' was meant that at every moment the individual should be scrupulous in eliminating any form of dirt that might come into contact with food. As it turned out, it came very near to being enforced as an ethical principle.[7]

These are indicative of the breadth dimension in the Marks & Spencer company-wide quality control effort; the company has made a conscious effort to educate and involve all categories of staff to help ensure high quality standards of its merchandise and service. At the same time, there is also an attempt to deepen this involvement. One example of this, though by no means the only one, is in fact quality circles.

The company has taken a serious interest in quality circles ever since the concept was 'introduced' into the U.K. in the late seventies. The technologists have been particularly active in promoting the quality circles idea to the suppliers. They organized briefing and training sessions for the latter and have in some cases been involved in setting up quality circles programmes in the plants. Towards the end of 1982 there were already fourteen manufacturers which had an active quality circles programme.

There are also quality circles in the stores, whose members are primarily sales assistants and supervisors. But the number of circles is still extremely small. There were less than ten active circles among the stores in the London area in mid-1982. From the interviews the author had conducted with a number of circle members and leaders, it seems that the movement had not really got off the ground. Management support, though forthcoming, was not strong and thorough enough. This was particularly noticeable at the store management level; many of the store managers and staff managers that the author has talked to are not familiar with the idea and do not seem to know how to support and facilitate its activities. There is also an apparent confusion between the nature and purposes of quality circles and the 'communication groups' in the stores which have been in operation for some time.

The communication groups constitute regular meetings of store staff consisting of representatives of every category/section of staff in the store. For example, a typical meeting is attended by the store manager, the staff manager, and a representative of each of the following: full-time sales assistant, part-time sales assistant, department supervisor, general office, warehouse, catering, and domestic services. The frequency of these meetings varies from once a month to once in 3 months, the average being every 8–10 weeks. It is usually the store manager or the staff manager who acts as the chairman, but there are also a substantial number of stores (over 50 in 1982) having other members of staff acting as chairman.

The communication groups meeting has no pre-set agenda as such and discussions may cover any aspect of store operation. Topics normally discussed range from choice of holiday dates, pension scheme, staff uniform, and the staff purchase system to customer complaints, staffing, training, inter-departmental relationships, etc. The meetings are valuable in providing an opportunity for representatives of different sections of the store to exchange ideas and to seek clarification from management of various policies and measures affecting their work. Concise minutes on a standard format are kept for all meetings and copies are sent to the personnel group at head office, where periodical summaries of the main points discussed by the 200-odd communication groups are prepared for review by senior management staff.

There is little doubt that these meetings have greatly enhanced two-way communication in the stores and, given the generally favourable organization climate prevailing in the company, the measure of success of the communication groups is indeed impressive. But the functions of the communication groups and quality circles are by no means identical; the former serves primarily to facilitate communication, while the latter, as pointed out above, constitutes a framework to enable small groups of rank-and-file employees to identify, study, and seek solutions to work-related problems *themselves*.

The company by no means equates communication groups with quality circles, nor is it attempting to substitute one with another. But it remains true to say that the immense potential of quality circles activities in contributing to the company-wide quality control effort is far from generally appreciated among the management staff. The fact that there is still a very limited development in the quality circles programme, despite a relatively mature system of communication groups, indicates perhaps that the company has still a considerable way to go as far as the depth dimension of company-wide quality control is concerned.

It should, however, be pointed out that the preceding analysis by no means implies that quality circles are the only criterion for company-wide quality control. But it does attempt to underline the fact that company-wide quality control is characterized by *in-depth* involvement of various levels of employees in the quality management effort and that quality circles constitute one such form of involvement. Marks & Spencer has yet to develop a comprehensive system as effective as the quality circles programme found in most enterprises fully immersed in company-wide quality control, notably in Japan.

## Surpassing the Japanese?

To the extent that most industrial enterprises in Japan have entered the stage of company-wide quality control, it is difficult to say that Marks & Spencer has surpassed the Japanese. But it is possible and meaningful to assert that Marks & Spencer has surpassed the Japanese in two specific senses.

In the first place, Marks & Spencer had begun its 'total' approach to quality management in the pre-World War II period, well before the Japanese began to learn from the West about quality control. In the second place, Marks & Spencer surpasses the Japanese in a more substantive sense, namely that, as a *retailer*, it has made a far more comprehensive and rigorous effort in quality control than any of its counterparts in Japan. Japanese *industry* is renowned for its quality control achievement, but not as far as retailing is concerned. The latter has still a lot to learn from Marks & Spencer and some of them, such as the retail chain giant, Daiei, look towards Marks & Spencer as their model. In this particular sense alone, Marks & Spencer can be said to have far surpassed the Japanese. It remains to be seen whether the latter will one day overtake its teacher, as they have already done in so many fields.

## Notes

1. Quoted in Rees, *op. cit.*, p. 144.
2. Lewis R. Goodman, 'Better human relations for better quality', *EOQC Quality, op. cit.*, p. 7.
3. A. V. Feigenbaum, *Total Quality Control: The Technical and Managerial Field for Improving Product Quality, Reliability and Reducing Operation Costs and Losses* (New York: McGraw-Hill, 1961), p. 1.
4. 'The inimitable magic of Marks', *Management Today*, September 1966.
5. See Chapter 4 above.
6. For a more elaborated discussion of the quality circles concept and its application, see K. K. Tse, *Harnessing Quality Circles for Higher Quality and Productivity: Lessons from Japan* (Hong Kong: Hong Kong Industrial Relations Association, 1981), and Mike Robson, *Quality Circles* (London: Gower Press, 1982). The quality circles concept is by no means applicable only to the manufacturing sector; in Japan, as well as in other countries catching on to the idea, it has been employed in all kinds of organizations; see, for example, the valuable work of Sud Ingle and Nima Ingle, *Quality Circles in Service Industries* (New Jersey: Prentice-Hall, 1983).
7. Published by Marks & Spencer p.l.c. 1981.

# PART III

# WHAT MATTERS MORE
# THAN PEOPLE?

## INNOVATIONS IN HUMAN RESOURCES
## MANAGEMENT

# CHAPTER 8

# Commitment to Good Human Relations—What it Means in Business

## It's People Who Matter
### (Lord Sieff)

The development of good human relations in industry is very important. I use the term 'good human relations in industry' rather than 'industrial relations' because we are human beings at work not industrial beings.

Good human relations develop only if top management believes in and is committed to their implementation and has a genuine respect for the individual. This is not something to be tackled from time to time, but demands continuous action.

Human relations in industry should cover the problems of the individual at work, his or her health, well-being and progress, the working environment and profit sharing. Full and frank two-way communication and respect for the contribution people can make, given encouragement—these are the foundations of an effective policy and a major contribution to a successful operation.

Most people appreciate being taken into confidence by management who must explain policies and development clearly. There is very little need for secrecy. At Marks & Spencer we try to ensure that all our staff are kept informed of proposed developments and that their views are taken into account. Unfortunately, much management tells employees as little, instead of as much, as possible.

Everyone should be informed of his or her progress or lack of it. Credit should be given for work well done. Then poor work can be frankly discussed and this stimulates people to work better, particularly if they know they have done well.

Fostering good human relations with employees means more than just paying good wages. Managers must be aware of, and react to, the problems of employees. Top management must know how good or how bad employees' working conditions and amenities are. They must eat in the employees' restaurants, see whether the food is decent and well cooked, visit the washrooms and the lavatories. If they are not good enough for those in charge they are not good enough for anyone.

At Marks & Spencer everyone enjoys the same amenities. I as chairman, when visiting the stores get the same morning snack, three-course lunch and tea as all the staff and generally eat in the staff restaurant. Everyone pays £1 a week for meals.

A policy of good human relations costs time, effort and money. Marks & Spencer's employees number 44,000 full and part-time, of whom over 1000 are in personnel. Some 850 of the latter are in staff management spread throughout the stores. Their priority is the well-being and progress of, on average, the 50 to 60 people for whom each is responsible; it is their job to train and help people to develop, to know their problems, seek their views and respond to constructive suggestion and worthwhile criticism. We invest much time training our commercial managers in good human relations for it is on them that our business relies for sensible day-to-day decisions about people.

Last year we spent £43 million [compared with a pre-tax profit of £176.8 million] on catering subsidies, medical and dental attention, non-contributory pensions and profit sharing for our staff. These benefits are for all, irrespective of position. Those who lead Marks & Spencer believe that money has been, and is, one of our best investments.

The senior board spend much time on personnel problems. It is a fundamental part of the good staff policy to be able unobtrusively and above all, speedily, to give help and advice where needed. The essence of any good scheme is prevention rather than cure. Legal requirements dictate a number of staff regulations, but the remainder should be reduced to a minimum and guidelines delegated to local management to act sensibly and generously in dealing with people. We tell them, 'If you are going to make a mistake, err on the side of generosity.' This instruction is rarely abused.

Our efforts have resulted in a stable staff, ready acceptance of change, high productivity and good profits in which all share—shareholders, staff, retired staff—and the community. Staff morale is high and the great majority care about the progress of the business, whatever their job.

There are a number of major companies, some unionized, some not, who implement successfully a policy of good human relations modified to suit their particular circumstances—GEC, United Biscuits, IBM, Standard Telephones and Cable are examples. You will find in these companies industrial strife is virtually non-existent, productivity, progress and profits are high, and everyone shares in the progress of the company.

A business cannot progress in isolation from the community in which it works and trades. Helping wherever possible to restore a healthy and prosperous environment is a responsibility which is not only good citizenship but is good for the business.

Today, many of us are concerned about the problems of inner city decay and unemployment. Most of us are part of city communities. For many years our staff have been jumping and jogging, swimming and slimming, racing and raffling to raise money for worthy local causes. Our managers are encouraged to play an active role in their communities.

Marks & Spencer donates substantially to medicine, the arts, research and other charities. But the cheque book is not enough. We second capable and experienced people to community projects. Their special skills contribute to solving some of the problems. We concentrate on projects to generate small new businesses and job opportunities and helping youngsters who cannot get jobs.

Since 1978, 42 of our staff have been involved in 37 schemes aimed at job creation, training unemployed teenagers; both in-company schemes and outside schemes in co-operation with the Youth Opportunities Programme of the Manpower Services Commission. Our seconded personnel return to us more capable to perform an increasingly important role in the business as a result of their outside experience.

If the leaders of industry cannot understand and pursue with patience and tenacity a policy of good human relations, then we must not be surprised if we wake up one morning to find ourselves members of a society that few of us want, where democratic values no longer operate and there is no freedom. Then we shall have only ourselves to blame.

(Excerpts from an article published in *The Sunday Times* of 13 December 1981.)

The above statement summarizes the essence of Marks & Spencer's approach to 'human relations in industry'. Depending on one's perspective, these passages may be interpreted in a variety of ways. They may not mean the same thing to, say, a unionist, a manager from another management culture, a chief executive in a strike-prone industry, an M&S competitor, an academic, a social critic, a fresh MBA, a Marxist, an unemployed worker. . . . Indeed, since I began my research on the company, I have shown the above article to numerous persons of diverse background to solicit their response. So far I have not yet come across two identical reactions. This, I think, underlines two important things. Firstly, there seems to be widespread misunderstanding, or failure to understand, what exactly Marks & Spencer means by good human relations in industry. Secondly, there is the difficulty, even with an adequate understanding of the foregoing, for many people to appreciate what this approach really entails in practical business terms. Underlying all these are deeper doubts, such as whether such an approach is compatible with core business values under capitalism, and if so, why has it not caught on elsewhere?

The following are illustrative of the range of responses I have come across:

(1)  scepticism as to whether it is put into practice;
(2)  regarding it as sheer paternalism of a prosperous family business;
(3)  alarmed by the 'investment' put in by the company, but would feel inclined to do the same if similar results could somehow be guaranteed; and
(4)  *the* answer to the British industrial relations disease.

It is not my aim to provide a 'correct' interpretation of the Marks & Spencer approach to employee relations. What I hope to accomplish in this part of the book is an analytical account of key aspects of the Marks & Spencer practice so as to enable readers to form a view of their own. In doing this I will attempt to place the M&S approach in the larger context of major contemporary trends in human resources management.

To prepare the ground for subsequent chapters, let me now briefly discuss the above views in turn.

### A Legitimate Scepticism

The first view is perhaps representative of those employees working in a management climate totally different from that of Marks & Spencer. It is a very legitimate scepticism. There are indeed many employers around who talk

about good human relations, but never practise it. Interestingly enough, Lord
Sieff has himself spoken eloquently on this point:

> Nearly everybody in top management says that they believe in good human relations.
> In fact, I have found that management can be divided into three groups—those who
> pay lip service to the idea but do not care a damn about it, those who believe in it but
> do not know how to implement it, and the small number who believe in it and
> implement the policy of good human relations successfully. Most top management
> does not appreciate what such a policy implies, certainly not what a total commitment
> to it entails. [1]

It might be difficult for someone with no previous experience of a 'good
human relations' environment to envisage what such an environment looks
like. But there are at least two sources of information that may enable one to
dispel some of the scepticism. First of all, there are the more quantifiable
indicators such as the ratio of personnel staff to employees, the number and
range of amenities and benefits and the aggregate costs of these. [2] On these
counts, Marks & Spencer easily emerges as a leader in the U.K. scene. The
second source, relating to the more qualitative aspects, requires a different
kind of validation. This can best be approached by talking to Marks & Spencer
employees at different levels in the hierarchy, as the present author and many
outside observers have done. One would find almost inescapably the general
pattern of feeling as something like this: that the company not only looks after
the staff well, but, more importantly, the staff feel they are being treated as
individuals; that they are given opportunities continuously to train and
develop themselves; that management is on their side, not against and above
them; and that they see very little gap between what top management preaches
and what is being practised. (Readers with acquaintances who are Marks &
Spencer staff are invited to validate these statements themselves.)

But perhaps the surest way of finding an effective answer to the doubts—
though this is not open to too many people—would be to work for the
company. An incidence of this has been recounted by Lord Sieff thus:

> Some five years ago I gave a talk to the Industrial Society of one university. The title
> was 'Human Relations in Industry'. Later at dinner, members of the audience said
> that they were glad to hear that industrial managers had a sense of social values, but
> they found it hard to believe that any business really practised such principles. Some
> eighteen months later I met one of them working at Marks & Spencer. I asked him
> how he was getting on. He replied, 'You really do it.' I said, 'Do what?' He answered,
> 'The operation is based on the principle about which you spoke to us some two years
> ago, but I really didn't believe it then.' [3]

### Paternalism: Myth and Reality

It is perhaps unfortunate that to most people Marks & Spencer is only a
paternalistic family business. To characterize its management as little more
than paternalism is I think a gross misrepresentation.

**A Business and Its Beliefs—the Ideas that Helped Build IBM**

Management at Marks & Spencer have a high opinion of other companies which practise good human relations. The Chairman and the Directors are fond of quoting the following remarks from Thomas Watson, Jnr., Chairman of IBM:

There is simply no substitute for good human relations and for the high morale they bring. It takes good people to do the jobs necessary to reach your profits goals. But good people alone are not enough. No matter how good your people may be, if they don't really like the business, if they don't feel totally involved in it, or if they don't think they're being treated fairly—it's awfully hard to get a business off the ground. Good human relations are easy to talk about. The real lesson, I think, is that you must work at them all the time and make sure your managers are working with you.

(From the book *A Business and its Beliefs*, by Thomas Watson, Jnr. New York: McGraw-Hill, 1963.)

Let us attempt to get at the root of the misunderstanding. It appears that the single most important factor could be that people from outside are often only able to observe the more visible aspects of the operation. The marvellous amenities and benefits that Marks & Spencer staff enjoy are very much talked about in trade journals and the popular press alike. Given the success of the company, people tend to reason thus: Making the Staff Work Hard + Giving Them Good Benefits = Paternalism. This in my opinion misses the most distinctive aspects of the Marks & Spencer approach to human relations, as I shall attempt to show in the following chapters. Consider for the moment briefly some of the points raised by Lord Sieff:

(1) respect for the individual at work;
(2) attention to all problems of individuals at work;
(3) full and frank two-way communication;
(4) recognition and motivation for effort and contribution;
(5) continuous training and development.

All these are important elements of the Marks & Spencer practice. But they are hardly conveyed, much less put into prominence, by such labels as 'paternalism'. I would argue that the welfare and benefits side of the company is best understood as 'hygiene factors' only—in Herzberg's use of the term—and that what distinguishes Marks & Spencer from most other companies which also have generous benefits schemes is their systematic approach and meticulous attention to the 'motivating factors' that affect employee behaviour.

The concepts of 'hygiene factors' and 'motivating factors' are taken from Frederick Herzberg, who distinguished in a classic study two sets of factors that *dissatisfy* and *satisfy* people at work respectively.[4] The two sets of factors, interestingly and significantly enough, are not the opposites of each other.

Dealing with dissatisfying factors does not turn them into satisfying or motivating factors. In general, the dissatisfying factors are things to do with the conditions of work, company policy and administration, salary, amenities, benefits, and physical conditions. He called these 'hygiene factors'. They are necessary (but not sufficient) conditions for successful motivation. The satisfiers are achievement, recognition, work itself, responsibilities and advancement. These he called motivators. Good hygiene deals with the question 'Why work here?'; only the motivators deal with 'Why work harder?'

In terms of 'hygiene', the standards of Marks & Spencer are certainly extremely high—and this has often been equated with paternalism. But what the company has excelled in above all is the 'motivating' elements, which alone could explain why their staff work so much harder and effectively than their counterparts in most other companies. (Chapters 12 and 13 will deal with the 'motivating factors' and Chapter 14 with 'hygiene factors'.)

## Investment in Good Human Relations

To many employers in the U.K. (or other parts of the world for that matter) the amount of investment in good human relations made by Marks & Spencer seems unacceptably high. Most would concede that they would never have the courage to make investment of this proportion. To a few others it might be held that although the stake is high, if the results were commensurate to those enjoyed by Marks & Spencer they might be tempted to put up the money. The trouble, however, is that the results could in no way be guaranteed.

The uncomfortable truth is that investment in good human relations is simply not susceptible to conventional cost–benefit analysis. It is, if anything, more of an act of faith. For one thing, most of the costs involved are not quantifiable or visible. How does one take into account the enormous management time and effort involved in an on-going basis? If a guesstimate were to be attempted, it might turn out to be larger than all the quantifiable accounts put together. As Lord Sieff has remarked:

> We discuss our personnel policies openly with other managements, some of whom think we must be mad to spend, as a Board, so much time on personnel work, to have so many people engaged in it and to spend so much money on it. I agree that perhaps we are mad but, looked at practically, our annual profit and loss account generally doesn't look too bad. In fact, those who lead Marks & Spencer have for a long time been convinced that without this investment in the care of people, we would not enjoy such success as we do.[5]

In another context he put it thus: 'Every single thing that we've done because we felt we had a moral obligation has also, within five or ten years, turned out to be good business, even though we didn't start out with that idea.'[6] For Marks & Spencer, the care and concern for people is anything but the end

FIG. 9. Marks & Spencer's flag store in Central London.

FIG. 10. Head Office, Baker Street, London.

FIG. 11. Over 14 million customers shop at M & S stores every week.

FIG. 12. A modern suburban store.

Fig. 13. The staff cafeteria.

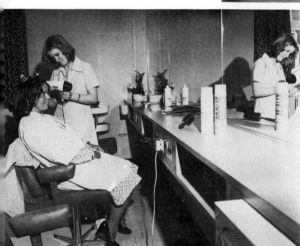

Fig. 14. The beauty salon.

Fig. 15. Chiropody treatment for sales floor staff.

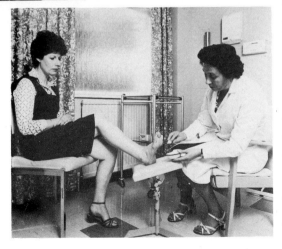

FIG. 16. The selector chooses and develops the range of merchandise for the department, is responsible for product innovation, the identification of new lines and for drawing up the specifications for manufacturers before a new line goes into production.

FIG. 17. Anticipation is the name of game, for the buying office works at least two seasons ahead of current production. The design teams must decide on what they believe the forthcoming fashion look will be. A crystal ball plays no part in their calculations. The visit fashion shows, exhibitions, yarn and fabric manufacturers and organisations such as the Cotton Council and the International Wool Secretariat.

FIG. 18. A machine commonly known as "Jaws" measures the strength and stretch of fabrics. Fabric is clasped into the machine and drawn apart under a load which is recorded on a graph.

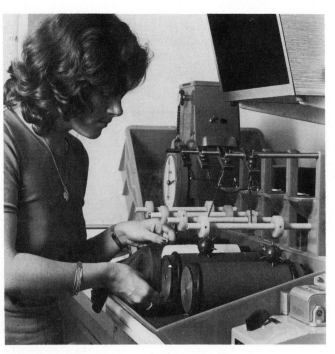

FIG. 19. A gadget which looks ⬛ a medieval weapon rotates acr⬛ fabric to cause deliberate sna⬛ The fabric's resistance to sn⬛ ging is measured on a sc⬛ and rejected if unsatisfactory ⬛ comes as no surprise that thi⬛ called 'The Mace Test'.

FIG. 20. Feathers can be a ticklish business. When they are used in duvets it is most important that the right type and amount are used, otherwise the bedding will be too hot or too cold.

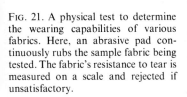

FIG. 21. A physical test to determine the wearing capabilities of various fabrics. Here, an abrasive pad continuously rubs the sample fabric being tested. The fabric's resistance to tear is measured on a scale and rejected if unsatisfactory.

Fig. 22. In the laundry room, sample fabric swatches, or the whole garment, are washed and dried under varying conditions—including tumble drying.

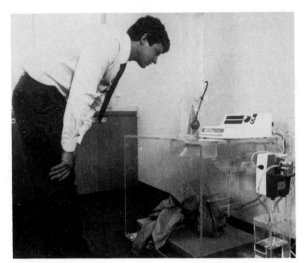

Fig. 23. Raindrops falling on your head may be acceptable. Raindrops penetrating a raincoat and wetting you are not. The raindrop test, in which water is dripped from a height onto a mesh cone which breaks up the water onto fabric, proves the shower-resistant qualities of the fabric. The flow of water represents an average shower. Storm conditions are not simulated as no shower-resistant fabric can be guaranteed to protect the wearer in very heavy rain.

Fig. 24. In this lab. temperature and humidity is carefully controlled to provide the standardised conditions essential to certain fabric tests. Most fabrics absorb moisture from the atmosphere. Therefore, if conditions were not constant, varying results would be obtained.

result of a conscious and deliberate calculation. It is rather a manifestation of the adherence to a simple principle integrated into the business by the founder, Michael Marks: 'As long as you put people first, you can't go wrong, even about making money.'

But whereas investment in good human relations cannot be the subject of calculation, it is nevertheless possible and profitable to think of human resources as an important asset of a company. Again, as with good human relations, most top management are also fond of speaking of their staff as human assets. But how many of them really see them as a vital asset? And if indeed they do, how many companies have a well-thought-out policy regarding the investment and deployment of these assets? To push the analogy slightly further, how many companies approach these assets as something which may appreciate in value over time?

Consider the following questions put together provocatively by Charles Handy:[7]

Can you or anyone else in your company answer the questions listed below?

- How much money was spent last year to recruit and select people? Was this expenditure worth the cost?
- Does your organization have data on standard costs of recruitment, selection, and placement which are needed to prepare manpower budgets and to control personnel costs?
- Was the actual cost incurred last year less than, equal to, or greater than standard personnel acquisition and placement costs?
- How much money was spent last year to train and develop people?
- What was the return on your investment in training and development? How does this return compare with alternative investment opportunities?
- How much human capital was lost last year as a result of turnover?
- How much does it cost to replace a key man?
- What is the opportunity cost of losing young, high-potential managers, accountants, engineers, etc.?

The following are compulsory:

- What is the total value of your company's human assets?
- Is it appreciating, remaining constant, or being depleted?
- Do your compensation and other motivation–reward systems reflect an individual's present value to the firm?
- Does your company really (I mean *really*) reward managers for increasing the value of their subordinates to the firm?

These questions are meant to be taken seriously—and literally—by any management aspiring to view human resources as an asset. The overriding significance of all this is that it is not money as such we are talking about in good human relations investment, it is rather the investment in instituting a management system (which might necessitate writing-off much of the existing ones) that elevates human relations as a cardinal value. This indeed is the lesson from Marks & Spencer.

## A Panacea to the British Industrial Disease?

Anyone with even a cursory knowledge of the U.K.'s industrial problems would hardly fail to recognize that 'industrial relations' ranks among the top of the list. British industry has long been on the decline, characterized by stagnant productivity and technological development coupled with low levels of profits and investment. In the meantime, incessant industrial disputes plague the entire economy, further depressing production, profits and investment. The vicious circle seems to be the only thing in industry which runs smoothly and majestically.

Nothing is a greater contrast to this deplorable scene than the Marks & Spencer empire. For a solid 100 years the company has been virtually free from any industrial dispute, and its uninterrupted growth in turnover, profits, productivity and management innovation has for decades been the envy of the nation.

Surely this is more than enough material for theorizing that Marks & Spencer has discovered the key to industrial harmony and business success. The panacea to the U.K.'s industrial disease, so the argument goes, is present right in the centre of every town, large or small, across the country. But why has not the patient responded?

For some industrialists, the answer is simple. As the managing director of one of Britain's largest heavy industries puts it:

> Marks & Spencer's Sir Marcus Sieff is always saying it is wrong to talk about industrial relations, it should be human relations. That is all very well when you are talking about pretty young girls selling clothes in a nice shop. It is a bit different when you are dealing with thousands of tough workers in a big plant.[8]

To some observers, such as Robert Heller of *Management Today*, it is due to the 'inimitable magic' of the company—magic that works for them, but cannot be transplanted elsewhere; 'the methods of Baker Street are no help to anybody outside'.[9] It seems, however, that the picture may not be as simple and mystic as it appears to be.

For example, one of the most distinctive features of Marks & Spencer is the conspicuous absence of trade unions. This alone distinguishes the company from the bulk of British industry. The company is not anti-union as such, but unionism simply finds it difficult to flourish in St Michael soil. In a sense, the company's attitude to trade unions may be characterized as a pre-emptive approach; managerial emphasis on good human relations has resulted in such exceptional working conditions and interpersonal relationships that probably few trade unionists would ever think of demanding or aspiring to. During my attachment to the company in the summer of 1982, one staff manager recalled:

> I was once asked by a local union official to organize a talk by him to the staff in the store. I made the arrangement for it, fully publicizing the event. When the time came,

I felt very sorry for him as no one had turned up. I subsequently took him to lunch in our restaurant amongst the sales assistants. He was shocked by the amenities in the store. I have never heard from him since.

To the extent that the trade union movement in the U.K. is predominantly 'economistic', the private welfare state of Marks & Spencer has of course little difficulty in shrugging off union activism. A colleague of mine at the Cranfield School of Management, who is both a great admirer of Marks & Spencer and a socialist, used to remark, 'With capitalism like this, you don't need to have socialism.' He also adds, however, 'the trouble is, unfortunately or fortunately, there is not too much capitalism like this around'.

To borrow an analogy from the study of the Third World economies, it may be said that British industry can be seen as characterized by a kind of 'dual economy'. On the other hand there is a small sector of companies with very progressive approaches to management; on the other hand there is the vast hinterland still very much dominated by antiquated, almost feudal, management philosphies and practice. The former constitutes more or less an enclave in an otherwise backward, retrogressive environment. Equally significant, progressive as the enclave may be, there is surprisingly little 'demonstration effect' observable. Just as the many metropolitan enclaves in most Third World countries have failed to bring 'modernization' to their underdeveloped countryside, the good human relations enclave in the U.K. has also had little impact on the larger sector.

This analogy may seem a bit far-fetched; but it does bring home the point that it is not realistic at all to speak of a panacea for U.K. industry in the form of a Marks & Spencer recipe. British industry could indeed learn a lot from studying Marks & Spencer, but it requires above all an integrated, holistic understanding of the company's philosophy and practice. Simplistic notions about the magical power of particular elements would only breed disillusion and inevitable frustration.

**WORLDS APART—A Glimpse at the Roots of Activism**

Like many parts of the Third World, advanced and sophisticated technology is sometimes combined with very backward labour relations. Hew Benyon, one of Britain's foremost industrial sociologists, has studied the 'roots of activism' in one of the U.K.'s most modern plants—Ford:

The shop steward in the car plant operates within the continuous world of the assembly line. The content of the work creates no relationship between him and the workers. They don't want his advice on how to attach the petrol tank to the car body; all they want from him is the regulation of the quantity of work that's demanded of them.

The steward on the trim-line will represent between 70 and 140 operatives depending on the speed of the line. Fluctuating line speeds, absenteeism and labour turnover all work against the development of a stable relationship between the steward and his members. On top of this the men he represents see themselves as small cogs, numbers; they hate their jobs and their life in the factory. One of the trim line stewards puts it like this:

The point about this place is that the work destroys you. It destroys you physically and mentally. The biggest problem for people is getting to accept it, to accept being here day in and day out. So you've got low morale from every point of view. You're inflicted with a place of work and you've got to adapt because it won't adapt to you. So morale is terribly low.

But you can build on this you see. You can't get much lower than hell and so you can increase morale through the union. Pull together sort of thing rather than dog eat dog. That's how I've found it on the trim. We're all in hell and you can get a bond out of that. We're all in it together like. That's where the union comes in.

The same steward describes his election:

Three years ago this place was in a very bad way. Ford's controlled everything. We had no steward on the line at the time. The lad who had taken it on broke down. The frustrations and the pressures were too much for him. I knew Eddie, I'd met him at some of the meetings and he told me to have a go. So I stood. Somebody had to do it. I didn't want to be a shop steward. That's the last thing I wanted when I came to the place first. I wanted to get on a bit. But I would see all the injustices being done every day so I thought I had to have a go. It wasn't right that they were having to take all the shit that Ford's were throwing.

Frank Banton also became active in the early days of the PTA plant:

When I came here first we had no representative. The old steward was recognized as a spokesman, but all the negotiations were done through the convenor. I knew that the lads were being brainwashed and kidded. The T&G was trying to organize the place and they were asking for volunteers—to work behind the scenes as it were. I volunteered and took up a job as a collecting steward. Eventually they persuaded me to take on the shop steward's job. I was pretty well known by that time and I was elected. I wanted to do it to look after the interests of my fellow workmen on the shop floor and to fight against these bastards here.

These two accounts summarize a wealth of experience. They contain the crucial elements of the emergent shop floor organization—conflict, sponsorship and a commitment to a humanistic collectivism, a strong desire to 'help your fellow man'. The structure of the shop stewards' committee in the PTA was created during a period of severe, continuous conflict, by a few activists who couldn't stand back and watch 'injustices being done every day'. This is not an uncommon pattern, but rather one which characterizes the entire history of the motor industry. Plants are unionized by men who stick their necks out and survive because of their mates' support.

The vast majority of stewards had no intention of becoming active when they walked through the gates at the start of their first day of work for the Ford Motor Company. The Ford Motor Company made them active.

(From Hew Benyon, *Working For Ford* (Penguin, 1973), pp. 187–9.)

## What It Means in Business

Let us recapitulate what has been discussed so far. We have seen what commitment to good human relations is *not*. It is not to be equated with or understood in terms of paternalism; it is not susceptible to cost–benefit analysis; it is not the panacea to Britain's industrial malaise. We have also indicated what it is and how it should be understood. Let us now put it more explicitly.

Good human relations entails 'putting people first', treating them as individuals, recognizing their capacity for responsibilities, trustworthiness, self-motivation, co-operative efforts, achievement and potential for development. It involves a holistic concern for the individual, emphasizing both the hygiene and motivating factors in the work environment and management culture. It takes the human resources of the company as critical assets—assets that appreciate in value over time from both employer's and employee's points of view.

Commitment to good human relations means significant investment by the organization in terms of time, effort and money. The return on the investment is necessarily intangible and will materialize only in the long run. A long-term perspective to human resources development is a *sine qua non* for good human relations.

The practice of good human relations also necessitates radical departures from conventional organization and job design. The organizational structure must be designed in such a way as to minimize the number of levels in the hierarchy, facilitate face-to-face interaction and frank and two-way communication among different organizational levels, ensure the maximum horizontal cross-fertilization and integration, and make possible the effective direction and coordination of the diverse functions and activities in the organization. In terms of job design the starting point is again the human element. Jobs are to be designed to fit the people, not the other way round, and this entails explicit consideration of the employees' intellectual and motor capabilities in work and work-place design so as to make for a more human work environment compatible with personal needs and aspiration.

Finally, good human relations entails a very unconventional, almost unique, leadership style. Pushed to its logical extreme it calls for a management style that approximates to Robert Townsend's ideal, set out in his celebrated work *Up the Organisation*. Paradoxically, Townsend has used two quotations from the Chinese philosopher Lao-tzu to epitomize this ideal.[10]

To lead the people, walk behind them.

As for the best leaders, the people do not notice their existence. The next best, the people honour and praise. The next, the people fear, and the next, the people hate.

When the best leader's work is done the people say 'We did it ourselves'.

No organization in the world—to the best of my knowledge and imagination—has reached this ideal. But from my study and observation of the management practice at Marks & Spencer, they are probably one of those few organizations which are working implicitly towards it. To be sure, they are still a very long way from this ideal. But it seems quite apparent that the practice of good human relations—in the most comprehensive sense of the term—is pushing them precisely in this direction.

In the rest of this Part we shall be examining aspects of the Marks & Spencer approach to people management and human resources development. In Chapter 12 the distinctive way Marks & Spencer conceives and implements the personnel function will be discussed. The revolutionary element in this approach is the attempt to integrate staff management and line management, flowing from the conviction that staff management will not be fully effective

## Leadership and Management: the M&S Approach

In an attempt to study managerial behaviour in retailing, P. A. Raveh in her doctoral research on Marks & Spencer has interviewed a large number of managers of different categories at 35 stores. The interview findings and analyses were presented in her unpublished Ph.D. dissertation, entitled 'Managerial behaviour in retailing', London Business School, 1977. The following are some of the remarks made by different managers:

The greatest compliment I can give my staff is to leave them alone to run their own sections.

It's not I who manage the store. It is many people who manage it. But they manage, hopefully, the way I would have done it.

If you have intelligent, well trained people, you are only wasting your time if you don't let them participate and make decisions with you. For 99% of the normal daily operations it is possible and necessary to use them and their abilities to your advantage.

I let the staff, and mainly the senior staff, make decisions and mistakes. This is the only way to operate, it's the only way to do things properly, because otherwise they don't think for themselves. All they would be doing is carrying out instructions.

I used to be a manager by setting example, and the staff don't want that. They want to do it themselves. I don't want the board of directors to come and show me what I should do. Provided that they did a good job in training me, I want to go away and execute things myself. The same is true for the staff. They want me to understand them, their hopes and aspirations, but that I let them perform themselves.

The fun for me is not producing the figures that the company wants. I find that fairly easy. The fascination for me is creating a team that automatically produces the figures. And that takes time.

In all likelihood, Robert Townsend could make a very good Marks & Spencer manager.

without enabling 'every manager to become a personnel manager'. Chapter 13 will take up the phenomenon of team management in some depth. It will be shown that the team approach at Marks & Spencer is not a management technique pure and simple, but more a defining characteristic of the management culture of the company.

The last chapter on the 'private welfare state' will give a systematic account of the 'hygiene factors', focusing in particular on a number of more innovative areas, such as preventive health service, profit-sharing, and the celebrated welfare committee. I have put this chapter at the end of this Part not so much to devalue its importance, but to put it in proper perspective.

## Notes

1. Lord Sieff, 'Co-operation or confrontation', The Royal Institution Discourse, 17 October 1975, p. 4.
2. See Chapter 12 below.
3. Lord Sieff, 'Social responsibility and wealth creation', speech delivered at the Headmasters' Conference, Edinburgh, 24 September 1980.
4. F. Herzberg, *Work and the Nature of Man* (Cleveland: World Publishing Co., 1966).
5. Lord Sieff, 'Co-operation or confrontation', *op. cit.*, p. 8.
6. Quoted in I. Murray, *The Shopkeeper—Profile of Lord Sieff*, undated.
7. Charles Handy, *Understanding Organisations*, 2nd edition (Harmondsworth: Penguin Books, 1981), p. 252.
8. Quoted by Eileen Mackenzie, 'Marksist approach to staff relations', *International Management*, June 1972.
9. 'The inimitable magic of Marks', *Management Today*, September 1966.
10. Robert Townsend, *Up the Organisation: how to stop the company stifling people and strangling profits* (London: Cornet Books, 1970), pp. 90–1.

# CHAPTER 9

# 'Every Manager a Personnel Manager'

Over the past decade, personnel management in many Western enterprises has been beset by a strange paradox. On the one hand there is the ever-growing importance of the personnel function, largely as a result of the increasing size and complexity of business organizations, changing patterns of employee behaviour and motivations, increased awareness of management–labour relationships and the multiplication of statutory regulations pertaining to employee relations. On the other hand there is the apparent failure of most personnel departments to tackle the rising tide of 'people' problems endemic in organizations of almost every description. The personnel specialists are confronted with a gigantic task, yet in most cases they have been utterly ineffective in delivering the solutions. What has gone wrong?

It seems that there are at least three major factors involved. First, although the human factor has become a critical element in survival and/or prosperity of many businesses, this has not always been recognized and appreciated by top managers. The personnel function has, more often than not, been (and still is) regarded as a 'cost', an 'overhead', or something which is important but peripheral to the main activities of the business.

Second, the growing specialization of the personnel function in many organizations has—paradoxically—rendered its contribution more and more dubious. The reason is simple: the personnel function is too important an area to be left to the personnel staff alone. The unnatural separation between personnel and line management and the centralization of personnel expertise in the personnel department must be seen as an important cause for its diminishing effectiveness.

Added to and closely bound up with the foregoing is yet another factor; namely, that the single most important source of personnel practitioners—line management—has in most cases not been properly equipped to carry out the personnel function. As most personnel specialists would agree, a very substantial and critically important part of the personnel function is best performed by line management—with the personnel staff acting only in a supporting role. The most effective personnel department is one which is successful in enabling line management to perform most of the personnel function adequately.

These are some of the fundamental problems afflicting personnel management in most organizations; having to live with one of them is bad enough, and in the nature of things they tend to come together. In this respect, the Marks & Spencer experience represents an encouraging departure from the norm. Indeed, the most distinctive elements of the Marks & Spencer approach to personnel management are precisely the following:

(1) 'Every manager a personnel manager'—that is, every member of staff with managerial or supervisory responsibilities is trained in, and expected to perform, a certain important personnel function.
(2) 'Every director a personnel director'—this implies that the personnel function—or more broadly speaking, good human relations—is not seen by the board as something 'important but peripheral' but as central to the basic philosophy and approach of the entire business. Board members responsible for no matter what area share the common responsibility for ensuring that the personnel function is properly executed.
(3) A strong, well-trained team of personnel staff to provide support, training, guidance and advice to management of various levels and to ensure that personnel skills constitute an important element in the career progression of all categories of managerial staff.

## The Personnel Group

In terms of the ratio of personnel to general staff, Marks & Spencer is among the highest—if not the highest—on the U.K. scene. Over the years the company has maintained a ratio of 1 personnel staff to every 50 to 60 staff in the stores. The ratio at the head office (which consists of less than 10% of total staff) is somewhat lower, about 1 to 70–90 staff. These ratios, however, understate the actual management time and efforts put into personnel work, as most of the line managers are also trained to perform some of the personnel function.

The personnel department (called 'group' at Marks & Spencer) is centrally organized, with a unified policy and system generally applied to all operations throughout the country. The personnel staff, however, is very much decentralized, with some 850 of the 1000-strong personnel group spread throughout the stores. Even at the head office the personnel staff is 'distributed' among the major functional groups (textile, food, distribution, building, etc.). But unlike many organizations which also have their personnel staff spread over the operating units, all of the personnel staff at Marks & Spencer are thoroughly trained under a common programme and centrally administered by the central personnel group.

Another major characteristic of the personnel function at Marks & Spencer is the fact that the personnel staff forms an integral part of a larger management team. For instance, the management team at the stores consists of four principal members: the store manager, the staff manager (i.e. personnel manager), the office manager and the warehouse manager (or warehouse foreman for smaller stores). The staff manager is an important member of this team which is responsible for running the entire store. Similarly, at the divisional level (the whole of the U.K. operation is divided geographically into 12 divisions, each with about 15 to 24 stores), the management team consists of a divisional executive, a divisional personnel manager, a divisional training manager, a divisional display manager and a divisional administrator. Again, the importance of the personnel and training elements in the team is very much underlined.

There is yet another aspect of personnel management which further distinguishes Marks & Spencer from most other business organizations; namely, the practice that the staff manager is also extensively trained in commercial management. This is a major innovation and has much to commend it. The rationale is as follows. In the same way as the line manager could benefit from personnel training so as to become a more effective and enlightened manager, it is believed that the staff manager's familiarity with the commercial side of the business could also greatly facilitate her/his work as a personnel manager. An indication of the intimate knowledge that the staff manager usually possesses on the commercial side can be seen in the fact that in those stores where there is no assistant store manager it is the staff manager who deputizes for the store manager in the latter's absence. This cross-familiarity of basic functional skills is an important factor underlying the effectiveness of the management teams at Marks & Spencer (see also Chapter 13 for further discussion).

These unique features point to a very important observation. The effectiveness of the personnel function at Marks & Spencer cannot be ascribed to the size of the personnel group (which is indeed large even in relative terms) or the quality of its staff alone. What is equally significant—if not more significant—is the strategic importance that is placed on the personnel function in the overall organizational structure, manifested in its organic relationship with line management as well as in senior management support and involvement. The figures that follow depict the strategic position of the personnel function in the company.

## How I See the Personnel Function

I was diverted into personnel management of a kind at an early stage in my career with Cadbury Limited. . . .

I found my personnel background relevant and valuable when I moved into general management and so I think it is worthwhile to encourage boards of directors to involve personnel management more fully in the strategic thinking of their businesses and to see personnel experience as an important element in the careers of those in senior positions.

The starting point is to decide within what kind of framework will industry be operating over the next 10 to 20 years. Where I would expect to see a difference emerging is in the way the personnel function will be organized. To some extent it will be a bought-in service on a consultancy basis, but within the organization it will form an integral part of a management team rather than being a separate staff activity. This presumes that we will have moved away from the traditional managerial pyramid towards a business team approach. Such teams will have the responsibility of running existing enterprises and developing new ones. They will be set up to carry out particular tasks and the tasks will determine the balance of individuals and skills in the team. Personnel skills must be in demand as an essential element in a rounded business team, but not in the sense of having someone who is exclusively preoccupied with personnel management. The team will be responsible for a business entity and so *each member must be a general manager first and a specialist second.* Apart from anything else such an approach would break down the rigid compartmentalization of large organizations which contributes to the arthritic state of British business.

What weight will be given to personnel at the level of the main board of the company which controls these separate divisions or enterprises? In the past one of the reasons why personnel has often failed to take its place at the company's top table has been that its contribution was seen to be important but peripheral to the primary issues of survival and growth. In the next 20 years we will be more dependent than ever not just on forecasting our future markets aright, but on guessing how the behaviour of individuals as customers and as employees will change and what constraints society and the pressure groups within it will exercise over the activities of our businesses. On these interpretations of the future we will build our plans and agree our aims. From there we have to develop patterns of organization which will enable those aims to be carried out; this means devising structures which encourage change, allow for individuality and operating autonomy and yet fit within a policy framework. All of this could offer great opportunities to managers with personnel training and experience and move the function nearer to the centre of the business stage.

(Source: Sir Adrian Cadbury, Chairman of Cadbury Schweppes Ltd, *Personnel Management*, April 1982, pp. 27–9; emphasis added).

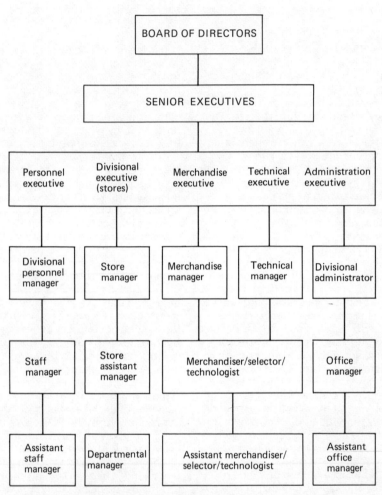

Figure 14   Simplified organizational structure, Marks & Spencer, 1982
(Source: Training Department)

From Figure 14 it can be seen that the personnel function occupies a prominent place in the overall organizational structure. The personnel staff are represented on all levels of the management set-up; they are instrumental in executing the personnel function, acting on an advisory and supporting role to all management staff, as well as ensuring that the human resources of the company are being used efficiently and effectively throughout the organization. Figure 15 takes a closer look at the central personnel group.

The central personnel group is located at the head office and is responsible for a wide range of activities. It is a team of well-trained and highly qualified

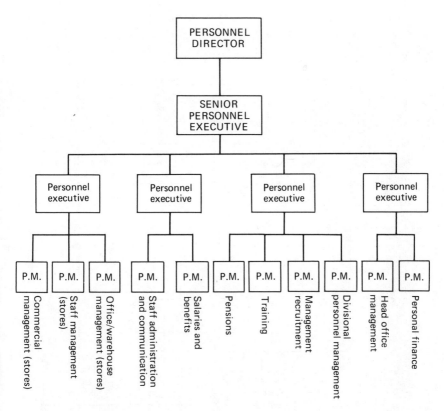

Figure 15   The personnel group at the head office; P.M. = personnel manager(s)
(Source: Training Department)

specialists, the majority of whom have also had extensive experience in commercial and other functions in the company in addition to the personnel one. It is significant to note that, as in other departments in the company, the *Note 1* higher one moves up the hierarchy the more varied is one's background experience likely to be. Almost as a rule, there is hardly anyone who reaches the position of personnel manager without having spent a number of years in other functions, while prospective candidates for further promotion within the personnel group would invariably spend a spell outside the group as part of the management development process. Even for relatively senior managers in the group, it is not uncommon for them to be promoted and transferred to an entirely different function.

This diversity in the sources of recruitment and career progression for personnel staff is highly significant in a number of ways. First of all, it brings the whole personnel staff more down to earth, and as a result there is far less danger of their being dismissed as 'those guys who know nothing about

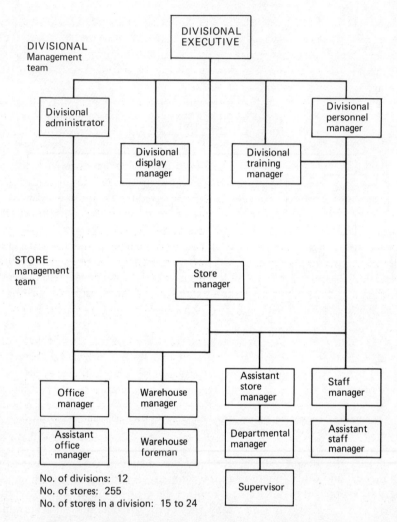

DIVISIONAL Management team

DIVISIONAL EXECUTIVE

Divisional administrator

Divisional personnel manager

Divisional display manager

Divisional training manager

STORE management team

Store manager

Office manager

Warehouse manager

Assistant store manager

Staff manager

Assistant office manager

Warehouse foreman

Departmental manager

Assistant staff manager

No. of divisions: 12
No. of stores: 255
No. of stores in a division: 15 to 24

Supervisor

Figure 16    Divisional management team and store management team
(Source: Personnel Group)

running the business'. Second, it enables them to gain more respect, and hence support, from line management as well as senior management; they tend to be more sensitive to, and realistic about, the operational requirements of the business and can better appreciate the problems, expectations, frustrations and priorities of their colleagues. Third, they are often in a better position to evaluate (and resist the temptation of) untried, sophisticated personnel systems and procedures which might sometimes turn out to be not only wasteful of scarce resources but also downright counterproductive.

Thus the personnel group is hardly a corps of specialists in the conventional sense, but is best conceived of as a group of managers with diverse background and experience who happen at be *at a particular time* engaged in full-time personnel responsibilities. This, in my opinion, constitutes one of the greatest strengths of the personnel staff at Marks & Spencer.

Figure 16 outlines the basic relationship between the management teams at the store and division levels. At each of the stores the staff manager, assistant store manager, the warehouse manager and the office manager report to the store manager, who in turn reports to the divisional executive. Under the divisional executive are the divisional personnel manager, divisional training manager, divisional display manager and the divisional administrator. The staff manager at the store is assisted and supported by the divisional personnel and training managers who spend most of their time at the stores within the division, although the former's direct responsibility is to the store manager. A similar relationship exists between the office manager and the divisional administrator. The store as such is run primarily by the store management team under the supervision and guidance of the divisional team, which provides the essential link between the stores and the head office. At both levels the team approach is very much emphasized—or more precisely, taken for granted.

It is interesting and significant to note the striking similarities between this management structure and the one envisaged by Sir Adrian Cadbury (see p. 131), who comes from a somewhat different industry but shares the same preoccupation with the personnel dimension in management. Sir Adrian has emphasized that in the years to come there will be a major transformation in the way the personnel function is being organized. He underlines three important elements in this transformation: first, the personnel function will form an integral part of a management team rather than being a separate staff activity; second, the team will be responsible for a business entity and so 'each member must be a general manager first and a specialist second'; and third, only such a team approach could possibly develop patterns of organization which would 'encourage change, allow for individuality and operating autonomy and yet fit within a policy framework'. In a fundamental sense, Marks & Spencer has been adopting for years an approach which is now being projected as the dominant trend in the decades ahead.

## Every Manager a Personnel Manager:
### Rhetoric or Reality?

Is it realistic to expect every manager to be a personnel manager? Is this feasible? practicable? desirable? What's left for the personnel manager to do when every manager is also a 'personnel manager'? What does it really entail

**The Job of a Staff Manager**

In a company publication intended for prospective management recruits, the job of the staff manager is described thus:

This personnel function is possibly the least well understood from outside the company. The Staff Manager's responsibilities are extremely wide-ranging. Most of the skills employed by the Store Manager are needed, but are applied with a different emphasis. The Staff Manager is responsible for all matters concerning employment, training, development and welfare. In addition, the Staff Manager controls the overall planning and organization of the store's staffing in order to achieve commercial objectives. In practice, the Store Manager and Staff Manager function very much as a team, contributing their combined experience and judgement to decision-making.

Like the Store Manager, the Staff Manager spends little time in an office. The role is best performed on the sales floor, in the stockroom, and in the staff restaurant, ensuring that the human resources of the store are being used efficiently, and that important priorities are dealt with first.

The Staff Manager also undertakes a counselling role in domestic matters where a member of staff may need advice. This is the historical function of the Staff Manager, and whilst the commercial and administrative aspects of the job have grown in complexity, we have been careful to preserve this special relationship. It is part of the Staff Manager's skill to be approachable enough to act as a successful counsellor when needed, whilst retaining the respect of the staff as a senior member of the management team. We see no contradiction in this dual function, but it demands personal maturity and judgement of a high order.

(From *Retailing and Much More: Careers with Marks & Spencer*, 1981, p. 9.)

when we say every manager should be at the same time a personnel manager? These are very real issues, and they defy simple answers.

Let us begin with a consideration of an extreme—though not entirely unjustified—view on the question. Robert Townsend, in a book quoted above, puts under the heading *Personnel (People VS.)* the following remarks:[1]

FIRE THE WHOLE PERSONNEL DEPARTMENT.

Unless your company is too large (in which case break it up into autonomous parts), have a one-girl people department (not a personnel department). Records can be kept in the payroll section of the accounting department and your one-girl people department (she answers her own phone and does her own typing) acts as personnel (sorry—people) assistant to anybody who is recruiting. She lines up applicants, checks references, and keeps your pay ranges competitive by checking other companies. . . . The trouble with personnel experts is that they use gimmicks borrowed from manufacturing: inventories, replacement charts, recruiting, selecting, indoctrinating and training machinery, job rotation, and appraisal programs. And this manufacturing of men is about as effective as Dr. Frankenstein was. As McGregor points out, the sounder approach is agricultural. Provide the climate and proper nourishment and let the people grow themselves. They'll amaze you. (Emphasis in the original)

Implicit in this comment is the distinction between two major aspects of personnel work. One of these focuses on the 'administrative' side, such as record-keeping, recruitment service, etc., which Townsend does not think is worth setting up a 'personnel' department to handle. As for the other aspect—the more creative, 'agricultural' approach of providing the climate and proper nourishment to let people grow themselves, Townsend seems to consider this too important to be left to the 'personnel' people to do. And as a result, he wouldn't mind firing the entire personnel department.

In all fairness, the 'administrative' side of personnel work has grown too large and complex to be dealt with in the way Townsend would have us follow. In addition to record-keeping and the like, there are at least the following functions to be carried out by personnel staff of some sort:

(1) administration of employment agreements;
(2) negotiation of industrial agreements;
(3) determination of wage and salary schemes;
(4) administration of welfare and benefits schemes;
(5) design and administration of selection and promotion mechanisms;
(6) development of career planning, manpower planning systems;
(7) administration of training and educational programmes;
(8) counselling service;
(9) advisory service on the application of behavioural sciences, etc.

Taken together, these require a group of trained staff to handle them properly and effectively; and to this extent Townsend's dismissal of the entire personnel department is unrealistic. But the main thrust of his argument lies elsewhere. *He is anxious to bring home the point that much of the personnel function conventionally conceived can be, and should be, performed by the line manager.* Unfortunately, however, he has not elaborated on this point.

From my study of Marks & Spencer, it strikes me that the following functions appear to be paramount for every member of the managerial and supervisory staff:

(1) knowing subordinates thoroughly, both as individuals and as groups, their strengths and weaknesses, their potential and limitations, their needs and aspirations;
(2) inculcating in subordinate staff the management style, values and norms of the company and reinforcing them in everyday activities;
(3) motivating subordinate staff, through a correct handling of expectations, capability, performance, and rewards;
(4) creating and maintaining a work environment for the efficient and effective application of the subordinates' efforts;
(5) continuously reviewing and appraising their staff's performance, progress and developmental needs and taking timely and appropriate action;

(6) consciously training and developing their staff on an ongoing basis to enable them to utilize fully their potential and progressively enhance their capability to contribute to the company's goals;
(7) facilitating two-way communication; in particular, effectively communicating to subordinate staff the goals, objectives and policies of the company/department/section, and reflecting their aspirations, ideas, frustrations, etc. to senior management;
(8) involving the subordinate staff as far as possible in decision-making affecting their work.

These are some of the functions implied in the phrase 'every manager a personnel manager'. In some companies, managers are expected to carry out these functions as part and parcel of their role as managers. But in most organizations one of the following situations is more likely to surface:

(1) that these functions are regarded as peripheral to the main tasks of the manager;
(2) that they are not recognized as important and necessary at all;
(3) that they are regarded as important, but beyond the capability of most managers to perform;
(1) that they are regarded as important, but left entirely to the personnel department to carry out.

Marks & Spencer, from my observations, seems to be one of those few companies which take these vital functions seriously and expect all their managerial staff to perform them as a crucial part of their responsibility as management. Throughout the organization, managerial staff—and to a large extent supervisory staff—spend a tremendous amount of time in activities related to these functions. During my attachment to the company I wondered at this aspect of management culture. In an attempt to arrive at a quantitative dimension of the phenomenon I asked several executives and managers to give an estimate of the proportion of time managerial staff (excluding personnel staff) spend on these activities. The 'guesstimates' I obtained ranged from 30% to 60%. (This may or may not be representative of the total management population in the company, but it does provide an indication of its magnitude.)

Simple and straightforward though these functions may appear to be, they are by no means easy to carry out. To put it in another way, certain prerequisites must be present for them to have a chance of being executed. First of all, all managerial and supervisory staff must be thoroughly convinced of their desirability and importance as part of their responsibilities. For this reason managerial staff at Marks & Spencer have to undergo a lengthy process of socialization into this basic philosophy of the company. Those who do not feel they could be at ease with such preoccupations, or that they do not possess the necessary inclination or aptitude for it, either leave the company at an early stage or become confined to sections of the organization where these skills are not so pertinent: which in most cases also means dead-end jobs. Those who successfully emerge from this process take these functions for granted, and consider them as an integral part of their managerial responsibility.

Second, the fulfilment of these functions has to be actively supported by the staff managers, who are generally more experienced and more extensively trained in these areas. There are also additional supporting resources from the divisional personnel manager and the central personnel group at head office.

Third, the attitude and practice of senior and top management are critically important. It would be extremely difficult, if not impossible, to expect front-line managers to carry out the functions we have identified if their superiors do not fully endorse or practise them themselves. What makes 'every manager a personnel manager' possible at Marks & Spencer has much to do with the fact that 'every manager's superior is also a personnel manager', culminating in 'every director a personnel director'. At Marks & Spencer every manager is evaluated and appraised on his/her effort and success in carrying out the personnel function, in addition to other criteria. As a rule, no matter how well one performs in other areas, an unsatisfactory record in personnel skills would almost inexorably severely limit the progress of one's career. Given the scarcity of managerial talent in British business this is a painful system to sustain. But the company's stubborn insistence has been duly rewarded: its senior and top management are almost without exception seasoned personnel practitioners, which in turn ensures the centrality of the personnel function in the organization.

## Top Management Involvement

The importance of this last point cannot be overstated. It has been emphasized above that the three most crucial factors affecting personnel management in any organizations are:

(1) a strong and competent personnel management team;
(2) 'every manager a personnel manager'; and
(3) 'every director a personnel director';

and that they are organically related to each other. The last factor which symbolizes top management commitment and involvement is the pivotal one. Only this can bring the other two into being, and without it the effectiveness of the other two would be drastically undermined. It is most unfortunate that this is often not appreciated by management, and this fact alone explains a lot of the 'failure' of the personnel function in many organizations.

## Pitfalls of Appraisal Schemes

Appraisal schemes usually have some or all of the following objectives:

(a) to provide a data base for the organization's inventory of people, skills and potential;
(b) to provide a mechanism for the proper assessment of performance by an individual so that he may be appropriately rewarded;
(c) to provide the individual with feedback on his performance and personal strengths and weaknesses;
(d) to help the individual and his subordinate to plan personal and job objectives and ways of achieving them.

All of these are desirable objectives, and forms can be devised which will, on paper, provide for the implementation of all four simultaneously. Unfortunately, as many organizations have discovered the hard way, the four are not psychologically compatible, and some of them, (c) and (d), extremely difficult to do well, even in isolation. Some of the reasons for this are:

(1) No individual is going to admit to deficiencies of any significance on a form which will provide data for future job assignment decisions. Yet, unless he genuinely accepts deficiencies, he will have no commitment to deal with them. This suggests that any piece of paper dealing with (c) and (d) should not be copied and should remain in the possession of the individual concerned, otherwise this part of the appraisal system will be seen as a control mechanism, not a developmental mechanism.
(2) The appraisal interview has little effect on performance improvement. Criticism arouses defensive mechanisms and does not improve performance. Praise is ineffective unless close in time to the behaviour. General commendation is discounted as politeness.
(3) Salary is a separate issue. Studies have shown that most individuals in large organizations do not believe that their salary is directly related to performance, but rather to such overall factors as length of service, seniority and qualifications.

The traditional appraisal procedure is not, therefore, very effective. From studies at a large number of companies there is now a consensus of recommendations:

(1) All the four objectives should be fulfilled by different means, at different times, and often by different people, with line management playing a primary role.
(2) Criticism improves performance only when:
    (a) it is given with genuine liking for the other person;
    (b) it is related to specific instances;
    (c) the subordinate trusts and respects the superior.
(3) Improved performance results when:
    (a) goal-setting, not criticism, is used. The goals are specific, jointly set and reasonable;
    (b) the manager is regarded as helpful, facilitating, receptive to ideas and able to plan;
    (c) evaluation of performance is initiated by subordinates, and as a prelude to further goal-setting, not appraisal.

(Adapted from Charles Handy, *Understanding Organizations* [Harmondsworth: Penguin Books, 1981], pp. 252–4.)

It is very common to witness top management paying lip service to the importance of the personnel function, but more often than not deeds do not measure up to words. Sometimes it is a matter of sheer hypocrisy, but in some cases it is a genuine failure of finding the right way to do it. It is apparent that verbal commitment is not enough; commitment materializes only to the extent of the actual time and effort allocated to the task. In this connection the following case reported by Douglas McGregor in a classic study is pertinent:

A staff group in a large company made a concentrated attempt several years ago to follow the 'manufacturing' approach to management development by creating an elaborate formal program and attempting to sell it to management. After some time this group became aware that the desired purposes were not achieved. The program was not operating well; most managers were not using the procedures or the forms, and there was rather generally a passive resistance to the whole field of management development.

Instead of concluding (as some management development staff groups have under these familiar circumstances) that the remedy was more 'selling' or a training program to teach management how to use the formal machinery, this group decided to start again using an entirely different approach. This involved just one activity: annual meetings of the president of the company with each of his immediate subordinates, individually, in which the subordinates reported in detail to the president on his activities and accomplishment in creating an environment conducive to the growth of his subordinates. Each individual reporting to him, and each individual at the second level below him, were discussed with the president in detail. The emphasis was on what the manager was doing to make it possible for his subordinates to further their own self-development. The president made it clear—not only in words, but also in action—that he held his own subordinates accountable for this managerial function, and that how well they fulfilled the responsibilities in these respects would make a substantial difference in their own rewards and punishments.

After a couple of years, the effects of this single activity were substantial. . . . The managers reporting to the president found that they could not fulfill this responsibility without encouraging a similar process among those reporting to them, and so the general emphasis upon accountability for management development began to move down in the organization. The managers themselves learned a good deal as they attempted to fulfill this new responsibility. This approach involved little formal machinery. Each manager was encouraged to develop his own methods for presenting to the president and his own ways of working with his subordinates to further their growth.[2]

This illustrates vividly the importance of top management involvement in the 'non-administrative' elements of the personnel function. Like the president in this company, senior management and the main board at Marks & Spencer spend an exceptionally large amount of time on similar personnel work. Indeed, personnel work—in the broadest sense of the term—is conceived of not so much as a 'function' but as a way of life, and as such it permeates the entire organization, from the board room to the sales floor. This of course is not something that can be achieved overnight, and has very much to do with the overall philosophy and values of the business consistently pursued over the different generations of management. This might well be one of the most 'inimitable' aspects of the company, but it does demonstrate the pivotal importance of top managerial involvement in the personnel function.

## Developing Human Resources

The readers may recall Charles Handy's questions mentioned in the last chapter:

(1) What is the total value of your company's human assets?
(2) Is it appreciating, remaining constant, or being depleted?
(3) Do your compensation and other motivation–reward systems reflect an individual's present value to the firm?
(4) Does your company really (I mean *really*) reward managers for increasing the value of their subordinates to the firm?

It scarcely needs me to point out that not too many companies take these questions seriously. The idea of human assets is often employed only in a purely figurative or, worse still, rhetorical, sense. As such, there is hardly any sensitivity to the issue that these assets could appreciate in value or be depleted. For most managers and employees, perhaps the only possible places where they can find mention of such terms as human assets are the chairman's reports or occasional speeches. This underlines much of the confusion and scepticism surrounding the efforts in continuously training and developing the employees. When mangement is not fully convinced of the possibility and desirability of increasing the value of the company's human assets over time, it is difficult to envisage any genuine commitment to the development of the human resources of a firm.

The third question is even more widely overlooked. As many companies have learned the hard way, having a pool of over-trained personnel in insufficiently demanding positions is far more disastrous than having inadequately trained staff. Training and development, to be rewarding for both the employee and the company, cannot be divorced from compensation and other motivation–reward systems, or more generally, from careful career planning for the employees. The key word in this question is the individual's *present* value to the firm, and this implies a three-step process: (1) training and developing the employee to successive levels of skills and competence; (2) providing the opportunities to exercise the newly acquired capabilities; and (3) rewarding him/her accordingly. Training and development, without due regard to all that entails in this process, may result in unrealistic expectations and frustrations, as well as depressed performance and morale.

The last question is a crucial one. It is easy to say—even to put into company policy statements—that every manager is to have the responsibility for training and developing the subordinates. But how many companies—or more precisely senior management—really make their immediate subordinates accountable for this function? For one thing, most motivation–reward systems are not designed explicitly to take this into consideration; managers are more often than not preoccupied with 'bottom lines' of various sorts, and hardly allow themselves to be detracted by the mundane business of training and developing their subordinates. The human assets approach brings home the moral vividly:

UNLESS top management really regards human resource as key assets of the business,

UNLESS it really commits itself not only to maintaining their existing value but to consciously and progressively increasing it over time,

AND UNLESS it takes trouble (and courage) to restructure the entire motivation–reward system in such a way as to ensure that every manager is accountable for the continuous training and upgrading of the subordinate,

There will NOT be much room for the training function in the minds of management staff at various levels, and a training department, however capable and professional, would hardly make a major impact on the organization.

With these considerations in mind we are now in a position to look at Marks & Spencer's practice from a proper perspective. Certain distinctive elements can be identified in their approach. First of all, training and development is considered a career-long process. Initial training—however extended and comprehensive—is seen as but the starting point of a long and continuous process. The company commits a huge proportion—by Western standards—of time, effort and resources in providing training for, and development of, the employees at various stages of their career, and training programmes, formal or informal, are closely integrated with career planning for the employee on the one hand and manpower planning of the organization on the other.

Second, there is full and total management support and involvement in the training function. In a way analogous to personnel work in general, it is by no means an exaggeration to say that every manager at Marks & Spencer is also a training manager. In my interviews with various categories of staff during my attachment to the company, some of the most frequently encountered remarks were, 'What I like most about the company is that they keep on training you and giving you new responsibilities', or 'The company really thinks that you should grow and develop and I never cease learning new things.' An executive put it more bluntly, 'M&S is like a university. The only difference is that everyone here is both a teacher and a learner at the same time.' (Come to think of it, this should perhaps not be so very different when one considers what is an ideal university.)

Third, as has been pointed out above, personnel skills, including the ability to train and develop one's subordinates, constitute an essential element in the company's motivation–reward system. The M&S managers do have their bottom lines to meet, but one of these is precisely that of the efforts and concrete results in performing the training function.

In what follows I shall briefly discuss three major aspects of the training function in the organization; namely, the use of working attachments as a principal training device, career and manpower planning, and the organization of the training department.

## Working Attachments

M&S has been well known for the meticulous planning and organization of its training programmes for different levels of its staff. Indeed some of the management training guides have been 'unofficially' used by other companies in the trade. But while it is difficult enough to draw up good programmes on paper, it is far more exacting to get them properly executed. Here the human factors, not systems and procedures *per se*, are of paramount importance.

In most of the training at M&S there are usually three major elements involved: courses/meetings, attachments, and assessment discussion. Courses and meetings are generally for conveying factual information and for presentation and discussion of particular skills or responsibilities. Assessment discussions, on the other hand, focus on a two-way feedback between the trainer and the trainee. The attachment programme, which is by far the most important part, provides extensive opportunities for the trainee to observe first-hand how various functions and duties are actually carried out on a day-to-day basis. By and large, no particular groups of staff are specifically designated to take on attachment trainees; everyone in the organization may be called upon to look after a trainee on attachment. In fact, for most managerial and supervisory staff there is a continuous stream of trainees assigned to them for various duration. To get a feel of what it involves, let us take an overall view of the training programme for the store manager (see Table 2).

The basic structure of training programmes for different functions in the stores (staff manager, office management, warehouse management, etc.) as well as those in head office (such as merchandising, distribution, technical and other supporting functions) is very much akin to this one, although the substantive contents as well as duration may of course vary considerably. A supervisor trainee, for example, would follow a fundamentally similar programme of roughly the same duration; a technologist or a selector, likewise, would have extensive attachment in different functions at head office as well as in the stores.

TABLE 2    OUTLINE OF TRAINING PROGRAMME: COMMERCIAL MANAGEMENT

| Approx. duration (weeks) | Details |
|---|---|
| 4 | Introduction to store.<br>Attachment to textile sales assistant.<br>Warehouse and stockroom familiarization.<br>Head office: introductory course. |
| 5 | *Textiles dept.*<br>Attachment to supervisor.<br>Divisional meeting: review of textile supervision.<br>Divisional course: introduction to management skills. |
| 8 | Sole responsibility for textile section. |
| 3 | *Foods dept.*<br>Attachment to sales assistant and supervisor.<br>Divisional meeting: review of foods supervision. |
| 7 | Sole responsibility for part of foods section. |
| 6 months | Total Stage 1. |
| 4 | *Head office attachment*<br>Various offices. To include methods of operation, basic systems and procedures.<br>Attachment to a buying department. |
| 1 | *Departmental management training*<br>Attachment to store manager. |
| 4 | Working attachment to staff manager; projects to include: staff analysis and payroll, utilization of staff, development of staff, welfare and personnel policy, service audit, hygiene control. |
| 12 | *Textiles department responsibilities*<br>Working attachment to departmental manager; projects to include: probing a department, forward planning and layout, shrinkage control, in-store sales promotion, quality control probe. |
| 2 | Working attachment to office manager. |
| 2 | Working attachment to warehouse manager.<br>Head office: management skills course. |
| 12 | *Foods department reponsibilities*<br>Working attachment to departmental manager; projects to include: probing a department, food merchandising, quality control probe, early morning reception of goods. |
| 4–8 | Attachment to store manager; assist in day-to-day running of store.<br>Head office: aspects of management course. |
| 16–18 months | Total Stages 1 and 2. |

Source: *Management Training Guide*. Training Department, Marks and Spencer, revised edition, August 1981.

Programmes involving attachments are by no means confined to the initial training of the staff; at different stages of one's career, attachments of various sorts may frequently be arranged. In an attachment one may be assigned to someone who is junior or senior to oneself, or at the same level. Attachments may also be arranged to outside companies—for example, suppliers of manufactured goods, banks, building contractors and even importers in another country. At the same time the company also makes available attachment facilities for outside organizations—again usually for training purposes—such as suppliers, the Civil Service, teaching institutions, overseas trading partners, etc.

As a result there is at a given point of time a high proportion of employees in the company under some sort of attachment programme; and if we take into account the number of people involved in receiving the trainees, the proportion is even higher. In this sense alone there is considerable substance in the remarks quoted above referring to Marks & Spencer as a university where everyone is teaching and learning at the same time.

As a training device the attachment programmes at M&S are probably one of the most well-developed and effective systems among major corporations in the U.K. It has apparently tremendous appeal to organizations genuinely interested in training and developing their employees. But it is also amply obvious that such a system may be extremely difficult to implement in most companies, if only because of the following considerations.

First of all, it entails a heavy commitment on the part of all levels of managerial staff to the training function. They must not, at the very least, regard the training responsibilities as extraneous to their work; but must be helpful, facilitating, and genuinely interested in and concerned about the trainee's well-being and progress.

In the second place, the overwhelming majority of the staff must themselves be well trained, competent and effective enough not to feel threatened by someone closely following their daily work. Indeed one of the principal—though not always articulated—obstacles for introducing attachment programmes in most organizations is apprehension on the part of many staff that their weaknesses and inadequacies might be brought to light. The staff at M&S are by no means infallible and there are indeed obvious shortcomings in their work, but they are on the whole so confidently efficient and effective, as well as receptive to criticism, that few, if any, of the staff have misgivings about the very pervasive attachment programmes. As one manager has put it: 'We are by and large very good. But we keep on improving the least efficient 20% of our operation. So we are not afraid of criticism, nor of ever becoming complacent.' Such an attitude of mind is a prerequisite for the success of company-wide attachment programmes.

Finally, the whole approach is yet another manifestation of the company's conviction and commitment to developing the human resources of the organization. As one director remarks, 'At M&S, training is not a function. It is a way of life, a way to make the organization work and grow.'

## Career Planning and Manpower Planning

It has been stressed above that training and development must be integrated with career planning for the employee on the one hand and manpower planning for the organization on the other. It has often been said that training and development is an act of faith on the part of top management in that one can never be sure of the likely returns to the investment on people. There is much truth in this, but why must it be so?

It seems that by far the most important cause is the fact that training and development is often divorced from career and manpower planning. One of most significant factors contributing to the success of the training function at Marks & Spencer is that the company has put in the same rigorous efforts on career and manpower planning as on training and development activities. Staff at Marks & Spencer are by no means a mere number in the company's computer memory, but an asset which is highly prized and attracts considerable attention and meticulous care right from the beginning. Systematic career planning is pursued with varying degrees of formality for different categories of staff. Formal career planning is least formal for both the lowest and highest levels of the organization structure. For the sales floor staff, for instance, it is generally the responsibility of the staff manager and the immediate superior concerned. Similarly, at the level of senior managers and above, the formality of career planning is less apparent, although in a sense more visible to other people in the organization. But for the trunk of the hierarchical structure, from supervisor/departmental manager right up to full managers, the planning of the career path for each employee is rigorously carried out. For example, for each category of store management staff, there is at the central personnel group a personnel manager known as category officer, who looks after the career development of every single member of staff in that particular category. Typically, a manager would be transferred to a number of stores of different operational scale and complexity and undertake a number of attachments to various functions at head office before being promoted to a higher grade. This is intended to maximize one's exposure to diverse areas of the business, to enable one to be more of a generalist than a specialist, to explore one's ability to cope with a variety of working conditions and environment, and to broaden one's horizon as part of the preparation for more senior positions. Every move by a manager is carefully planned and executed; it represents the intersecting point of two distinct but interrelated processes: career planning and manpower planning.

As a rule the company does not recruit management staff from outside, except in highly specialized fields. The company trains and develops its own management staff through the recruitment of management trainees who have only a few years' working experience or are fresh from universities; appointment to management positions is almost entirely through internal promotion. As a retail business—although the reader should by now be fully convinced that it is far more than a retailer—its proportion of graduate managers is extremely high. At the same time the turnover rate of management staff is exceedingly low—certainly one of the lowest on the U.K. scene. In a way this simplifies the task of manpower planning since it could rely heavily on the internal source of supply for managerial staff. But more importantly it substantiates the company's claim and commitment to the development of human resources, in a way that few companies in the West are prepared to pursue.

---

**Across the Atlantic: Promotion from Within**

In 1972, when John D. deButts became the chief executive officer of the American Telephone and Telegraph Company, he took a job that by most standards is considered to be the largest managerial job in the world of business. The work force of AT&T numbers almost one million employees (it is larger than the U.S. Army), and it has $80 billion in assets. How does someone come to head a corporation the size of AT&T? Although it often looks like a haphazard process, in many cases it is the result of careful planning on the part of the individual and the organization. It took Mr deButts thirty-six years and twenty-two jobs to reach the top. He joined AT&T straight out of college and quickly began to move up. He was transferred from one functional area to another so that he would become broadly familiar with the business. He eagerly sought out such transfers, realizing that *the 'only' way to get to the top was to have a broad range of knowledge.* For its part, AT&T, which is committed to promotion from within, constantly assessed the performance of Mr deButts and asked his bosses to report on his promotability.

During most of his career at AT&T, the desire of Mr deButts for an excecutive position and the needs of AT&T for well-trained top managers seemed to mesh well. Although no formal joint career planning took place between deButts and the members of top management he developed several sponsors in top management who saw to it that he made the appropriate moves. However, one day in 1958 deButts got what he described as 'the shock of my life'. He was offered the position of general manager of New York Telephone's Westchester office. This represented a demotion, and he could not understand why he was being punished. He called a number of friends in top management to find out what was going on. He was told to take the job even though he did not want to. He did so, and years later learned that the move was brought about by the president of AT&T who wanted to test deButts' suitability for the top job. He passed this test with flying colors and years later the experience paid off with the presidency of the company.

(Adapted from D. A. Nadler *et al., Managing Organizational Behaviour* (Boston: Little, Brown and Co., 1979), p. 40; emphasis added).

## Training and the Trainer

Another major innovation in the training function at Marks & Spencer manifests itself in the organization of the training department. We have already emphasized that a very substantial part of training is carried out informally— through on-the-job training and working attachments, for example. As far as formal training is concerned, a unique feature is observable in the organization of training personnel. Roughly speaking, there are three major foci of training activities. First, training of sales assistants in the stores, which is the responsibility of the staff manager and her supporting staff. Second, training of managerial staff for store operations, which is coordinated by the training department of the central personnel group at head office. Finally, training of head office staff, which is conducted primarily by the respective functional groups. It is in the organization of the training department of the central personnel group which we find a distinctly innovative feature.

The training department, headed by a training manager, is an integral part of the central personnel group. It had in 1982 34 full-time training personnel plus supporting staff. Among the 34 trainers (of which 12 are 'in the field' with the divisions), over 90% are on *temporary* assignments for 1 or 2 years. They are mostly relatively young managers who have been in the company for 4–5 years. At the same time, they are usually outstanding managers who have distinguished themselves in their previous jobs and have been identified as having potential for further promotion. They stay in the training department for 1–2 years, after which they would be transferred back to the stores or to other head office functions; only a small number of them stay in the training department for a longer duration. It is training staff like these who are held responsible for running and monitoring the training programmes for store management personnel. However unconventional this arrangement may appear, there are a number of most apparent advantages.

First of all, the bulk of the training staff is fresh from the field. They are likely to have a more intimate knowledge of the actual operational and managerial requirement than any specialist training staff; and as they have been selected for their proven track record, they tend to command more credibility in the eyes of the trainee. The importance of this can hardly be over-emphasized, as one of the critical factors affecting the outcome of any training programme is the trainees' *perceived* competence and practicality of the trainers. Numerous training programmes have failed elsewhere, largely as a result of the dichotomy of 'theory' and 'practice' as seen by the trainees.

Second, the direct involvement of managers with recent line experience contributes significantly to the design and execution of the training programmes. It makes possible a quicker and clearer identification of training needs as shaped by the ever-changing competitive environment, and the first-hand knowledge of business operations these trainers possess also renders the execution of the training programmes more realistic and effective. What is more, these practitioner–trainers are particularly sensitive to the reinforcement requirements in day-to-day operations for what are being communicated in the training sessions. It scarcely needs to belabour the fact that one of the greatest frustrations for training staff in most organizations is that most, if not all, of what is being conveyed in the training sessions is not being reinforced at all when the trainees are back in their jobs.

Third, the organization of the training department with a substantial input from line management reduces considerably the proportion of specialist training staff. There is, to be sure, a number of experienced training personnel in the department to provide the basic orientation and some element of continuity of the department's work, and the trainers are by no means 'untrained' as they also receive training prior to actually appearing before the trainees. But the emphasis on non-specialist personnel is indisputably apparent. The company as a whole is well known for its very critical appreciation of specialists in whatever functions (this in fact partly explains its guarded approach towards computerization) and in training the conviction is that the more specialist the training staff, the more likely would they become divorced from the 'users' in the field. It reflects perhaps another instance of the company's preoccupation with the integration of staff and line management.

Finally, the training department's set-up itself may be seen as an important training device. Managers on temporary assignments to the department undergo a unique training experience: more thorough understanding of the company's training philosophy, participation in the design of training programmes; first-hand experience of the problems, frustrations and satisfaction in executing the training function; exposure to and acquisition of training techniques; and critical assessment of the training impact on operations. All these constitute a valuable part of their own training and development within the organization. It should not only enable them to appreciate better the training function in the years to come but should also make them more aware of the potential impact training could have on the organization. From a longer-term perspective it is envisaged that managers—and senior managers—with training experience are more likely to make a training-conscious manager, which is what the company would like every manager to be.

## Notes

1. Robert Townsend, *Up the Organisation*, pp. 132–3.
2. Douglas McGregor, *The Human Side of Enterprise* (New York: McGraw-Hill, 1960), pp. 203–4.

# CHAPTER 10

# 'Nobody's Perfect, but a Team Can Be'

In management circles it is fashionable nowadays to show one's allegiance to the team approach to management. At the apex of the organization there is supposed to be a top management team. Below that level, divisions or departments are said to be run by management teams. Across a number of functional units, it is common to have teams of various descriptions such as task force, working parties, committees, etc. Within a department there can be diverse team-like groupings ranging from work teams, autonomous working groups, employee participation teams, quality circles and the like. In such organizations it appears as though teams of various sorts have taken over the management of the business, or, as one management writer has put it, 'where individuals have failed, the teams are now in command'.

All this has been a relatively recent phenomenon. What has made for the sudden upsurge in interest in the team approach? What do the teams mentioned above have in common? In what sense are they management *teams*? What exactly are the ingredients of an effective management team? This chapter attempts to clarify some of these issues in the light of Marks & Spencer's experience in team management.

Let us begin with the first question—Why this upsurge of interest in the team approach? Fundamentally speaking, it is possible to trace it to the limitations of the individual in two major respects. First, owing to the growing complexity of the modern organization with its accompanying functional differentiation and specialization, the amount of professional knowledge an individual may possess is proportionately less and less significant; more and more tasks require the joint effort of a large number of personnel with diverse expertise. The team, in many instances, represents an attempt to integrate the specialized knowledge of different functional areas essential to the completion of a specific task.

The other aspect stems from the limitations of the individual in terms of personnel qualities. For a long time we have naively expected to find in management staff a whole cluster of personality traits that few individuals ever possess. We have searched in vain for *the* ideal manager; the personal attributes expected of him can hardly be found in single individuals—but it may be possible to find them all in a team of people. Few writers have captured this phenomenon more eloquently than Antony Jay, author of the well-known book *Corporation Man*. In an article in the *Observer Magazine* bearing the same title as this chapter, Jay has written:

> For too many years the search for successful management has been seen almost exclusively as a search for the right individual. Corporations have been preoccupied with the qualifications, experience and achievement of individuals. Yet all of us know in our hearts that the ideal individual for a given job cannot be found. He cannot be found because he cannot exist.
>
> Any attempt to list the qualities of a good manager demonstrates why he cannot exist; far too many of the qualities are mutually exclusive. He must be highly intelligent and he must not be too clever. He must be highly forceful and he must be sensitive to people's feelings. He must be dynamic and he must be patient. He must be a fluent communicator and a good listener. He must be decisive and he must be reflective; and so on. And if you do find this jewel among managers, this paragon of mutually incompatible characteristics, what will you do when he steps under a bus, or goes to live abroad for the sake of his wife's health, or leaves to take up a better job with your principal competitor? But if no individual can combine all these qualities, a *team* of individuals certainly can—and often does; moreover the whole team is unlikely to step under a bus simultaneously. This is why it is not the individual but the team that is the instrument of sustained and enduring success in management. A team can renew and regenerate itself by new recruitment as individual team members leave or retire, and it can find within itself all those conflicting characteristics that cannot be united in any single individual. It can build up a store of shared and collectively-owned experience, information and judgement that can be passed on as seniors depart and juniors arrive. And it can be in 10 places at once.[1]

These two factors have been the major impetus behind the changing emphasis towards the team approach to management; but while these driving forces are powerful enough, the record so far is by no means filled with unqualified success. In fact, in many instances the very attempt to introduce team management creates more problems than it solves. Before we examine the exceptional achievement of Marks & Spencer, it is instructive to consider two major innovative attempts at team building. The first is associated with the now popular term 'matrix organization' which represents a systematic approach to the integration of diverse functions in an organization. The second is typified by Dr Meredith Belbin's seminal work on team roles which endeavours to specify the constituent personal qualities for different members of an effective management team.

## The Advent of the Matrix Organization

Each era of management evolves new forms of organization as new problems are encountered. Earlier generations of managers invented the centralized

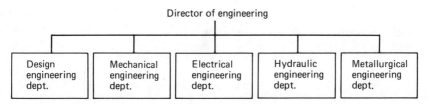

Figure 17    Functional organization

functional form, the line-staff form, and the decentralized product division structure as a response to increasing size and complexity of tasks. The matrix organization grows out of the organizational choice between project and functional form. Taking an engineering firm as an example, a functional organization may be depicted as shown in Fig. 17. As the number of personnel in the organization multiplies and the complexity of jobs/projects to complete increases, the functional organization may experience considerable strain. And as the company and customers become increasingly interested in end results— that is, the final product or complete project—there is the pressure to establish responsibility in someone to assure such end results.

An alternative form of organization is the project organization (Figure 18). But full project organization may not be feasible for a number of reasons. For example, the project may not be able to utilize certain specialized personnel or equipment full time; also, the project might be of relatively short duration. Moreover, highly trained professional personnel generally prefer to be allied organizationally with their professional group; they feel that if their superiors are professionals in the same field, they will be more likely to appreciate their expertise at times of salary advances, promotions, training and development, etc.

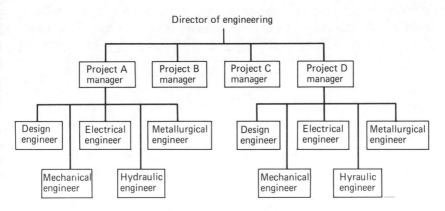

Figure 18    Project organization

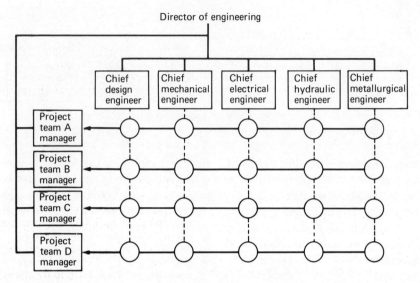

Figure 19　Matrix organization

The matrix organization represents a mixed functional and project organizational structure. This structure reflects a matrix-type set of relationships among the various functional units in support of a number of specific projects (Figure 19). In the matrix organization each project manager is assigned a particular group of personnel from each function, depending on the nature of the project and the type of functional expertise needed, for the duration of the project. This constitutes the basis of the project team.

In addition to project responsibility the project manager has authority over those functional groups assigned to his project. When the project has been completed these groups are reassigned to their respective functional units, or to other active projects. Consequently, members of a matrix organization must be able to work with different teams of people and be adaptable to applying their specialized talents to different project settings. The matrix organization constitutes an ingenious, flexible and dynamic approach to integrate diverse functional expertise in an organization in the form of project teams. It has proved to be an effective means for achieving organizational efficiency that calls for individual specialized knowledge and skills combined with receptivity to change and willingness to function in a hectic environment at an accelerated pace. With increased emphasis on end results and goal accomplishment, there can hardly be any doubt that increasing use will be made of some form of matrix organization in most businesses.

One of the most intriguing aspects of a matrix operation is that it is far more than a change in organizational form. Some of its most distinct characteristics

**Matrix Organization Made Simple**

The identifying feature of a matrix organization is that some managers report to two bosses rather than to the traditional single boss; there is a dual rather than a single chain of command.

Companies tend to turn to matrix forms:

(1) when it is absolutely essential that they be highly responsive to two sectors simultaneously, such as markets and technology;
(2) when they face uncertainties that generate very high information processing requirements; and
(3) when they must deal with strong constraints on financial and/or human resources.

Matrix structures can help provide both flexibility and balanced decision-making, but at the price of complexity.

Matrix organization is more than a matrix structure. It must be reinforced by matrix systems such as dual control and evaluation systems, by leaders who operate comfortably with lateral decision-making, and by a culture that can negotiate open conflict and a balance of power.

In most matrix organizations there are dual command responsibilities assigned to functional departments (marketing, production, engineering, and so forth) and to product or market departments. The former are oriented to specialized in-house resources while the latter focus on outputs. Other matrices are split between area-based departments and either products or functions.

Every matrix contains three unique and critical roles: the top manager who heads up and balances the dual chains of command; the matrix bosses (functional, product, or area) who share subordinates; and the managers who report to two different matrix bosses. Each of these roles has its special requirements.

Aerospace companies were the first to adopt the matrix form, but now companies in many industries (chemical, banking, insurance, packaged goods, electronics, computer and so forth) and in different fields (hospitals, government agencies, and professional organizations) are adapting different forms of the matrix.

(From Stanley M. Davis and Paul R. Lawrence, 'Problems of matrix organizations', *Harvard Business Review*, May 1978, p. 134.)

are far from being generally recognized and appreciated by companies adopting the matrix form, such as:

(1) a dual chain of command, which implies necessarily a dual control and evaluation system;
(2) a non-hierarchical situation where managers have two or more bosses, high levels of responsibility and low formal authority;
(3) a reporting relationship that gives equal power to project/task responsibilities and functional/people requirements of the organization.

Without anticipating our discussion of the Marks & Spencer experience below,
it is instructive to note that matrix management presents some radically new
demands and challenges for the organization and the individuals in it, notably
the following:

(1)  establishing individual as well as team objectives and accountabilities;
(2)  bringing together different people with different opinions and back-
     grounds to make decisions;
(3)  eliciting and encouraging the airing of problems and differences of opinion;
(4)  sensitivity to those situations that require others to make decisions;
(5)  open-mindedness about changing plans and objectives when confronted
     with new information;
(6)  encouraging decisions through a synthesis of ideas rather than authority;
(7)  'brainstorming' ideas in a decision-making situation;
(8)  testing for understanding and commitment to decisions, goals and objec-
     tives before implementation; and
(9)  trying to influence others through competence and knowledge rather than
     authority and status.


## A Team is More than a Group of Individuals

We have seen that in the matrix organization personnel from different
functional areas are represented in a project team. To the extent that the
accomplishment of project/task requires the given range of functional expertise, this constitutes the *necessary* condition for productive team effort. But is
this *sufficient* to enable the team to work effectively and efficiently? The answer
is categorically in the negative. Managers with experience in team work know
in their heart that a lot more is required; but behavioural science researches in
management teams are still too rudimentary to offer a comprehensive and
satisfactory answer. An important advance, however, has been made by Dr
Meredith Belbin of the Industrial Training Research unit at Cambridge, who
has devoted over a decade to the study of the conditions that made for
successful management teams. The findings are fully documented in his recent
book, *Management Teams: Why They Succeed or Fail*,[2] which, according to
Antony Jay, is 'the most important single contribution of the past decade to our
understanding of how human organizations work, and how to make them work
better'.[3]

Dr Belbin's crucial perception is that all members of a management team
have a dual role. The first role, the functional one, is obvious: as in the case of
a project or matrix organization. But the second role, what Dr Belbin has called
the team role, is much less obvious, and yet critical to the successful functioning
of the team.

In a sense we have all been dimly aware of such team roles ever since we first started to work in teams: we know, for instance, that Peter is always coming up with bright ideas; that Noel is always anxious to get decisions finalized and tasks allocated; that Martin tends to pour cold water on other people's proposals; that Paul is meticulous about details. What is more, we know that Peter, Noel, Martin and Paul are likely to show these same characteristics whatever team they are in—the new project team, the task force on cost reduction, the social committee, the quality circle. . . . Moreover, on further reflection, there cannot be all that many characteristic roles that crop up again and again.

It is these enduring characteristics, these team roles, that have been the subject of Dr Belbin's research. Through extensive and meticulous experimentation with working teams, Dr Belbin has isolated and identified just eight roles as the only ones available to team members.[4] These eight roles are:

Chairman
Shaper
Plant
Monitor–evaluator
Company worker
Resource investigator
Team worker
Finisher

## Chairman

The Chairman is distinguished by his preoccupation with objectives. He may be at least reasonably intelligent, but not in any sense brilliant: it is rare for any of the bright ideas to originate with him. He is much more remarkable for his 'character': his approach is disciplined, and it is founded on self-discipline. He often has what is called 'charisma', that is, ability to move others without the overt exertion of authority. He is dominant, but in a relaxed and unassertive way.

In a meeting it is the Chairman who clarifies the team's objectives and sets its agenda; he identifies the problems for the group's consideration and establishes priorities, but does not attempt to dominate the discussion. His own early contributions are more likely to take the form of questions than assertions. He listens, he sums up group feeling and articulates group verdicts, and if a decision has to be taken he takes it firmly after everyone has had his say.

His instinct is to trust people unless there is very strong evidence that they are untrustworthy, and he is singularly free from jealousy. He sees most clearly which member of the team is strong or weak in each area of the team's function, and he focuses people on what they do best. He is conscious of the need to use the team's combined human resources as effectively as possible. This means he is the one who establishes the roles and work-boundaries of the others and also who sees gaps and takes steps to fill them.

## Shaper

While the Chairman is the social leader, the Shaper can be seen as the task leader. His principal role is to give a shape to the application of the team's efforts. He is always looking for a pattern in discussion, and trying to unite ideas, objectives and practical considerations into a single feasible project, which he seeks to push forward urgently to decision and action.

The Shaper is full of nervous energy; he is outgoing and emotional, impulsive and impatient, sometimes edgy and easily frustrated. He is quick to challenge, and quick to respond to a challenge. He often has rows, but they are quickly over and he does not harbour grudges.

Only results can reassure him. His drive, which has a compulsive quality, is always directed at the group's objectives but he, more than the Chairman, sees the team as an extension of his own ego. He wants action and he wants it now. He is personally competitive, intolerant of woolliness, vagueness and muddled thinking, and people outside the team are likely to describe him as arrogant and abrasive. Even people inside the team are in danger of being overwhelmed by him on occasions, and he can make the team uncomfortable; but he makes things happen.

## Plant

The Plant received his name when it was found that one of the best ways to improve the performance of an ineffective and uninspired team was to 'plant' this team role in it. The Plant is the team's source of original ideas, suggestions and proposals: he is the ideas man. Of course others have ideas too: what distinguishes the Plant's ideas is their originality and the radical-minded approach he brings to problems and obstacles. He is the most imaginative as well as the most intelligent member of the team, and the most likely to start searching for a completely new approach to a problem if the team gets bogged down. He is much more concerned with major issues and fundamentals than details; indeed he is liable to miss out on details and make careless mistakes.

He is thrustful and uninhibited in a way that is fairly uncharacteristic of an introvert. He can also cause offence to other members of the team, particularly when criticizing their ideas. His criticisms are usually designed to clear the ground for his ideas and are usually followed by his counter-proposals.

The danger with the Plant is that he will devote too much of his creative energy to ideas which may catch his fancy but do not fall in with the team's needs or contribute to its objectives. He may be bad at accepting criticism of his own ideas and quick to take offence if his ideas are dissected or rejected: indeed, he may switch off and refuse to make any further contribution. It can take quite a lot of careful handling and judicious flattery (usually by the Chairman) to get the best out of him. But for all his faults, it is the Plant who provides the vital spark.

## Monitor–Evaluator

In a balanced team it is only the Plant and the Monitor–Evaluator who need a high IQ, but by contrast with the Plant, the Monitor–Evaluator is a bit of a cold fish. In temperament he is likely to be serious and not very exciting. His contribution lies in measured and dispassionate analysis rather than creative ideas, and while he is unlikely to come up with an original proposal, he is the most likely to stop the team from committing itself to a misguided project.

Although he is by nature a critic rather than a creator, he does not usually criticize just for the sake of it, but only if he can see a flaw in the plan or the argument. He is slow to make up his mind, and likes to be given time to mull things over, but his is the most objective mind in the team.

One of his most valuable skills is in assimilating, interpreting and evaluating large volumes of complex written material, and analysing problems and assessing the judgements and contributions of the others. Sometimes he can do this tactlessly and disparagingly, which does not raise his popularity, and he can lower the team's morale by being too much of a damper at the wrong time. Although he is solid and dependable, he lacks jollity, warmth, imagination and spontaneity. Nevertheless he has one quality which makes him indispensable to the team: his judgement is hardly ever wrong.

## Company Worker

The Company Worker is the practical organizer. He is the one who turns decisions and strategies into defined and manageable tasks that people can actually get on with. He is concerned with what is feasible, and his chief contribution is to convert the team's plans into a feasible form. He sorts out objectives, and pursues them logically.

Like the Chairman, he too has strength of character and a disciplined approach. He is notable for his sincerity, his integrity, and his trust of his colleagues, and he is not easily deflated or discouraged; it is only a sudden change of plan that is likely to upset him, because he is liable to flounder in unstable, quickly changing situations.

He is a bit obsessed with stable structures, and is always trying to build them. Give him a decision and he will produce a schedule; give him a group of people and an objective and he will produce an organization chart. He works efficiently, systematically and methodically, but sometimes a little inflexibly, and he is unresponsive to speculative, 'airy-fairy' ideas that do not have visible immediate bearing on the task in hand. At the same time he is usually perfectly willing to trim and adapt his schedules and proposals to fit into agreed plans and established systems. If anyone does not know what on earth has been decided and what he is supposed to do he will go to the Company Worker first to find out.

## Resource Investigator

The Resource Investigator is probably the most immediately likeable member of the team. He is relaxed, sociable and gregarious, with an interest that is easily aroused. His responses tend to be positive and enthusiastic, though he is prone to put things down as quickly as he takes them up.

He is a member of the team who goes outside the group and brings information, ideas and developments back to it. He makes friends easily and has masses of outside contacts. He is rarely in his office, and when he is, he is probably on the phone. His range and variety of outside interests can lead him, like the Plant, to spend too much time on irrelevancies that interest him: nevertheless his is the most important team role to preserve the team from stagnation, fossilization and losing touch with reality.

## Team Worker

The Team Worker is the most sensitive of the team—he is most aware of individuals' needs and worries, and the one who perceives most clearly the emotional undercurrents within the group. He also knows most about the private lives and family affairs of the rest of the team. He is the most active internal communicator; likeable, popular, unassertive, the cement of the team. If someone produces an idea, his instinct is to build on it, rather than demolish it or produce a rival idea.

He is a good and willing listener and communicates freely and well within the team, and also helps and encourages others to do the same. As a promoter of unity and harmony, he counterbalances the friction and discord that can be caused by the Shaper and the Plant, and occasionally by the Monitor–Evaluator. He particularly dislikes personal confrontation and tends to try and avoid it himself and cool it down in others.

When the team is under pressure or in difficulties the Team Worker's sympathy, understanding, loyalty and support are especially valued. He is an exemplary team member, and though in normal times the value of his individual contribution may not be as immediately visible as most of the other team roles, the effect is very noticeable indeed when he is not there, especially in times of stress and pressure.

## Finisher

The Finisher worries about what might go wrong. He is never at ease until he has personally checked every detail and made sure that everything has been done and nothing has been overlooked. It is not that he is overtly or irritatingly fussy—his obsession is an expression of anxiety.

The Finisher is not an assertive member of the team, but he maintains a permanent sense of urgency which he communicates to others to galvanize them into activity. He has self-control and strength of character, and is impatient of, and intolerant towards, the more casual and slap-happy members of the team.

If the Finisher has one major preoccupation it is order; he is a compulsive meeter of deadlines and fulfiller of schedules.

If he is not careful he can be a morale-lowering worrier with a depressive effect on the rest of the team, and he can too easily lose sight of the overall objective by getting bogged down in small details. Nevertheless his relentless follow-through is an important asset.

### USEFUL PEOPLE TO HAVE IN TEAMS

| Type | Typical features | Positive qualities | Allowable weaknesses |
|---|---|---|---|
| Company Worker | Conservative, dutiful, predictable. | Organizing ability, practical common sense, hard-working, self-discipline. | Lack of flexibility, unresponsiveness to unproven ideas. |
| Chairman | Calm, self-confident, controlled. | A capacity for treating and welcoming all potential contributors on their merits and without prejudice. A strong sense of objectives. | No more than ordinary in terms of intellect or creative ability. |
| Shaper | Highly strung, outgoing, dynamic. | Drive and a readiness to challenge inertia, ineffectiveness, complacency or self-deception. | Proneness to provocation, irritation and impatience |
| Plant | Individualistic, serious-minded, unorthodox. | Genius, imagination, intellect, knowledge. | Up in the clouds, inclined to disregard practical details or protocol. |
| Resource Investigator | Extrovert, enthusiastic, curious, communicative. | A capacity for contacting people and exploring anything new. An ability to respond to challenge. | Liable to lose interest once the initial fascination has passed. |
| Monitor–Evaluator | Sober, unemotional, prudent. | Judgement, discretion, hard-headedness. | Lacks inspiration or the ability to motivate others. |
| Team Worker | Socially orientated, rather mild, sensitive. | An ability to respond to people and to situations, and to promote team spirit. | Indecisiveness at moments of crisis. |
| Finisher | Painstaking, orderly, conscientious, anxious. | A capacity for follow-through. Perfectionism. | A tendency to worry about small things. A reluctance to 'let go'. |

(From R. Meredith Belbin, *Management Teams: Why They Succeed or Fail* (London: Heinemann, 1981), p. 78. Reprinted by permission of William Heinemann Ltd.)

## Team Roles: Some Management Implications

It is obvious that not every team must necessarily consist of eight members. It is possible, and often desirable or necessary, for a team member to perform more than one role. The important thing is that, from Dr Belbin's research findings, the successful team usually has each of the eight roles covered by at least one member of the team. Readers with management team experience may draw their own conclusions from the discussion of team roles above. The following are some of the implications which deserve special attention:

(1) When putting a team together, be sure to select a group of individuals who could cover all the team roles. This assumes that one must have an intimate knowledge of each member's strengths and weaknesses as well as his preferred team roles.[5]

(2) If one of your existing management teams is not working very well, try to analyse it in terms of the eight team roles. Try to see if you can identify the major gaps and ensure that you fill them with appropriate team members.

(3) Whenever you are yourself being enlisted in a team, try to examine its composition in terms of team roles. Bring it to the attention of the one who puts the team together if it is out of balance. If nothing can be done about the membership, try at least to mobilize some of the members to fill the apparent gaps.

(4) When you are staffing a department or any operating unit, do not focus only on the head of the group; focus on building a team which has a wide team-role coverage. The importance of this cannot be overstated; witness the countless incidences in which an individual may perform extremely well in a certain team but becomes utterly ineffective in another setting.

(5) In building a team, pay special attention to the *Chairman* and the *Plant*. While not exaggerating the role of the Chairman, think of it as critical: he must be an inspiring and commanding figure who generates trust and looks for and knows how to use ability. A successful team also needs one strong *Plant* who is highly intelligent, creative and a source of original ideas. It is a must to get these two roles filled by the right persons. (Caution: too many *Plants* in one team may be counter-productive; such a team is most likely to be highly inefficient, spend too much time in abortive and destructive debate and be extremely difficult to manage, or to get things done.)

(6) Successful teams are also characterized by a membership which offers a good spread in team-role coverage. The Chairman has a special responsibility for ensuring that there is a good match between the members' personal characteristics and their roles in the team. Weaknesses can be compensated for by self-knowledge: this applies as much to the individual as to the team. A Chairman should always be on the look-out for any imbalance and it should be remembered that a single admission to a team can change the fortunes of a group, while a single subtraction from the team can have an

equally momentous effect in the other direction unless the balance is re-established.

## Management Teams: Marks & Spencer Style

Let us now consider the management teams at Marks & Spencer. It should be pointed out right away that Marks & Spencer has not explicitly adopted the matrix form of organization. Nor has it built its management teams employing Dr Belbin's framework of team roles. But, as I shall demonstrate below, the remarkable effectiveness of its management teams can be understood precisely in terms of the rationale underlying the matrix organization and team role theory.

For analytical purpose—and for this purpose only—we shall take up the discussion of the matrix organization and the team roles in turn. In a significant sense the store management structure at Marks & Spencer is a type of matrix organization. The organization of the divisional and store management teams depicted on p. 134 of the previous chapter can be understood in terms of a matrix (Figure 20). This organization chart represents a more realistic approx-

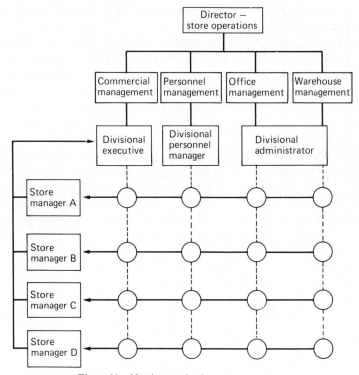

Figure 20   Matrix organization: store management

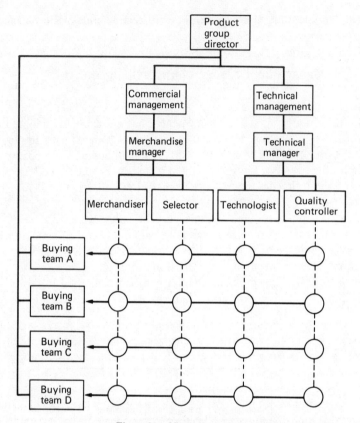

Figure 21    Matrix organization: buying office

imation of the actual reporting relationships than the previous one (Figure 16). For instance, in the previous chart it is *implicit* that the members of the store management team have two 'bosses'; in the matrix chart, on the other hand, the dual chain of authority is very much *explicit*. This constitutes a distinctive characteristic of the store management structure at Marks & Spencer. At the store level the management team has a relatively high degree of autonomy in running the operation and the members of the team all report directly to the store manager. But the initial training, subsequent assignments and career progression of these same members are divisionally—and in effect, centrally—administered by the divisional team and the category officer at head office. As far as performance planning and appraisal is concerned, it is the *joint* responsibility of the two bosses, i.e. the store manager and the relevant divisional manager, thus recognizing the imperative of having a dual system of control and evaluation corresponding to the dual chain of authority.

In another context, at head office another form of matrix organization is observable. Most of the head office staff are organized into buying teams, known as buying offices, responsible for designing, selecting and procuring different lines of products. For example, in the textile group there are buying offices looking after children's wear, ladies' underwear, ladies' fashion, men's garments, etc. The organization of the buying team is very much a manifestation of matrix management (Figure 21). In each of the buying teams there are at least four principal members; for some teams there may be two or more persons representing one function. They work as a team in executing the buying office's functions. The team is usually headed by a senior member of the group who is usually from the commercial side. Again, it is apparent that the team members have two 'bosses' at the same time (even though, as in the case of store management, the term 'bosses' at Marks & Spencer does not have the usual connotations as in most other organizations). The characteristic mode of decision-making in the team is by consensus. When there are differences of opinion each member tends to influence the other by reasoning, competence and knowledge rather than status and authority. This is made possible and greatly facilitated by one important fact—namely, that all team members have gone through the same extended training programme and possess a working knowledge of the other members' functional areas as a result of the attachment programme. This vital point cannot be overstated. In a significant sense each member is a generalist first and a specialist second. This enables a more *organic* integration of the members' functional roles in contrast to a mechanical combination of individuals thrown together in a 'team'. To underline this phenomenon, it is possible to postulate two polar types of teams in matrix organizations: at the one end is the 'organic' team characterized by a high degree of cross-fertilization and 'organic solidarity'; at the other end is the 'mechanic' team with a low level of mutual knowledge of the team members' functional roles. Diagrammatically this may be presented as in Figure 22. Largely as a result of the organizational structure and carefully designed training programmes, management teams at Marks & Spencer approach more closely the polar type of 'organic' teams.

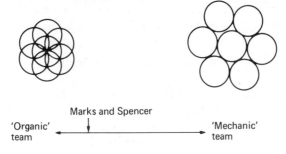

Figure 22    Two polar types of teams

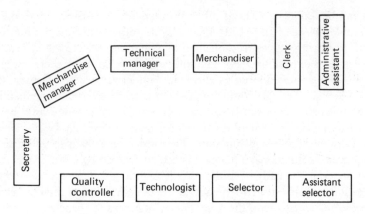

Figure 23   A typical buying office layout: foods group

There is yet a further factor contributing to the effectiveness and solidarity of the buying team. This concerns the physical arrangement of the buying offices. It is apparent that team performance hinges very much on close interaction and communication of the team members. The buying office design reflects this concern by putting all the team members into a single office instead of having the commercial and technical personnel located in different offices. Typically, a buying office looks something like Figure 23. Such a layout has been designed to maximize the contact of the constituent members. Although the composition of the team remains relatively constant over time, the membership of the team may change from time to time. Typically few individual staff stay in the same team for more than 2–3 years; they may be transferred to other teams partly because of organizational requirements or more commonly as part of the training and career development process. But for a given functioning team, there is intimate contact among its members, which facilitates continuous consultation (each is within 'shouting distance' of another), collective decision-making, mutual awareness of functional requirement and routines, and the fostering of a team spirit.

## Can Team Roles Be Trained?

It is interesting and significant to note that although Dr Belbin has referred to Marks & Spencer as a classic case of 'winning teams in industry', the company's team-building efforts have evolved and developed quite independent from Dr Belbin's work on team roles. But from hindsight, it appears that their effectiveness can in part be understood and appreciated in terms of team-roles theory.

Simply put, most management teams at Marks & Spencer seem to have a wide coverage of the eight team roles. How do they manage to achieve this? Part of the reason may be attributable to their recruitment policy, and part of it has much to do with the nature of the training their staff receive. As far as recruitment is concerned, the company's rigorously formulated and meticulously executed policy helps ensure that only individuals with certain requisite personality traits are selected. For example, for management trainees the company looks consciously for such personal qualities as being articulate, analytical, resourceful, versatile, sociable, and possessing self-discipline, drive and imagination. The company employs elaborate interview and testing procedures to ensure that it identifies the right individuals to recruit. This applies just as much to commercial as to technical and other functional personnel.

The recruitment and selection exercise at Marks & Spencer is extremely time-consuming and 'management-intensive' and the recruitment cost per employee is apparently much higher than that in most companies of comparable size and complexity. But the result is that the candidates who emerge from the elaborate screening are those who possess the personal attributes consistent with and compatible to the management culture of the company. Viewed from another angle, they are individuals who have the *potential* to be *trained* into a relatively large number of team roles, such as Chairman, Shaper, Company Worker, Team Worker, etc. The emphasis here has been on training potential; that is, possessing the necessary inclination, aptitude and requisite personal qualities.

I have indicated above that one of the distinctive characteristics of the training programme at Marks & Spencer is its emphasis on providing the trainees with a broad exposure to the different functional areas of the business. An additional defining characteristic of such a programme is its implicit but effective training of the staff concerned into a broad range of team roles. For instance, all trainees are socialized into the role of the Chairman through leadership training and 'training by modelling'—that is, close observation of various chairmen at work during the attachment programmes. At Marks & Spencer, to be a manager means at the very least an effective chairman. In a similar way, trainees obtain an insight into the requirements of a Team Worker, especially in their attachments to the staff/personnel manager.

In the training programmes there is also the emphasis on 'project' assignment with the trainees taking the initiative to identify a problem area, probe into it and formulate a strategy to tackle it—elements of the Shaper's role. Management at Marks & Spencer places a premium on the ability 'to give a shape to the application of a team's efforts', the ability to unite ideas, objectives and practical considerations into a single, feasible project. At the same time, the management culture of the organization also demands the prospective manager to be a Company Worker whose distinct traits are being practical, systematic, methodical and result-oriented—in a word, a practical organizer.

Although it appears that the roles of the Plant and the Resource-Investigator may seem to have more to do with in-born talent and personality traits, there is ground to believe that training and experience may at least to some extent affect the effectiveness of these two roles. While it is true that to be a creative and original thinker is something that can hardly be taught, it is possible through better knowledge and appropriate exposure to a broad range of the business to furnish the potential Plant with more 'raw materials' to exercise his ingenuity. Assuming there is a reasonable number of Plant in the management staff of the company, the fact that they have a broad knowledge of the business is likely to make them more productive creative thinkers.

This is similarly true for the Resource-Investigator. Through the extensive working attachment programmes, staff at Marks & Spencer typically have a wide network of contact throughout the organization. Whenever they are confronted with a problem they are in a privileged position to tap the resources of diverse functional departments within the organization to tackle it. The Resource-Investigator is by nature outgoing, sociable, and has masses of outside contacts; but when there is an on-going programme of planned staff mobility throughout the organization, even people with less inclination as the classic Resource-Investigator may be able to develop the type of contact and outside resources that they may utilize when needed.

It is more difficult to say that one can be 'trained' to be a Monitor-Evaluator, in Dr Belbin's sense of a dispassionate, cool-headed critical analyst. But the management training of the company does stress the skills in assimilating, interpreting and evaluating large volumes of complex materials, especially sales-related statistics and the ability to analyse multi-faceted problems and assess the judgements and contributions of the others. Finally, as far as the Finisher is concerned, the M&S operation is known for its thoroughness in detail management—an area that is unsurpassed in the U.K. scene. Staff at all levels—board members included—are expected as a part of their duties to master the finest details of the respective operation.

Two things must be emphasized at this point. Firstly, when training is mentioned in the preceding discussion it refers not only to formal training programmes as such but also the more important career-long training process intercepted by working attachments of various kinds. Secondly—and this is very important—by emphasizing that the training process contributes to socializing the staff into a variety of team roles, it is not, however, intended to imply that most M&S staff are comfortable in all of the team roles. What has been underlined is the fact that the nature and type of training the staff receive has been instrumental in enabling most of them to be familiar with a relatively large number of team roles, perhaps three or four, which makes them somewhat more versatile in terms of team roles. It is perhaps being a 'generalist' in another sense. Broadly speaking, it can be observed that at M&S the higher one moves up the management hierarchy, the more all-round one may be in terms of team roles, bearing in mind that the 'ideal' manager is one who has all the team role attributes present in one single person.

## The Double-versatile Team Member

We may now pull together our discussion of matrix organization and team roles in an attempt to get at the secret of success of the M&S teams. We have emphasized that the member of a team has a dual role: a functional role and a team role. In some organizations of considerable complexity the matrix form provides a useful framework for integrating a range of functional roles in a matrix team. We have also underlined some of the prerequisites for the proper functioning of matrix organization, such as dual chain of command *accompanied* by dual system of evaluation, open and consultative management style, etc. But even when all these necessary conditions are present—which is already by no means easy to obtain—there may be difficulties in getting the matrix teams to function properly if the team roles are entirely left out of the picture.

Here the classic problems may appear something like this: in a certain team the necessary functional roles may be well represented but the team roles as discussed above may not be adequately covered by the individuals forming the team. Alternatively, there may be a team which has a broad coverage of the team roles but falls short of some of the requisite functional roles. More generally speaking, how to design and construct a team that *simultaneously* meets the requirements of both functional and team roles constitutes one of the most intriguing aspects of team-building. This is also one of the most critical factors determining the fortunes of management teams in industry. It is here that the M&S experience of team work offers the most valuable insight.

In a significant sense the effectiveness of the M&S management teams hinges on the company's success in enabling most of its staff to have a relatively high degree of versatility in terms of functional as well as team roles. The M&S staff are to a considerable extent a 'generalist' in both dimensions. This makes it possible to combine and recombine the teams in a way that almost automatically ensures meeting both the requirements of functional and team roles, even in spite of the fact that the concepts of team roles are not being employed explicitly. This is perhaps another aspect of what Robert Heller has referred to as the 'inimitable magic' of M&S. But if our analysis has been substantially correct, then maybe it is not as mystic as the word 'magic' implies—though nonetheless 'inimitable'.

The M&S investment in training and in creating the conditions for effective team work has been gigantic and amazingly long-term, but the payoff, as we have seen, is equally spectacular. In practical business terms it enables the company to acquire a unique competitive edge which goes a long way to explaining the enviable record of the company's success.

# Notes

1. Antony Jay, 'Nobody's perfect, but a team can be', *Observer Magazine*, 20 April 1980. An abridged version appeared in *Hong Kong Manager*, December 1982.
2. London: Heinemann, 1981.
3. Jay, *op. cit.*
4. Dr Belbin was able to arrive at these team roles by finding a unique human laboratory and being able to work in it for 7 years, forming his hypotheses, testing, discarding, revising and re-testing until he was able to produce a remarkable study of the anatomy of teams with a quite unusual volume of experimental evidence to support it. The unique laboratory was the Administrative Staff College at Henley, Oxon, which runs an internationally famous 10-week course for successful middle-managers with board potential.
5. Dr Belbin has developed a powerful and convenient questionnaire (consisting of seven questions) which can be used to ascertain an individual's preferred team role. It is included as an appendix in his book *Management Teams: Why They Succeed or Fail, op. cit.*, pp 153–7.

# CHAPTER 11

# 'A Private Welfare State' or A Theory Z Organization?

Welfare is something which, like love itself, is always changing its opportunities and demands. There is no end to what is required in a happy marriage and in good labour-relations, simply because human nature and general circumstances are always changing in relation to each other.

Israel Sieff, ex-Chairman, Marks & Spencer

It has already been emphasized that the popular image of Marks & Spencer as a paternalistic company is highly misleading. It is misleading in the sense that it obscures some of the most crucial aspects of the 'good human relations' which characterize the company; the discussions in the preceding two chapters may perhaps have shown why this is so. This does not, however, imply that all the fabulous fringe benefits, amenities and welfare schemes so much associated with the paternalistic label are fictional or insignificant. What has been emphasized is the fact that they should best be understood only as 'hygiene factors' and thus put into their proper perspective.

I introduced the term 'hygiene factors'—as distinct from 'motivating factors'—in Chapter 9. Let us elaborate on this slightly. In a series of much-quoted researches on a large sample of salaried employees, Frederick Herzberg studied in considerable depth the factors involved in providing job satisfaction and job dissatisfaction. He has produced the interesting and highly significant result that the factors affecting job satisfaction (and motivation) are *separate and distinct* from those that lead to job dissatisfaction. That is to say, 'the two feelings are not opposites of each other'. The opposite of job satisfaction is not job dissatisfaction but, rather, *no* job satisfaction; and similarly the opposite of job dissatisfaction is not job satisfaction, but no job dissatisfaction. Figure 24 summarizes Herzberg's major findings. Herzberg calls those factors contributing to job dissatisfaction 'hygiene' factors, and those contributing to job satisfaction 'motivators'. The analogy of hygiene is employed to highlight the fact that the presence of these factors is only a prerequisite, but no guarantee, for good health.

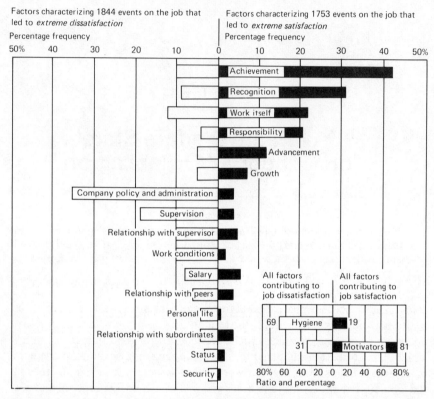

Figure 24    Factors contributing to satisfaction and dissatisfaction. (Source: Frederick Herzberg, 'One more time: how do you motivate employees?' Harvard Business Review, *On Management*, (New York: Harper & Row, 1975), p. 367)

In industrial settings the 'hygiene factors' deal with the question 'why work here?', while only the 'motivators' deal with the question 'why work harder?' The welfare and benefits a company offers have their places only as elements of 'hygiene factors'.

To amplify this point, it may be appropriate to mention another well-known motivation theory: Maslow's concept of hierarchy of needs. Maslow has postulated that there is a hierarchy of needs for individuals in most organizations. Figure 25 shows this diagrammatically. Again, it is apparent that the welfare aspects of an organization—however generous and glamorous—may satisfy only some lower-order needs of an individual.

All this is highly relevant for our consideration of Marks & Spencer as a 'private welfare state'. It reiterates the point that the welfare dimension is but one of the elements of 'good human relations'. It also brings home very vividly the crucial importance of the line manager in motivating the employees and

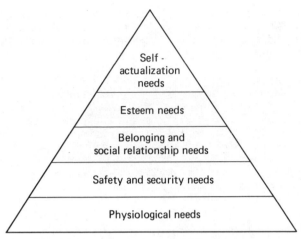

Figure 25    Maslow's concept of hierarchy of needs

satisfying their higher-order needs—*something which can in no way be left to the personnel staff alone.*

In what follows we shall be looking at how Marks & Spencer *care* for their people. No attempt will be made to provide a comprehensive list of benefits that they offer to the staff. Rather, the emphasis will be on a number of more innovative measures which manifest the company's meticulous concern for the well-being of the individual.

**Marksist Approach to Staff Relations: An Outsider's View**

Susan Rogers settles comfortably under a hair drier in an attractive beauty salon. An attendant brings her a three-course lunch on a tray. The menu includes tomato soup, lamb chops with potatoes and green beans, followed by nut-and-raisin cake. After her short, dark hair is styled, Susan goes into a private dressing room, where perfumed soap, talcum powder and hand cream are available. Then she returns to her job downstairs behind the stocking counter at the Marks & Spencer Ltd.'s (M&S) shop in central London.

The luxurious lunch-time treatment is all part of a package of fringe benefits that the U.K. food and clothing store chain offers all its 34,000 employees. The paternalistic pampering is linked with above-average pay and an effort to get all employees, and even their families in some cases, involved in the operation of the business.

For example, Susan Rogers had her hair done for only 75 cents. Her lunch, plus mid-morning coffee and biscuits and a substantial afternoon tea of sandwiches and cake, costs only 25 cents. For 30 cents Susan could have had a chiropody treatment for her tired feet. If she has to rush from work to a cocktail party, she can shower and dress in the pink-tiled washroom. During her rest periods she can relax in a soft arm chair in a beautifully decorated lounge, with wall-to-wall carpeting.

Employees get free attention at M&S' medical department. If they are ill, special consultants and convalescence are paid for by the company. Free dental treatment is offered twice a year. All employees automatically come under a company pension plan. They work five days a week, receive a minimum holiday of three weeks.

The Marks & Spencer combination of good management and modern paternalism commands respectful admiration among fellow-retailers. Robert Werner, president of Grope Docks de France, one of France's biggest supermarket chains, describes Marks & Spencer as 'une très belle affaire'.

A British competitor says: 'They are probably the best retailers in the world, even including the U.S. And their good management naturally includes good relations with their employees.' He admits that other firms have followed the Marks & Spencer lead in providing meals, hairdressers and fancy washrooms, but they cannot match the Marks & Spencer welfare programme.

Marks & Spencer executives are eager to convert others to the 'Marksist' philosophy of human relations. They already support their 600 principal suppliers with over $2.5 million worth of technical services, laboratories and scientific and styling experts every year.

Now M&S has set up a welfare and productivity section to help suppliers improve their staff amenities and employee relations. They send in teams of experts to make recommendations, train staff people, plan building changes.

There are enthusiastic converts. Park Cake Bakeries Ltd improved its canteen and staff facilities and added a staff relations officer; it claims this decreased labour turnover by 30% and improved quality standards. Adria Ltd., a stocking manufacturer in Northern Ireland, made similar improvements and added a welfare officer; it reports staff turnover fell from 47% to 25%, resulting in an annual saving of $40,000 in recruitment and training.

'Marks & Spencer is willing to pay for—and indeed insists on—the sort of facilities and working conditions they give their own people', says C. J. Spackman, divisional director of Bovis Fee Constructions Ltd. This firm has handled all Marks & Spencer construction and redevelopment since 1926. And on all M&S building sites there are canteens serving hot food, showers with hot water and lavatories.

## Caring for People Means Much More than Welfare

During an interview with the present author, a senior executive remarked: 'We care for our people, not just provide them with benefits.' This statement epitomizes the essence of the Marks & Spencer approach to staff welfare. Caring for the employee is the end; welfare and benefits are *some* of the means. The starting point has been—as it should be—human relationships, not things. The implications are that 'welfare' is above all a manifestation of the concern of the needs and well-being of the individual, and that it materializes primarily to the extent that the line manager, the staff manager and top management are genuinely concerned about them.[1] The staff restaurant, for instance, has been one of the much-envied amenities enjoyed by Marks & Spencer employees. As a staff benefit the quality of its service is renowned and probably unsurpassed anywhere in the U.K. But the circumstances that prompted management to pioneer this service almost half a century ago have been less well known. The following recollections by Israel Sieff, ex-chairman and co-architect of Simon Marks, were revealing:[2]

> One day I was in one of our stores and I asked a girl to pack something up for me—she had no idea who I was, and assumed I was an ordinary shopper. As I asked her to get the things ready, Simon, who was with me, glanced at the clock and saw her lunch-time had already begun. 'Don't you start on that,' he said, 'or you'll be late for your lunch.' 'Oh,' she said, 'that's all right, it doesn't make any difference, I won't be having any lunch.' 'Not have any lunch?' I said. 'It's very bad for you going without food in the middle of the day. Why aren't you having any lunch?' 'I can't afford it,' she said.
>
> We were very shocked. We were doing our best with our wage scheme—one of the first things Simon had done when in full control of the firm as Chairman was to start drawing up a wage structure for the business as a whole—and we knew that what we were paying was not to be ashamed of. That night I sat up late with Simon talking. We came around to the conclusion that even if we paid wages which in the majority of cases were as fair and generous as general trading conditions could stand, and even if in the typical case we could feel morally satisfied with what we were doing, there would still be cases in which individuals, possibly because they had extra demands made upon them at home—brothers and sisters out of work, an invalid brother, or some problem of that kind—would so wish to scrape the last farthing to take home that they would go without their lunch or tea. There was only one thing that could cope with this, and that was to provide a hot meal at a cost so low that an employee would have to recognize it as uneconomical not to pay for it and eat it. Out of that chance encounter with a girl in the store developed an expansion of our whole welfare apparatus, which was started by Flora Solomon and her acolytes.

It is this underlying concern for the staff's well-being that spurs the company to pioneer one benefit measure after another which not only far exceeds statutory requirements for employee welfare but also goes well beyond what the competitors in the trade are ready to offer their counterparts. It is also out of this concern that a basic principle for the design and maintenance of staff amenities has been evolved, namely, 'if they are not good enough for those in charge they are not good enough for anyone'.

In the 1930s, as Israel Sieff recalled, the company's concern for the employees' welfare did not make them popular in all quarters. Marks & Spencer was among the small minority of companies who were not only actively interested in the pay and working conditions of their own employees but also in those of men and women who worked for the companies that supplied them goods and services.

In the thirties [wrote Israel Sieff] we announced that we were instituting an inquiry into wages in our *suppliers'* factories. One manufacturer told us fiercely that this was the first occasion he had encountered which a customer was asking a manufacturer to raise wages. Simon promised him that it would not be the last.[3]

The following incident is again instructive:

We arranged with a building firm for the construction of a new store. Just after work began a few of us went to have a look at how things were going. It was raining—raining very hard. The tarpaulins which had been put up to shelter the men were not doing a proper job—the men looked wet and miserable. We said to the builder, 'Why don't you put up a shed where the men can come in the morning and change into working clothes, and bring a spare pair of trousers they can change into if they get soaked?' We found the men had no proper lavatory, and that they were eating their midday meal of sandwiches in the shelter of the half-constructed walls. We asked for a temporary building as a dining-room, and we got them lavatory accommodation.

Some weeks later the Chairman of the firm, an MP, came to see me. He told me with pride that our store would be available for opening several weeks ahead of schedule: productivity of labour on that site had gone up by some almost sensational proportion, and that the casual labour turnover had dropped significantly. We congratulated him.

When I look back, it is the record of doing, or at any rate trying to do, things for the people who worked for us that gave me most pleasure, that and the faith that those who came after us will continue to do the same, and for the same reasons.[4]

The last remark is particularly pertinent. From time to time companies may have the good fortune to have a benevolent top executive who may do marvellous things for the staff. But to be able to sustain a philosophy of meticulous care for the employees over generations of management is an achievement of an altogether different magnitude. It requires—among other things—the transforming of such a philosophy into a core value of the business, fully embraced by all levels of management.

## The Welfare Committee

The welfare committee is a Marks & Spencer institution which does have a paternalistic flavour, but nevertheless reflects its holistic concern for the employees' welfare. We have seen that the staff manager is given broad authority to act sensibly and generously in dealing with people. Local store management were instructed that 'when dealing with human beings, if you are going to make a mistake, err on the side of generosity'. Even so, there are still problems which cannot be dealt with locally or regionally and need a decision from the head office. One of the devices to deal with such problems is the welfare committee. The committee was set up in 1934 and has met weekly without a break since, over 2000 times. On average, eight cases are referred to the committee weekly. Most cases are concerned with special help because of accident or sickness either to the employees or their families. This may mean loans or grants, long leaves of absence, perhaps reduced working hours, soemtimes legal or medical advice and assistance.

The following are examples of the kinds of cases handled by the committee:

(1) A young male employee's father died suddenly in the U.S.A. The following day he was on an aeroplane bound for America, with enough pocket money to meet expenses. When he returned to work he was asked to repay only the amount of money he would have spent on his local vacation.

(2) Another employee, who had been working in a store warehouse for only 14 months, fell and broke his leg, and complications developed. The company paid his full salary for many months until he has officially registered as disabled and granted a government pension.

(3) Another case involved an unmarried salesgirl who had a baby and a dependent mother to support. The company paid her wages for 2 years while she was looking after the baby, and it still paid her full wages when she started to work again for only 3 hours a day.

(4) An employee's husband was seriously ill and she was granted a long leave of absence with full pay to nurse him. When he died the committee paid for a week's seaside holiday for her and her daughter.

A striking feature of the welfare committee is that it has an open-ended budget, and there is no formal limit of its expenditure. There are nine members in the committee; not one of them is on the board. It has, however, complete autonomy to deal with all cases of hardship and disaster. It takes its own decisions and makes suggestions which are rarely turned down.

In a sense the welfare committee provides a safety net—no-one with serious personal difficulties should feel that he or she has nobody to turn to. The committee gives an immediate decision in 90% of the cases and in any event all cases are dealt with speedily and the individual concerned is informed of the decision, or told what further information is required, in a matter of days. The company takes great pride in this institution which it thinks helps ensure that top management never loses sight of the original philosophy of caring for the employees.

## Occupational Health Care

Perhaps by far the most innovative element of Marks & Spencer's welfare schemes is in the field of preventive health care. Indeed, the company has for decades been the internationally acknowledged mentor of occupational health services.

The beginnings of the company's health service dates back to the 1930s. A remarkable personnel manageress, Flora Solomon, was partly responsible for encouraging Simon Marks to pioneer a scheme whereby medical doctors attended the stores regularly. The service was further expanded after the war, with much emphasis on hygiene standards, and the number of store doctors grew until every store had a visiting doctor. Today the company operates one of the most comprehensive and imaginative health care systems for its employees.

Broadly speaking, the design of health services at Marks & Spencer has been shaped by three underlying assumptions:

(1) that the responsibility for health maintenance is not the monopoly of the medical profession, but also of government, the employer, the family and the individual;
(2) that it is the employer's responsibility to protect the employees against any health hazard which may arise out of their work or the conditions in which it is carried out;
(3) that it is the employer's obligation to contribute to the establishment and maintenance of the highest possible degree of physical and mental well-being of the employee.

In trying to maintain and improve the health of the employees, Marks & Spencer has two advantages. Firstly, the business is a *relatively* non-hazardous operation. Secondly, the Board is willing to invest much in financial and manpower resources in pursuit of the objective.

The health services department, headed by a chief medical officer, comprises medical, dental and nursing personnel as well as physiotherapists and chiropodists. There are seven doctors, each of whom is involved in a broad range of duties. There are another seven part-time medical officers, each of whom covers a number of stores. All other stores have a contract doctor, who is usually a local family doctor.

In addition, the health services department is staffed by professional physiotherapists and chiropodists. In the physiotherapy section there is a senior physiotherapist and two part-time physiotherapists. As for chiropody, there are one full-time and two contract chiropodists in the head office and every store has a visiting chiropodist.

A special feature of the preventive health care provided by the department is specific screening examinations. Because of the high proportion of female staff in the company, two screening examinations have been given special attention; namely, screening for cancer of the breast and screening for cancer of the cervix (neck of the womb). Breast screening was offered to women aged 34 and over and to age-eligible wives of male staff. The screening takes place every 15 months in the store and comprises clinical and x-ray examination of the breasts. Between 1976 and 1980, 69 cases of cancer had been detected, a rate of 4.4 per 1000 women screened.

As far as screening for cancer of the cervix is concerned, the company was the first national organization to institute this facility. The scheme offers cervical smears to all female employees as well as to wives, irrespective of age. These smears are repeated routinely once every 2 years. Of the 62,987 women screened between 1968 and 1979, 170 cases of cancer were spotted. They were all referred to gynaecologists and had a cervical biopsy performed.

In addition, the department provides such services as pre-employment health checks, health re-checks (for those with problems detected at the pre-employment health checks), age-related checks, special health checks for employees in special areas, such as food handlers, cold storage warehousemen, etc. It also provides imaginative management health checks for all members of management aged 35 and over. The department's personnel are also heavily involved in a number of committees, such as fire, health and safety committee, hygiene committee and welfare committee.

Finally there is the much envied dental service, which has been running for over 40 years, well before the introduction of the National Health Service which began to provide free dental treatment in 1948. Today the department still runs a dental clinic at Baker Street which caters for the needs of the 4000-strong head office staff. In addition, a dental inspection is arranged every 6 months by the inspecting dental surgeon for the staff of all stores. The inspection is intended to monitor the state of health of the whole mouth and not just the teeth. The attendance at the inspection has been over 90% for the past 10 years and the quantity of treatment required has steadily fallen. In 1973 a dental health education scheme was launched when a preventive approach to dental disease was first attracting the attention of the public, mass media and the dental profession. The scheme was first tried experimentally in two divisions in the company. It consisted of illustrated talks given at every store by oral hygienists. Since 1975 it has been extended to all stores, involving 17 part-time oral hygienists. The scheme has been instrumental in reducing the plaque index and gingival index of the staff. The programme is being constantly updated to keep the message interesting and effective. Quizzes, competitions and group counselling with the opportunity to disclose plaque, with instructions on its removal, are some of the recent innovations. (Incidentally, the author—during his attachment to one of the London stores—benefited from the treatment and advice of a company-appointed dentist and oral hygienist.)

## Sharing of Prosperity: Marks vs. Marx?

One of the central contradictions of capitalism is the private ownership of capital. In crude Marxist terms the owners of the means of production constitute the bourgeoisie in the society, while those who do not own any

## Who's Health? Who's Service?

Consistent with the company's policy of close integration of staff and line functions, the health services department at Marks & Spencer is by no means simply a service department in the conventional sense. The medical personnel is expected to have a full understanding of the objectives of the company, the nature of the business, its demands and challenges, the larger socio-economic context of occupational health and the company's resources and limitations in promoting health care among its employees.

The company speaks of 7 Cs in the effective fulfilment of the Health Services Department's role:

(1) *Clarity of objectives*   The objectives of the department and those of specific schemes should be clearly defined and implemented.
(2) *Commercial awareness*   Health services cannot function in a cosy vacuum. Members of the department must be aware of the current socio-economic state of the business as well as the nation's as it affects their resources, the people who are their concern and therefore their activities.
(3) *Customer knowledge*   Just as commercial colleagues must know their customer, the doctors must know theirs. Customer knowledge implies knowledge of the job descriptions, pressures and problems. The interaction of individuals and groups within the company's structure follows on naturally from the second criterion. Therefore, when an individual presents with a problem, each doctor asks himself the question—Can this patient be himself a presenting symptom of a more widespread departmental problem rather than only a sick individual?
(4) *Competence*   Careful selection of occupational health personnel should ensure good standards. However, further training is necessary to acquire more knowledge relevant to the worker's health and the work environment.
(5) *Confidentality*   To do the job effectively, those in an occupational health service must have the confidence of all levels of the work force. This depends, not only on the competence of the doctor, nurse or whoever, but also on the confidentiality of the consultation.
(6) *Commitment*   It almost goes without saying that all in Health Services should believe in the company's broad personnel policy and in the objectives of the service, and translate this belief into a very full range of activities. In Marks and Spencer this degree of commitment requires a nucleus of full-time professionals to co-ordinate our activities throughout the company as well as to take part in them themselves.
(7) *Communication*   Even if they fulfil all the other criteria, members of Health Services are wasting their time and many other people's if they don't or can't communicate. Within the company this means effective communication, listening as well as talking—to the patient, personnel group, technologists, other service groups—whoever the right person is at the time. It also means liaison with family doctors, other occupational health services personnel, hospitals and many other outside organisations and individuals.

(Source: 'Occupational health services in Marks & Spencer', mimeographed; Health Services Department, 1982, p. 8.)

means of production, but are obliged to sell their labour power in the market place, make up the proletariat. Although profound changes in the operation of capitalist economy have taken place since Karl Marx's days, the basic source of class division and class conflict, according to the Marxists, has remained fundamentally the same. The capitalist economy, so the argument goes, is still class-ridden and the capitalist enterprise is inexorably bound up with the irreconcilable contradiction between capital and labour.

The capitalist class, to be sure, also recognize the division of interest between the shareholders and the bulk of the employees. In the past two centuries numerous attempts have been made to win the working class over to the side of the owners of capital. Some of these are ingenious and appear to have produced results, while others are self-defeating or even disastrous. Marks & Spencer, being a capitalist enterprise, has also made serious attempts to reconcile and integrate the interests of shareholders and the employees, and one of the means to this end is the introduction of a profit-sharing scheme for its employees.

In his announcement of the scheme to the shareholders in 1977, Sir Marcus J. Sieff, then chairman of the board, remarked:

> Your directors feel that it is important for our staff to be able to have a greater share in the future prosperity and profitability of this business and in a way which gives them a community of interest with our shareholders. Employees and shareholders alike inevitably share the risks of a business; similarly they should both have a stake in the success of that business. . . . This will increase staff involvement in the business and should ensure that the interests of shareholders and employees will be even closer than they are today.[5]

In 1977 a profit-sharing scheme was introduced to provide for the issue of shares to all staff employed by the U.K. company who have completed 5 years' continuous service. Both full-time and part-time employees are entitled to participate, except for temporary seasonal and casual staff. Each year the board in its discretion decides in the light of current profits the number of shares to be distributed to the employees. The minimum profit level below which no amount will be made available for the scheme was set at £100,000,000 pre-tax for the U.K. operation. (The actual pre-tax profits for the years between 1978 and 1982 were £118, £162, £174, £181 and £222 millions respectively.)

After the board has decided on the amount of shares to be distributed, the allocation to the qualifying employees is based on a simple formula; that is, in proportion to the total taxable remuneration they receive in the financial year concerned. In another words, if an employee's remuneration is 0.1% of the total remuneration of all qualifying staff, he will be entitled to 0.1% of the shares distributed. Typically, a sales assistant earning £4000 a year in 1981–82 may be allocated about 120 shares for the year. The amount of shares distributed and the number of qualifying employees for the years between 1978 and 1982 are shown in Table 3.

TABLE 3   PROFIT-SHARING SCHEME, 1978–82

|  | 1978 | 1979 | 1980 | 1981 | 1982 |
|---|---|---|---|---|---|
| Amount of shares distributed | £1.9 m | £2.7 m | £3.1 m | £3.2 m | £4.2 m |
| Number of qualifying employees | N.A. | N.A. | 19,291 | 19,566 | 21,086 |

The following extracts from a company leaflet may serve to indicate what the company intends the profit-sharing scheme to mean to the average staff:[6]

– Why does the Company have Profit-Sharing?
   Profit-Sharing was introduced to enable United Kingdom Staff to become shareholders of Marks and Spencer Limited. The Board wishes longer serving staff to have greater involvement in the Company's prosperity and profitability.
   Staff who are eligible and who are issued with shares become part-owners of the business in which they work.

– What is a share?
   The ownership of the Company is divided into equal portions called shares; each one represents a relatively small amount of money. An individual normally becomes a shareholder by purchasing shares through a stockbroker.
   Shareholders are entitled to a portion of the Company's profits and are paid a Dividend according to the number of shares they own. They may vote at General Meetings called to discuss Company affairs.

– Who qualifies for Profit-Sharing?
   All full and part-time United Kingdom staff who have completed five years unbroken service by the end of each financial year.

– Once I qualify, do I automatically receive shares every year?
   Shares may be made available for the schemes each year, provided that the Company's United Kingdom annual pre-tax profits are over £100 million. Profit-Sharing is always subject to the Board's discretion and current Government legislation.

– Can I take cash instead of shares?
   No. The Rules do not allow for the value of the shares to be taken in cash.

– Does the issue of share affect any of the other benefits I receive?
   No. Employees' Profit-Sharing is quite separate from salary and other benefits. It is an additional benefit for longer serving staff.

– Am I paid a Dividend on my shares?
   Yes. Whichever scheme you belong to, you will normally be paid a Dividend in the same way as other shareholders, usually in January and July. You should receive your first Dividend payment in the January after your initial share allocation.

– Will the value of my shares increase?
   The value of the shares of a company depends mainly on how well the company is doing and the state of the national economy. This means that their value can increase or decrease.

– Who administers Profit-Sharing?

Trustees have been appointed by the Board of Directors to administer the schemes. The Trustees are directors and members of staff who must ensure that the schemes are run correctly and fairly according to the Rules.

Each year the Board of Directors decides how much money to make available for Profit-Sharing and the Company then pays this to the Trustees to purchase shares for the staff.

– Can the schemes be altered or terminated?

The principal detailed Rules can be altered or amended only with the approval of the shareholders at a General Meeting. The Board can terminate the schemes at any time, in which case no further shares would be issued.

It is difficult to ascertain the extent to which the profit-sharing scheme has contributed to the integration of the shareholder's and the employee's interest. Suffice it to point out that the scheme is but one element of a well-considered approach to nurture a sense of belonging and loyalty to the company.

## Who Owns Marks & Spencer?

The 1300 million ordinary Marks & Spencer shares are owned by some 235,000 shareholders. Most are small private investors, with seven out of ten owning less than 2000 shares. The biggest single shareholder is the Prudential Corporation, which owns slightly less than 7% of the total. The directors of Marks & Spencer own less than a half of 1% of the total equity of the Company; 22,000 members of staff have become shareholders through the company's profit-sharing scheme.

## A Theory Z Organization?

The preceding discussions have highlighted aspects of the Marks & Spencer approach to staff welfare. Together with the other three chapters in this Part, the analyses have perhaps given a relatively comprehensive picture of the 'good human relations' the company aspires to maintain. Here let us take an overall view of our discussion thus far.

It should be amply apparent by now that the popular paternalistic label attached to the company is strikingly misleading. The company's 'employee relations' are indeed unique in many respects. In fact they are so unique that they are sometimes likened to the Japanese company. This again, in my opinion, is equally misleading though not without some apparent justifications. Let us consider what William Ouchi—author of the best-selling book *Theory Z: How American Business Can Meet the Japanese Challenge*[7]—has said about the typical Japanese and American company (Table 4). Ouchi also emphasized that not only the elements of the respective models, but also the ways in which these elements fit together to form a working system, merit close attention.

TABLE 4    TYPICAL U.S. AND JAPANESE COMPANIES COMPARED

| Type J organizations (typically Japanese) | Type A organizations (typically American) |
|---|---|
| Lifetime employment | Short-term employment |
| Slow evaluation and promotion | Rapid evaluation and promotion |
| Non-specialized career paths | Specialized career paths |
| Implicit control mechanisms | Explicit control mechanisms |
| Collective decision-making | Individual decision-making |
| Collective responsibility | Individual responsibility |
| Holistic concern (for the individual) | Segmented concern (for the individual) |

Employment is typically short-term in American companies. It is not uncommon for companies to have an annual turnover of 50% and even 80–90% in some years; even at managerial level, turnovers of 25% per year are not unknown. Rapid employee turnover necessitates speedy evaluation and promotion. In such organizations people tend to operate without depending on or consulting others. No-one else is likely to know of, or care about, their problems or be around long enough to follow through collaborative responsibilities.

The typical career path in American firms is highly specialized. A lifelong career with a current employer cannot be counted on. To maintain marketability to other companies a high level of specialized skills that can fit in to any company must be maintained. The typical American organization is thus a set of individuals of widely different talents, skills and aspirations. Such people are in an important way strangers to one another. Nothing can be left to an unspoken mutual understanding or to the imagination, since both probably will differ. Thus mechanisms of control become explicit and formal, losing all of the subtlety and complexity that can exist in co-operative life. The obsession with individualism in American society also has its marks on corporate life. Individual decision-making follows naturally from individual responsibility and accountability. Similarly, the typical American company's concern for the individual is highly segmented. Employment is primarily a monetary contract; there is hardly any holistic concern for the employee.

The above description may seem a far cry from the Marks & Spencer operation, and it is tempting to go to the other extreme to assert that Marks & Spencer approaches the typical Japanese company. In fact, the company appears to approximate more closely yet another type of organization—what Ouchi has captured as type Z. The following description of the type Z organization deserves to be quoted at some length[8]:

Type Z companies tend to have *long-term employment*, often for a lifetime, although the lifetime relationship is not formally stated. The long-term relationship often stems from the intricate nature of the business; commonly it requires a lot of learning-by-doing. Companies, therefore, want to retain employees, having invested in their training to perform well in that one unique setting. Employees tend to stay with the company, since many of their skills are specific to that one firm with the result that they could not readily find equally remunerative or challenging work elsewhere. (This perhaps explains in part the low staff turnover rate at Marks & Spencer.) These task characteristics that produce the life-long employment relationship also produce a *relatively slow process of evaluation and promotion.* Here we observe one important adaptation of the Japanese form. Type Z companies do not wait ten years to evaluate and promote; any Western firm that did so would not retain many of its talented employees. . . . However, promotions are slower in coming than at Type A companies.

*Career path* in Type Z companies display much of the 'wandering around' across functions and offices that typifies the Japanese firm. This effectively produces more company-specific skills that work toward intimate coordination between steps in the design, manufacturing, and distribution process. An employee who engages in such 'non-professional' development takes the risk that the end skills will be largely non-marketable to other companies. Therefore, long-term employment ties into career development in a critical way.

Typically Type Z companies are replete with the paraphernalia of modern information and accounting systems, formal planning, management by objectives, and all of the other formal, explicit mechanisms of control characterizing the Type A. . . . In a Type Z company, *the explicit and the implicit seem to exist in a state of balance.* While decisions weigh the complete analysis of facts, they are also shaped by serious attention to questions of whether or not this decision is 'suitable', whether it 'fits' the company.

In Type Z organizations, the *decision-making process is typically a consensual, participative one.* . . . This participative process is one of the mechanisms that provides for the broad dissemination of information and of values within the organization, and it also serves the symbolic role signaling in an unmistakable way the cooperative intent of the firm. . . .

In Type Z companies, the *decision making may be collective,* but the ultimate responsibility for decision still resides in one individual. . . . This combination of collective decision making with individual responsibility demands an atmosphere of trust. Only under a strong assumption that all hold basically compatible goals and that no one is engaged in self-serving behaviour will individuals accept personal responsibility for a group decision and make enthusiastic attempts to get the job done. . . .

Type Z companies generally show *broad concern for the welfare of subordinates and of co-workers as a natural part of a working relationship.* Relationships between people tend to be informal and to emphasize that whole people deal with one another at work, rather than just managers with workers and clerks with machinists. This holistic orientation, a central feature of the organization, inevitably maintains a strong egalitarian atmosphere that is a feature of all Type Z organizations.

It is amazing to observe the close similarities between what has been described here as Type Z organization and the Marks & Spencer operation. This serves to underline a critical point; namely, that holistic concern for the employee— which many outside observers reckon to be nothing more than 'welfare'—is an integral element of a particular management philosophy and approach. The implication is that the so-called 'private welfare state' at Marks & Spencer cannot be understood and properly appreciated in isolation from its broader management culture; it is part and parcel of a distinct management philosophy which has yet to find widespread acceptance in Western enterprises.

## Notes

1. There are plenty of examples in which the employing institution does offer excellent benefits but its management does not really care about the employees as individuals. Some government departments, for instance, fall into this category.
2. Israel Sieff, *Memoirs* (London: Weidenfeld & Nicolson, 1973), p. 158.
3. *Ibid*, p. 186.
4. *Ibid.*, pp. 186–7.
5. 'Employee share schemes', the chairman's report to the shareholders, 9 June 1977.
6. 'Profit-sharing: an explanation'. Marks & Spencer leaflet, 1982.
7. New York: Addison-Wesley, 1981.
8. *Theory Z: How American Business Can Meet the Japanese Challenge* (New York: Addison-Wesley, 1981), pp. 71–9.

PART IV

# WHAT CAN A BUSINESS CONTRIBUTE TO THE COMMUNITY?

## AN ACTIVE CORPORATE CITIZEN

CHAPTER 12

# Beyond Charity: Serving the Local Community

Philanthropy has a history perhaps as long as human society itself. The birth of corporate philanthropy likewise dates back to the beginnings of the Industrial Revolution. The nature and form of corporate giving, however, has come a long way since. Today, most corporations with a sizeable staff would feel obliged to contribute to charities of some sort. Indeed, the concept of philanthropy has given way to an entirely new term—corporate citizenship; an active and responsible corporate citizen is expected to render part of the corporate resources to enhancing the well-being of the community in which the business operates.

The forms of corporate giving have also undergone profound changes. The cheque book is by no means the only form; nor has it been always the most effective one. Staff involvement has become a major feature in charity fund-raising. Companies also find that they can make valuable contributions by putting their special technical or managerial expertise in the service of community causes. Increasingly active corporate citizens find themselves involved in a wide range of novel activities such as seconding staff to community projects, launching of new products/services catering for social rather than commercial needs, participating in neighbourhood environmental conservation, providing training for socially disadvantaged groups, and the like.

Alongside the above changes the mechanism of corporate giving is also being transformed. Owing to the size and complexity of the charity budget, few large companies can afford to follow the old-fashioned routines by which appeal letters simply drift through the company to the board. Coupled with inflation, rising costs and difficult economic conditions, most top managers would admit that the responsibility they have to use all the funds available to them efficiently ought logically to extend to the resources given by the company to deserving causes. It needs to be managed properly, using all the skills and imagination of modern management.

Marks & Spencer has been a major charity donor for decades. It is also one of those companies who have recognized that the cheque book is by no means enough. Each year hundreds of its staff across the country take part in a whole range of fund-raising activities and other community projects. More significantly, the company is actively involved in a large number of schemes ranging from job creation schemes such as the London Enterprise Agency and Leeds Business Venture to training for unemployed young people, such as Project Fullemploy or Transition to Working Life.

In what follows I shall briefly discuss the company's charitable giving and other fund-raising activities. This is then followed by a more detailed review of the company's multi-faceted involvement in local communities. The next chapter will focus on yet another unique form of contribution by the company to a national cause—giving a hand in the recent drive to streamline the British Civil Service.

## The Cheque Book . . .

Marks & Spencer has been a major charity contributor for decades. In the 1982–83 edition of *The Times 1000*,[1] the top 15 U.K. charitable corporations for the previous year are as shown in Table 5. The company has a set of very explicit guidelines for charity allocation. For instance, it is a matter of policy not to make cash donations to charities pertaining to animals and buildings (an exception to the latter is the National Trust). Nor does it favour supporting popular charities which the company reckons to be 'wealthy' in terms of

TABLE 5   TOP U.K. CHARITABLE
ORGANIZATIONS, 1981

|  | Donations (£) |
| --- | --- |
| Marks & Spencer | 1,205,000 |
| British Petroleum Co. | 1,149,000 |
| Shell U.K. | 929,000 |
| ICI | 720,000 |
| Unilever | 700,000 |
| Rank Xerox | 600,000 |
| BOC | 596,000 |
| Distillers Co. | 505,000 |
| Rio Tinto-Zinc Corpn. | 414,000 |
| Esso Petroleum Co. | 400,000 |
| Boots Co. | 316,000 |
| Imperial Group | 286,000 |
| Kodak | 283,000 |
| S. Pearson & Co. | 266,000 |
| General Electric Co. | 262,000 |

sources of funds. It does not, for example, contribute towards cancer research which is a 'popular' charity, but it does actively support cancer relief, which is a relatively neglected area. It is also the company's policy to limit its donations to overseas-oriented charities.

The bulk of the charity budget goes to four major areas; namely, medicine, education, welfare and the arts. In 1981–82, for instance, the proportion of allocation is something as follows:

| | |
|---|---|
| Medicine | 18% |
| Education | 12 |
| Welfare | 10 |
| The arts | 20 |
| Others | 40 |
| | 100% |

Apart from cash donations there is also a variety of non-cash contributions to charities of different sorts. The most notable of these are fashion shows organized on behalf of the requesting organizations. The models for the shows are almost as a rule sales assistants rather than professionals. The proceeds of the shows go to the charities while Marks & Spencer pays for the venue and the total cost of the event. Over forty such shows are sponsored each year in different parts of the country. So popular is this form of fund raising that the current waiting list stretches over 2 years.

In addition, both the management and the staff are actively encouraged to take part in a whole range of fund-raising activities for local or national causes. They range from jumping to jogging, swimming to slimming, racing to raffling; the house magazines are filled with impressive accounts of contributions by the staff at different local stores.

## . . . Is Not Enough

Although the company is a leading charity donor, it takes most pride in its other contributions to the community. Over the recent decade the company has become increasingly involved in a number of new ventures initiated and designed to deal with some burning issues afflicting the urban centres in which they trade. By far the most significant ones of these pertain to jobs creation on the one hand and training for the unemployed youth on the other.

The post-war years have witnessed a steady dwindling of the British economy. Economic depression has been accompanied by social problems on a massive scale. A high level of unemployment, sustaining well over 10% in recent years, threatens to become a permanent fact of life. Not only is the absolute number of unemployed phenomenal but the rank of long-term unemployed (out of work for over 2–3 years) is persistently on the rise. Joblessness, like other social ills, has an uneven impact on different localities and social strata. Some of the cities are more badly hit than others and within the urban area the inner city tends to experience the most stress. Similarly, certain social groupings, such as the young school-leavers, the less skilled workers, the coloured population, have more than a proportional share of misfortune under the current recession.

By most standards the problems are gigantic. What can a business do to alleviate any of these? 'Not much' is likely to be the only answer. Indeed it is. But to the management of Marks & Spencer this answer is true but inadequate. The company believes that it can play a part in the nation's effort to confront these problems. M&S consider it as much a responsibility of an active corporate citizen as it is an enlightened self-interest. As Director David Sieff has remarked,

> Today's problems are at our front doors. The high street cannot be insulated from the social decline and economic distress of the back streets. In particular localities, the problems may be vandalism, blighted urban areas, racial tensions, poor housing, declining industries and mass unemployment. The scale is bewildering and the solutions beyond the resource of government alone: the problems must be shared. But it is my belief that the process of wealth creation through individual initiative—a concept which is familiar to us—can play a vital role in remedying many of society's ills. The responsibility we have, both as citizens and as businessmen, is to recognise the imperative need to help in the local communities in which we live and trade.
>
> Some principles which guide us as a business are curiously relevant, like the attention we give to good human relations and uncluttered administration. The budding entrepreneur could find such principles helpful to start and expand his own embryo business. Similarly, a better informed young person will discover a more acceptable working world than just from hearsay and the prejudiced views of others—a world that does not owe them a living.

Elaborating on how the company could contribute, David Sieff continues:

> Firstly, we must concern ourselves with helping to stimulate the growth in numbers of people starting and developing businesses, because they are the source of new employment opportunities.
>
> Secondly, we must concern ourselves with the training of young people for the world of work, by showing them how wealth is created and how they, their mates and the country, benefit.
>
> Thirdly, we give financial support through a charity budget and we shall continue to give our customary and substantial support to charities.
>
> But a cheque book is not always the best answer. Secondments of staff—and we have 12 people on various full-time assignments throughout the country—are often more critical to the success of a project than straight financial support.
>
> For to give practical and positive help to the community in which we trade is not only the right thing to do but is good for the future of our business.[2]

## St Michael has a Halo

When Brixton erupted for the first time last April the warehouse foreman of the local Marks & Spencer store stood outside the store all night. The rioters left it alone. Nobody was surprised: 20% of Marks & Spencer workers at its Brixton branch are black, including that brave foreman. Britain's most successful department store chain does more than most firms for some of the country's saddest urban areas. Other inner-city firms need to follow its lead.

In July, another riot hit Brixton High Street on a busy Friday afternoon. Two police cars were ablaze outside M&S. While some other stores quickly pushed their customers out into the streets and closed up, the M&S manager, Mr Philip Morris, locked the doors, took his customers and their children upstairs to the staff lounge, gave them tea and turned the place into a temporary crêche. When the rioting died down, he arranged transport home for his stranded customers.

Not even M&S, of course, is safe from hooligans and next time (in the riots which some of its managers fear will be repeated this summer) the company might not escape unscathed. But M&S is determined to give good service to Britain's multiracial population.

Few companies have a bigger stake in preserving the life of Britain's high streets, and its bosses realise that healthy high streets depend on healthy back streets. In the past decade, since the Victoria tube train line brought Brixton within 15 minutes' ride of Oxford Street, many shops have closed there. More have shut since the riots. M&S, holding on, is now at the centre of the 'I'm backing Brixton' committee of local traders (with Lambeth council support and £100,000 to spend from the environment department). Mr Morris has become a community worker as well as a manager, and chief cheerleader for Brixton.

Back at M&S headquarters in Baker Street, the company has devised schemes to help small businesses in the inner cities and to train youngsters when they leave school. Eighteen M&S employees are currently on secondment to community projects, such as Fullemploy, which gives dead-end kids some clerical and retail skills. This year M&S will spend £1.25 m on community work and charities.

A drop in the bucket, of course, compared with the money needed to tackle the festering inner cities. But a marker for the many other companies which make money out of Britain's high streets. M&S, after all, is making a sensible long-term investment in its market place.

(Source: *The Economist*, 20 February 1982.)

## Job Creation and Youth Training

Since mid-1978, 32 of M&S staff have been involved in 35 schemes in different parts of the country aimed at job creation and training unemployed young people. These include both in-company schemes as well as outside schemes in co-operation with such agencies as Manpower Services Commission. At any one time these schemes have involved full-time secondment of up to fifteen members of staff and part-time of a further six. They have been drawn from executive, managerial and supervisory grades; secondments generally range from 3 months to 2 years. As a matter of policy, only the best of staff are considered for secondment; all of the returning secondees have a change of job, many of them a promotion. To the secondees the experience outside the company is as much a part of training and development as serving a community cause. Most of them return to the company more mature and seasoned than previously and in some cases become more self-critical of themselves and of the company. The following cases adapted from a special report by the editorial staff of *St. Michael News* may enable the reader to obtain a feel of what is being involved.[3]

**Stephen Hartley: Helping to turn dreams into reality**

Previously store manager of Castleford and Pontefract, Stephen Hartley was on secondment for 2 years to a project aimed at job creation. He served as the Executive Director of the Leeds Business Venture which was started by a group of local industrialists to encourage the development of small firms in the city.

Leeds has probably suffered more than most with the decline of traditional industries such as textiles and engineering. But conversely many of those people who have been made redundant decided to act positively with their severance money. The dream is to start their own small business.

'For many of them it's the chance to take the plunge with their own business—whether it's designing a new product or ways of improving production', Hartley explains. 'But often it's the lack of business know-how that stops them in their tracks, that and where to go for help and the fear of how much advice is going to cost.' These prospective entrepreneurs may have difficulties in registering a jingle, or preparing a cash forecast that will impress the bank into lending them some money. It is these basic questions and other more complicated ones that Hartley tries to solve. He acts as the link between the individual, who probably has no more than half an idea, and the team of LBV experts from accountants to marketing men.

During his first year with the venture Hartley has had more than 200 enquiries and has helped more than 34 firms to establish themselves. They range from a flag manufacturer to a redundant engineer who now exports aluminium sculptures to America.

**Pauline Grant: In the front line**

A supervisor at Dalston store, Pauline Grant was on secondment with Full-employ as an instructor.

Fullemploy was set up in 1973 by a group of London employers to help disadvantaged young people from inner city areas. It is directly aimed at young people who are used to being in the back row at school. There were only four students to one instructor so, for the first time in their lives, they found themselves in the front row instead of the back.

The aim of the 13-week course is entirely practical; to provide both commercial and social skills with either a clerical or retail business bias. There are now six Fullemploy courses under way in Britain, and Pauline is a full-time instructor at the only retail course in the south London base, teaching such subjects as stock control, cash handling, basic English and personal decision-making.

Work experience with various retailers is a valuable part of the course and culminates in an intensive 2-week job-hunting programme.

Pauline admits it's been as much an education for her as for her class: 'I came to Marks & Spencer straight from school, so their way of working was all I knew. Being involved with Fullemploy and meeting other retailers has widened my perspective enormously—it has made me more appreciative and sometimes critical of my own company.' She added: 'It's not just the students who feel more mature after the course; I do too.'

## John Ross: Breaking down barriers

John Ross is general foreman at Glasgow Sauchiehall Street store on second-ment as a working coach in the Transition to Working Life scheme. The courses conducted under this scheme are as much about learning to live in the community as getting a job. The scheme was set up in 1979 for young people who encounter difficulty in settling into stable and satisfying work. Left to themselves the youngsters can become resentful over lack of job opportunities, and easily discouraged.

The working coaches, who are ordinary men and women from the shop floor, provide a valuable link with the adult world and working experience from someone who is not parent, teacher or social worker. 'Many of these kids come from second or third generation unemployed', said John, 'and have no idea what it's like in a working environment at all. They see it as an extension of school.'

Outings to offices, shops and factories are a constant surprise to the kids. 'Most of their contact with adults comprises being told to shut up, move on or being threatened with the police! Going to factories or shops and meeting people who are happy to talk about their work and seeing that a job can be a two-way exchange—not just one person jumping to another's orders—is an education for them.'

Being able to talk frankly and on their terms is the most valuable asset a working coach can offer. John Ross is clearly able to do this—he's a down-to-

**How to be a Good Corporate Citizen**

To many companies there is a vast gulf between posting off a cheque to a community organization and sending it someone to help. Sending a person usually means a much greater degree of commitment and involvement—the file cannot be marked 'closed' the moment the cheque is signed. Moreover, the amount of money involved is frequently more than a straight donation, because people's time, especially where specialist or managerial staff are concerned, is expensive. Perhaps it is for these reasons that so many fight shy of a formal programme to make employees available for community service.

Nonetheless, the advantages to the firm are considerable. Employees who are actively engaged in community projects are a valuable source of information on what is happening in the outside world. And a number of companies have now begun to realize the immense potential that secondment offers as a means of developing broader skills in specialist staff.

IBM (U.K.), in a policy document on its secondment programme, lists the benefits to all three parties in the agreement—the charity, the employee, and the company—as follows:

The employee gains an opportunity to
- practise and test business skills in an alternative environment
- develop previously unused skills
- develop a lasting interest in social problems
- encounter different concepts, ideals, priorities, values, cultures, and ways of life.

The receiving organization gains:
- expertise and experience it could not otherwise afford to buy in
- a fresh approach to a problem
- a contact in a different field of work which may be helpful in the future.

The seconding organization gains from:
- the increased experience and broadened approach of its secondees
- the easing of promotional log-jams and manpower imbalances
- an opportunity to influence realistic community planning
- general approval that employees give to such enlightened company initiatives
- keeping its goals and values in step with those of the rest of the community.

The good private citizen is one who gives of himself to the benefit of the community at large. How better can the good corporate citizen give of itself by giving the time of its people?

(Source: David Clutterbuck, *How to be a Good Corporate Citizen* (Maidenhead: McGraw-Hill, 1981), pp. 28, 37; reprinted by permission of McGraw-Hill.)

earth man with a lively sense of humour who quelled his initial fears of facing a group of sullen teenagers by taking out his newspaper and reading it. 'It was one way of getting them to talk to me.'

Over the last 5 months John has built up a good relationship with the group, becoming personally involved with all of them and their hopes of finding a job. This personal involvement extends in some cases to their families. So much so that one schoolteacher sent a boy's report to him because he was more interested than the father!

## A Corporate Community Worker

Few other companies have perhaps involved themselves as extensively in the local community as Marks & Spencer has done. In a significant sense the company has been acting like a corporate community worker. It is an active supporter and a ready source of help in a wide spectrum of community affairs.

But not unlike other social or community workers, the problems at hand are complex and immense. To the extent that the social worker's role is 'reformist' in nature, the same can perhaps be said about Marks & Spencer's effort. What they have been addressing themselves to might well be only symptoms of deeper societal ills. The latter, however, are apparently beyond the means and imagination of the company to tackle. It is fair to say that given the existing politico-economic framework, the company has done far more than most other companies in discharging its responsibility as a corporate citizen.

## Appendix

## Marks & Spencer Involvement in Job Creation and Youth Training Schemes

### Job Creation

1. *London Enterprise Agency*
   The aim was to encourage the start-up and expansion of small firms in London and to give advice where needed so that jobs could be created or saved. It provides business counselling, marketing and viability studies, and other services to small businesses. One of M&S managers sits on the management committee and technical advice is freely available to 'clients' of the agency.

2. *Leeds Business Venture*
Modelled on the London Enterprise Agency, it is a consortium of local firms which launched the venture in September 1980. A M&S manager has been seconded for 2 years.

3. *Leicestershire Business Venture*
Similar to the Leeds venture, with Corah, a major M&S supplier taking the initiative. M&S has seconded a manager for 2 years as Director.

4. *Wandsworth Business Resource Centre*
A small firm creation agency sponsored by the local authority and staffed by seconded managers from different companies. A M&S manager was on secondment for 18 months.

5. *Action Resource Centre*
A national organization, registered as a charity, and funded by nearly 200 companies. It acts as a broker in arranging secondments, bringing business skills to community projects. M&S is represented on its Advisory Council and has seconded a manager to be a senior executive at ARC head office.

6. *Lambeth Industries*
A project sponsored by the local authority providing premises for 27 small firms and workshops in a converted factory. A M&S manager serves on the management board.

7. *Operation Goodwill—Glasgow*
A workshop and retail shop in the Maryhill area of Glasgow, renovating and selling furniture and domestic equipment. It has grown into a viable business employing a large number of formerly unemployed young people. M&S seconded a manager to set up the retail operation.

8. *Hackney Business Promotion Centre*
A local authority initiative to help small business start-ups. A staff manager was seconded for 8 months to develop a job opportunity programme for young people.

9. *Islington Small Business Counselling Service*
An advisory service for small businesses staffed by seconded managers from a number of major companies. An administration manager from M&S was seconded for 1 year.

10. *Hackney Fashion Centre*
A project aimed at providing marketing and technical resources to the small local garment-manufacturing business. M&S provided a seconded manager for 1 year.

## Youth Training Schemes

1. *Project Fullemploy*
The project aimed at helping young people (age 16–19) of normal intelligence, but so disadvantaged as to lack any qualifications, to become responsible and employable members of society. Most of these young

people had no chance of getting a job. Many had opted out of school long before the statutory leaving age. Some have been in trouble with the police. Most have unstable domestic backgrounds. Practical courses (13 weeks' duration) were run for these youngsters. M&S seconded a manager to help run the courses.

2. *Operation Springboard—Camden Town*
Six months' work experience and life skill training for recent immigrant youth. A partnership between seconded business managers and educational instructors sponsored by Community Relations Council. M&S seconded a staff manager for 8 months to set up the scheme and provided a manager part-time to co-ordinate work experience opportunities with local industry.

3. *Transition to Working Life—London, West Midlands, Glasgow*
This is a 'working Coach' scheme sponsored by the Grubb Institute. It links unemployed school leavers with working men and women who act as the coaches. Each group of trainees meets once a week over a 6-month period and is basically a workshop discussion group about attitudes to work, value of qualifications, work experience, life in general. M&S provides supervisors and warehouse foremen as coaches for 6 groups at Islington, Dalston, Wolverhampton, Walsall and Glasgow.

4. *Trident Trust*
Trident has a three-pronged approach, involving adventure training, community service and work experience for those in their last year at school. M&S supports Trident financially and in addition seconded for 2 years a senior personnel manager to the scheme in the Borough of Brent.

5. *Burnbake Trust—Southwark*
A training workshop for young offenders which aims at commercial self-sufficiency. A practical alternative to prison. Backed by the Home Office, sponsored by private citizens, it has a low recidivism rate. One of M&S managers was seconded for 18 months to run this project.

6. *Islington Schools Project*
A project to enquire into better job-matching for school leavers in an area notorious for mis-matching. A M&S staff manager was seconded for 18 months.

7. *Target—Tower Hamlets*
A training workshop in wood and metal skills providing training for up to 100 young people. Sponsored by local Council with support of IB and Queen Mary College. A catering manager from a M&S store was seconded to help set up a catering training unit.

8. *Lands and Workshop—Hammersmith*
Community workshops providing training for 60 young people. A M&S manager was seconded as a part-time management Board member and another was seconded full-time to run the office and to instruct in office skills.

9. *Youth Opportunities Programme of the Manpower Services Commission—Work Experience on Employers' Premises*
The company was providing over 1,000 places per annum in 230 stores for unemployed school leavers under this scheme. A comprehensive training programme, including life skills, was followed by each trainee.

The company was also actively involved in designing and implementing a new Youth Training Scheme (costing the Government £1 billion a year) which replaced the Youth Opportunities Programme in 1983.

## Notes

1. *The Times 1000*, 1982–83 (London: Times Books Ltd., 1982), p. 117.
2. Source: Publicity Group, Marks & Spencer.
3. *St. Michael News*, April 1981.

FIG. 25. Foods will be dissected, analysed and criticised by technologists and other buying department staff, and sometimes members of the Board, including the Chairman. If the food sampled meets with the approval of the company's sternest critics, it is safe to assume that the company's customers will buy and enjoy the same products.

FIG. 26. Food must also be tested and tasted at various stages of production.

FIG. 27. Test kitchens contain a variety of conventional equipment which simulates as closely as possible the items available in any home. Here, new recipes are tried out and existing lines cooked so that technologists can check on flavour and eating quality.

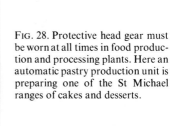

FIG. 28. Protective head gear must be worn at all times in food production and processing plants. Here an automatic pastry production unit is preparing one of the St Michael ranges of cakes and desserts.

FIG. 29. The technologist's work may involve worldwide travel as well as visits to suppliers throughout the UK, and most of the working week will find any technologist on a factory floor or walking around a farm. But looking at food at the source of production is only part of the role.

FIG. 30. All St Michael goods are distributed to stores through a simple integrated transport network set up exclusively for Marks & Spencer by independent contractors.

FIG. 31. More than 200,000 people are engaged in the production of St Michael goods. Many suppliers have been associated with Marks & Spencer for thirty or forty years, sharing in the expansion of business and growing from small firms to large organisations.

# CHAPTER 13

# The Rayner Scrutinies: A Hand in Streamlining the Civil Service

We have seen in Chapter 12 the involvement of various levels of M&S staff in promoting a wide range of community causes. They have made an admirable contribution by devoting their entrepreneurial resources and meticulous hard work to serving local communities. In this chapter we shall look at yet another way Marks & Spencer makes available its accumulated experience of progressive management to the larger community in which the company operates. This is associated with the work of Sir Derek Rayner, vice-chairman of the company, in playing a prominent role in the current drive by the Thatcher government in streamlining the Civil Service.

When Mrs Thatcher came to power in Spring 1979 the Conservative Party's election manifesto had committed her to the 'reduction of waste, bureaucracy and over-government'. Within scarcely a week in office she succeeded in persuading Sir Derek Rayner, then Joint Managing Director of Marks & Spencer, to act as her adviser on improving the efficiency of the Civil Service. Since then, Sir Derek, part-time and unpaid, had been leading the Prime Minister's crusade against bureaucratic waste and inefficiency. Mrs Thatcher's vision has been, in the words of an outside observer, 'to make British Government more like Marks & Spencer . . . to trim the civil service into something approaching the lean, efficient, customer-oriented operation that is the fond image of Sir Derek's high street stores'.[1]

Not everyone has expected miracles from Sir Derek's new role. Indeed, scepticism abounds as to whether significant and long-lasting results would be forthcoming. After all, it was not the first time that businessmen of various distinctions were brought along to advise the government. In the last Conservative administration Mr Heath brought in six businessmen—of whom Sir Derek was one—and most of them gradually 'peeled off'.[2] There was, and still is, widespread scepticism that there is really any place for a businessman from outside trying to alter and influence the way Whitehall operates.

Moreover, the recent record of successive governments' attempts to stream-line the Civil Service had been—to say the least—miserably disappointing. The last major attempt was the Fulton Commission, appointed in 1966 by the Labour government to undertake a service-wide study with the object of fundamentally reorganizing and strengthening the state bureaucracy. The Commission enquiry resulted in a series of well-prepared reports and the establishment of a new department—Civil Service Department (CSD)—to carry out the reforms and to lead the quest for more efficient government. The CSD had failed on both counts (and was subsequently dissolved in 1981, after 13 years of existence). A similar fate had met with Mr Heath's brainchild—Programme Analysis and Review (PAR)—launched with great zest in the 1970s. In any case the British Civil Service, as the *Economist* observed, 'has a genius for finding a piece of grit, turning it into a pearl, an irrelevant pearl, which is then ignored'.

It is still too early to assess the full impact of Sir Derek's anti-bureaucracy crusade. Sir Derek himself, modestly and realistically enough, had spoken of a 10-year horizon to bring new life into the antiquated Service. But the 3 years since his assignment began have already ushered some remarkable and unpre-cedented changes in Whitehall. The 'Rayner shock' is being felt throughout the entire Service; 'Raynerism'—that is, scrutinies of particular aspects of central government work—has become a byword in the language of the Civil Service, Parliament and the Press.

By the end of 1981 there were clear signs that scepticism had begun to give way to considered optimism. Peter Hennessy, who had been following closely the whole exercise, was making the following remarks in September of that year:

> Is Sir Derek Rayner about to succeed where Lord Fulton and several others have failed by pulling off the first real reform of the Civil Service for 100 years? The signs are that the joint managing director of Marks and Spencer, who doubles as the Prime Minister's part-time adviser on the elimination of waste, is on the brink of doing just that.[3]

The very fact that 'Raynerism' has become a central focus of public attention and debate is by itself significant. As Andrew Likierman of the London Business School and an adviser to the House of Commons Select Committee on the Treasury and Civil Service put it:

> In the political arena, to have 'ism' attached to one's name is a mark of rare distinction, and in the field of government efficiency 'isms' are in notably short supply. Yet within a short period of his appointment, Sir Derek Rayner's name has become part of the Civil Service vocabulary.[4]

## Achievements So Far

Like most 'isms', Raynerism has its share of controversy. To some critics the scrutinies are nothing more than manpower cuts in disguise; to some others it is 'an unnecessary distraction from the main business of government to deal with candle ends'; whilst to yet others it is the long-overdue intervention of a true professional to curb the notorious profligacy of an outdated bureaucracy. David Allen has perhaps given the most authoritative definition of Raynerism so far: 'Raynerism is aimed at encouraging greater economy, efficiency and effectiveness in the use of the very substantial resources consumed in running the many essential businesses of government through *better management from within*' (emphasis added).[5]

In a White Paper on the Efficiency in the Civil Service, presented to Parliament by the Lord President of the Council in July 1981,[6] the following summary of achievements was reported:

> The scrutinies undertaken by departments with the help of Sir Derek Rayner have made a substantial contribution to the process of critical examination. Since June 1979 there have been 68 scrutinies of particular activities at a cost of about £1 million. This year there will be about 40 more. Savings possibilities of around £190 million a year (11,000 staff) have been identified so far. Ministers have already taken firm decisions to save some £90 million a year plus £28 million once and for all.
>
> These scrutinies have meant getting down to where the work is done, with the examining officers mastering the complexities and detail; free to question all aspects of the activity (to the point of challenging its very existence); and then, unfettered by committees and hierarchy, reporting direct to Ministers. They have tapped the initiatives and ideas that exist at all levels and have produced reports for action.
>
> Tasks are being simplified, functions reduced or cut out, office networks streamlined, procedures improved, methods brought up to date with new business practice and technology. Much of this results from the day to day work of line managers, but a great deal flows from review of functions by Ministers, scrutinies, service-wide reviews, and the work of specialised personnel.

## A Herculean Task

While conscious efforts have been made to quantify savings and costs and to curb any possible exaggerated claims, it is amply apparent to Sir Derek and most observers that at the end of the day the achievement of the whole exercise cannot be expressed in numbers alone. The hallmark of Sir Derek's success, if every attainable, would be a fundamental transformation in the management culture of the Civil Service. What Sir Derek and his colleagues at Whitehall have set out to do is to inject professional management into the Service. That is to say, to ensure that civil servants at various levels in charge of financial and manpower resources are capable of deploying and making use of these resources as effectively and efficiently as the best managers outside the Civil Service are doing. In other words, the objective is to ensure that ministers and other ranks in the Civil Service are accountable not only in the political sense (which itself is often vague and obscure), but also in the managerial sense, i.e. in terms of their capability in managing the resources under their control. The latter aspect, as most commentators recognize, has for too long been ignored as a central criterion in evaluating a civil servant. As an editorial in *The Times* put it[7]:

> At the heart of . . . the scrutinies of the civil service . . . is a theme which is both obvious and yet, compared to past British practice, revolutionary: that good government means good administration, and that therefore efficient policy implementation is as important as policy formulation. Most of the present generation of top mandarins have advanced in a tradition which emphasizes skills at policy advice to ministers rather than administrative management. . . . But the private citizen or businessman, who pays heavily for his bureaucracy, also wants good administration. Permanent secretaries must now place increased emphasis on this, in their training programme, in promotion criteria, and in themselves setting an example to line management.

Sir Derek's job, put in these terms, is indeed a Herculean task. It takes a man of exceptional courage and confidence—in himself as well as in those who work with him—to accept such a challenge.

Crudely speaking, it is possible to distinguish four major, overlapping phases of Sir Derek's work thus far:

PHASE I—Securing top management support and commitment, namely, from the Prime Minister, the Cabinet, and the senior Civil Servants. This extended roughly from June 1979 to mid-1980.

PHASE II—Working closely with the Ministers to launch scrutinies projects on selected aspects of central government work. Late 1979 to present.

PHASE III—Building on the success and momentum of the scrutinies, launching a series of service-wide reviews: on statistical services in 1980/1; on administrative forms in 1981/2; on supporting service in R&D and allied scientific establishments in 1981/2.

PHASE IV—Formulating and instituting 'lasting reforms'; that is, radically changing some of the well-entrenched rules and procedures which inhibit effective management in government. 1981 to present.

## Commitment from the Top

During the first 10 months of his assignment much of Sir Derek's effort had been centred around securing commitment and support from the upper echelons of the Civil Service. Political will from the top—but not simply from the Prime Minister alone—was seen as one of the most critical prerequisites for any progress of the exercise. Sir Derek had been in the Service before, and he knows the mandarin game. As one of the team of businessmen brought in by Mr Heath in 1970 his assignment then was to reorganize defence procurement; he became the first Chief Executive (i.e. Permanent Secretary and Accounting Officer) of the resulting Ministry of Defence Procurement Executive in 1971/73. From his experience in government he formed the view which he still holds, that the Civil Service is well capable, and has the potential ability, to reform itself, but this capability is often impeded by obscurity about objectives, by a lack of sense of purpose and commitment to change.

Sir Derek politely declined Mrs Thatcher's initial suggestion to look across the government departments as a whole. It was not only because he had little faith in elaborate investigations as often conducted by full-dressed royal commissions and committees of inquiry, but more importantly, it was due to his conviction that in the past too much attention had been focused on identifying what is wrong while not enough imagination and ingenuity was placed on 'making things happen'. As he put it in a BBC interview ('Platform One', 24 January 1980): 'There is nothing new about the identification of what is wrong. It is lack of action that follows it, and I very much regard it that my real role is ensuring that action is taken.' The 'identification of what is wrong' might perhaps be adequately carried out by a competent team of investigators, but to ensure that action is properly taken requires an entirely different approach and line of attack.

Sir Derek's effort in securing top management support culminated in the preparation of a Cabinet paper modestly entitled *The Conventions of Government* but containing some strikingly radical proposals. Unfortunately it is a classified secret document and will remain so until 1 January 2011. However, the central thrust of the paper can be discerned from the following proposals put foward:[8]

(1)  A full assessment of the running cost of central government, with a detailed breakdown, ministry by ministry, showing which parts of the machine are absorbing the most people and funds, plus a requirement on departments to pay for the accommodation (offices, storage etc.), transport, telecommunications, stationery and other 'common services'. For example, departments will be asked to pay current market rents on Crown-owned properties to make them aware of the value of the assets in their charge as well as of the recurrent costs of maintaining such assets.

(2)  A shortening of the Whitehall hierarchy to avoid duplication of effort and to achieve a clearer sense of personal responsibility. Greater delegation of financial reponsibility to those managers who determine and incur the expenditure, and making them more accountable for their decisions.

(3)  Career planning to ensure that Civil Servants appointed to senior posts have demonstrated their ability to manage manpower and money.

(4)  Accelerated promotion and extra financial rewards for those who have saved money and shown a capacity to stick their necks out and take risks.

(5)  An obligation on permanent secretaries to give an annual account to their ministers of their stewardship of the department resources.

(6)  Better working conditions for staff at all levels and the removal of confusing, conflicting or burdensome instructions on officials in executive and clerical positions.

To the extent that these objectives can be achieved in any degree, they can hardly be construed as a chase after numbers in manpower cuts and the like. They set out in broad outline the basic directions of the Rayner efforts. It was on these basic objectives that Sir Derek had been spending the first 10 months of his assignment in formulating and getting the Ministers to agree. In the end, he had the full-fledged support of the Prime Minister and apparently a very substantial number of the Ministers.

## The Scrutinies in Action

Simultaneous to his efforts in securing commitment and support from the top, Sir Derek initiated in the latter half of 1979 a series of study projects, which have since been known as 'Rayner scrutinies'.

The so-called 'scrutinies' are simply critical, in-depth investigations of specific aspects of government work by an official (or team) from the department concerned with a view to producing concrete measures for improving the effectiveness and efficiency of that function or activity. It is the well-tried Marks & Spencer technique of the laser beam rather than the arc light. The subjects for scrutiny are chosen by the department, in consultation with Sir Derek. The examining officers (mostly assistant secretaries or principals, young and dynamic) selected to carry out the inquiry are encouraged to 'question all aspects of work normally taken for granted'; they are free to examine the specific part of their department's functions in detail, seeing such colleagues and making such visits as are necessary within their own departments, consulting other departments and going right outside the government where appropriate. They are armed with three simple yet radical questions: Why is this work done at all? Why is it done as it is? How could it be done more efficiently and effectively at less cost?

Each scrutiny conducted under the Rayner plan follows a tight time schedule, and is usually completed within 90 days. Typically, the first 3 weeks are devoted to working out the study plan, which lays out the specifics of the WHAT and HOW to study. This is to be reviewed and approved by Sir Derek and the Minister concerned. Half-way through the study, a synopsis of findings is prepared, indicating the progress of the study, special difficulties encountered and the final plan for the rest of the study. At the end of the 90-day period a report is submitted which goes directly to the Minister and Sir Derek, in contrast to previous practice such as that of Programme Analysis and Review (PAR) in which 'too many senior civil servants could get at its findings before they reached ministers, erasing all traces of radicalism in favour of Whitehall's preferred virtues of moderation and compromises'.

The report thus prepared represents only the initial phase of a chain of action. On receipt of the report it is then the responsibility of the Minister to evaluate its recommendations and to produce an 'action document, within 3 months. The document is usually prepared by senior officials in the Ministry who in most cases are also responsible for personally supervising the implementation of the action programme. The completed 'action document' is again submitted to the Minister and Sir Derek and, once approved, its implementation will be closely monitored and Sir Derek is to report the progress directly to the Prime Minister. The entire exercise, as is apparent, is singularly action-oriented.

> The reasoning behind the scrutiny programme [explains Sir Derek] is that ministers and their officials are better equipped than anyone else to examine the use of the resources for which they are responsible. The scrutinies therefore rely heavily on self-examination. The main elements are the application of a fresh mind to the policy, function or activity studied; the interaction of that mind with the minds of those who are expert in the function or activity; the supervision of the ministers accountable to Parliament for its management and the resources it consumes; and the contribution of an outside agency in the shape of my office and me.[9]

The operational instructions that the team of scrutineers received are characteristic of the Marks & Spencer style:[10]

> Officials should seek solution to problems. Their reports should offer, at the very least, the outline of the practical changes necessary; they should not dump the problem, without solution, on their minister's doorstep. The purpose is not simply good analysis of what is, but preparation for action.
>
> Scrutinies should not be conducted as desk studies. Nor should interviewing be confined to top people and HQ. There is no substitute, whatever the nature of the function or activity under study, for going and seeing it. Officials should not rely on paper to get the study going, so:
>
> (1) Don't write around, talk around;
> (2) Don't assume that you know anything until you've been to see it—start where the work takes place;
> (3) Regard paper [sic] which you write as the product rather than the medium of the study.
>
> Given the right approach, staff will go out of their way to be helpful. The message is that you are neither Smart Alecs nor 'Assistant Waste Finders General'—your role is not accusatory or inquisitorial, but that your department and others have an opportunity to look at a piece of administration with the enthusiastic backing of ministers, from the Prime Minister down.

All this sounds simple and straightforward enough; but the power of such a common-sense approach is not often appreciated simply because it is seldom put into practice. The following report from *The Sunday Times* is instructive:[11]

> One day last autumn, the social security office at Hoxton, in London's East End, had an unnerving experience. It was not simply that Sir Derek Rayner had arrived, along with Norman Warner, a middle-rank official in the department of health and social security. The staff had some days' warning of their visit—a luxury, by the way, Marks and Spencer staff do not enjoy before Rayner descends on *them*. What caused the stir was the way Rayner and Warner went to work.

They studied every detail of that office at work. They watched as staff talked to claimants; they saw forms filled in, calculations checked and cheques printed. They came, they saw—and they were horrified.

What struck Rayner about Hoxton? 'The complexity of rules', he said. 'I think they are incomprehensible to ordinary people. Secondly, because they are so complicated and because of the lack of experienced staff, enormous checking is needed. This is inefficient and bad for morale, so you get a high staff turnover—which means more inexperienced staff whose work needs checking and so on.' (The staff turnover at Hoxton is 45% a year.)

'There were two old machines for printing Giro cheques. Both broke down while I was there. And most cheques had to be met with two cheques, because of an upper limit per cheque of £30. Most payments are for more than this. So you would see one cheque for £30 and another for two or three pounds.'

Clapped-out printing machines in Hoxton are a far cry from the glamour of 'Whitehall'. Or are they? Britain has 700,000 civil servants, costing around £6 billions a year to employ. All bar 5,000 or so are engaged in the execution rather than construction of policy. The great majority are scattered around the country, grappling—like Hoxton—with the everyday grind. *It follows that any attempt to improve government efficiency must be built on those minutiae.*

It was *obvious* from Hoxton that most forms could be shorter, most claims dealt with more simply. *Obvious*, that the £30 cheque limit was absurd. *Obvious* that many claimants could be, and would prefer to be, paid by post. *Obvious*, in short, that, in Sir Derek's words, 'the way we pay out Social Security benefits is an antique piece of administration'.

Such has been the basic approach of the Rayner method: getting down to where the work is done, asking the obvious questions, getting the people who are doing the job to reflect on what they are doing, drawing out their ideas and suggestions, and working out action programmes with the involvement of those who are to implement them.

It has been pointed out that Sir Derek has relied primarily on the internal resources of the departments in carrying out the scrutinies—'I didn't want to set up a bureaucracy to deal with a bureaucracy'—it is perhaps not surprising that most of the difficulties encountered in the process are also internal to the Service. To begin with, the selection of problems to be studied had not been without complications. It sometimes took protracted discussion just to get the department to agree on a study programme, and in some instances Sir Derek has had to assert his position. 'One of the important things in these discussions', he reflects, 'is that I have the strong backing of the Prime Minister and her senior colleagues and they all know it.' Even then, the first-round projects were all politically 'safe'. It was only in the second and subsequent rounds of scrutinies that substantially more serious and 'sensitive' issues were tackled.

But more importantly, there was the formidable obstacle in the belief that 'people may suffer as a result of proposing economies'. It was generally felt that putting forth recommendations in improving efficiency and reducing waste may not always be popular with senior management and that there could be considerable personal risk for Civil Servants daring to do so. Even in the course of the scrutiny, Sir Derek came across officials carrying out the study who made such remarks as: 'We do not know if we will be promoted for carrying out what you want us to do, or whether we will be promoted if we carry out what some of our senior colleagues may prefer' (BBC interview, 24 January 1980). What is more, attempts to improve efficiency usually have much wider implications, some of which may not always be pleasant for those in charge. The following is by no means an untypical complaint from someone down the line: 'Well, what could I do in my case, because the rot exists at the top in my section of the department. There's slothfulness and incompetence near the top. And unless that is challenged, then I don't think we will alter our pattern' (quoted by Robert McKenzie in the above-mentioned BBC interview).

To the extent that 'slothfulness and incompetence' is epidemic in the management hierarchy, such scepticism—or even cynicism—may indeed be prevalent in the Service; and this is by no means easy to overcome. It calls for exceptional resolve and impetus from the top for it to have a chance of being dispelled. But precisely because of the problems at various management levels, determination and enthusiasm at the very top may not be felt by the people at the other end. Sir Derek was painfully aware of the dilemma, and at the very early stage of the exercise he knew that two things must be done. In the short run, the scrutiny teams must be fully backed and tactfully 'protected'; the practical results of the study may to some extent help to overcome fear and cynicism among their colleagues. For this reason Sir Derek attempted to limit the number of scrutiny projects to a scale that he could personally supervise. 'It is my determination', he has said, 'that everybody appointed to do a scrutiny will be known to me personally, and I will speak with them personally about what they find and I will, where necessary, go with them and find out what is going on.' To obtain results he found that he had to throw the full weight of his authority and personal resources behind the projects carried out under his banner.

In the longer run, what is required is more fundamental changes in the management structure of the Service, towards the direction of making management skills and effectiveness a central element in the evaluation and promotion of Civil Servants with management responsibility, or simply put, 'making sure that people are promoted because they take action, not because they avoid taking action'. This is in fact another major area of Sir Derek's work which is now commonly referred to as 'lasting reforms' (see below).

## Service-wide Reviews

The scrutiny projects were started towards the end of 1979; by mid-1980 preliminary results were coming in. Building on the very positive response of these projects, Sir Derek began to initiate a series of service-wide reviews—that is, reviews of specific functions common to most departments. By 1982 three major service-wide reviews had been completed, covering respectively:

(1) statistical services,
(2) administrative forms, and
(3) supporting service in R&D and allied scientific establishments.

In what follows, the review of administrative forms will be briefly discussed to highlight the nature and significance of these efforts.

Few governments in the world have been immune to the Parkinsonian disease of swelling bureaucracy—least of all the British Civil Service. According to official estimates the volume of paper consumed by the Treasury has been increasing by 8% on a regular basis; 'they were treating it as if it were air and just came in'. To the average Briton, central government manifests itself not so much as devoted individual Civil Servants but more often as an ocean of paper. Consider the following facts revealed in the *White Paper on Administration Forms* following the service-wide review:

(1) Some 2000 millions [sic] forms and leaflets are issued by the government each year, that is about 36 for each man, woman and child in the country.
(2) The cost for departments in issuing these forms is huge, totalling more than £1000 million each year.
(3) The cost to the form-fillers is also considerable though more difficult to quantify; but in every instance examined during the review costs to business of filling in forms are found to be greater than the costs of departments in processing them.
(4) Many forms are written in language few people understand. This not only can be a considerable irritant to the recipient of the form, but can cause him/her to lose benefits or fail to exercise rights or responsibilities.

The recommendations contained in the White Paper are equally striking—and revealing:

> Of the 93 different kinds of forms reviewed, half of them are to be redesigned and over a quarter to be withdrawn altogether.[12]

The question of administrative forms does not normally inflame the imagination of the politician, the academic or journalist commentator; they are, however, a crucial instrument in government's relations with the public. Good forms allow information to be conveyed and obtained more accurately and concisely than could be done by other means. Potentially they could help administration to work efficiently, economically and fairly. On the other hand, bad forms cause problems and incur avoidable costs (to the public and user departments). They can damage relations between the government and the public and undermine whatever efforts Civil Servants—particularly those in local offices—try to make to provide an efficient and helpful service. As the review brings home quite vividly, 'government forms will never please everyone but much more can be done to improve them; complex administration cannot be expressed through simple forms but more streamlined administration should result in fewer and better forms'.

One of the fundamental causes for the uncontrolled proliferation of administrative forms has been the widely held and very erroneous attitude towards the *cost* of forms. There are two distinct and separate costs involved with a form: the cost of producing it, and the cost of using it. Hitherto, emphasis on control has been directed at production costs since they are direct and visible. However, these costs have only been controlled within the much larger expenditure on stationery generally. And as a *stationery* item, they rarely attract the attention of any senior officials. No department has up to the time of the review been able to produce guidelines which balance the costs of using a form with the costs of producing it.

But while it is important to ensure that forms are procured in the most economical way, production costs as such—as the review findings demonstrate—constitute but the smallest element in the overall cost of forms. The cost of forms in use is far greater. 'Cost in use' includes the cost of staff to issue forms and to check them and correct and query them when they are returned incomplete or containing errors; the cost to the public who have to use them; and postage costs. For example, one typical form studied during the review cost only 3 pence to produce but £2 for the department to check and correct.

The review has shown that, for good forms, the costs in use are often very large but necessary. But bad forms waste time and money unnecessarily. It is very commonplace for officials to hold that these costs are an inevitable consequence of using a form and therefore they rarely consider them before they introduce, design or review a form. This may be partly because forms are an integral part of administrative systems and, as such, costs in use are difficult to separate out from the cost of processing. However, the review findings have convincingly established the case that costs in use must henceforth be gathered by the departments concerned so that informed decisions about the introduction, design and continued use of forms can be made.

Another major flaw common to thousands of forms issued by the departments is in the language in which the forms are prepared. Many forms are complex and difficult to understand because they are written in language which is 'legalistic, lengthy and intimidating'.

This is not because [as T. L. Lonsdale explains] the officials who create the forms are trying to confuse the recipient. . . . But forms become self-protecting because the officials try hard to avoid being criticised for failing to inform the citizen of his or her rights or responsibilities. Some officials also find difficulties in understanding the procedures of which the forms are part! Problems such as these are rarely identified before a form is introduced into use because few forms are tested with those who fill them in. Consequently error rates of 30% or more are common.[13] (For example, application for citizenship 48%, tax returns 47%, application for hill land compensation 50%.)

The message from the review is clear: that departments must ensure that forms are simpler, more intelligible and work as they are intended. This means avoiding jargon, using plain English, delivering the 'good form of plain words', and testing the forms as far as possible before they are introduced to check that the public can understand them and that staff can process them efficiently.

This is again a simple lesson; and again there are fundamental administrative principles involved. The significance of the review, as an editorial in *The Times* puts it,

> is the commendable insistence that the *needs of the consumer* be elevated in the minds of the producer of forms. Too often hitherto they have been drafted in Whitehall with little consultation either with the customer public or even with the civil service who have to deal with costly confusions arising from impenetrably legalistic prose and sloppy layout. . . . Henceforth we are promised more prior costing and pilot-testing of new forms, and senior civil servants will be encouraged to go out and consult the sharp end of government[14] (emphasis added).

In the business world, the 'needs of the consumer' are paramount; it is in government administration that they tend to be persistently suppressed and ignored. The question of administrative forms is but one of the many areas of government work in which the citizen is entitled to receive a good service, and the civil service has an obligation to give the possible 'value for money' to the taxpayer.

It would of course be naive to expect that the century-old habits of the Civil Service could be changed overnight, but the Service-wide reviews and individual scrutinies conducted so far have clearly challenged the fundamental outlook and approaches to government work in a way that has never occurred before. The Rayner shock has made its impact; it remains to be seen whether 'lasting reforms' will be forthcoming.

## How Lasting Will the Reforms Be?

It has been emphasized that at the very beginning of the whole exercise Sir Derek has attempted to secure agreement and commitment from the top Whitehall officials on a number of broad objectives for reforming the state bureaucracy. Having succeeded in doing that, he then set in motion a series of scrutinies and reviews which, however, were on a much lower and practical level than the objectives. The idea was that the tightly scheduled and controlled studies could be expected to produce concrete and immediate results in a relatively short span of time. This could be profoundly important for a number of reasons. First of all, it strikes a hard blow to the widespread fatalism among civil servants that things cannot be expected to change; the Rayner efforts demonstrate forcefully that, given the political will and determination from the top, a lot can be done to change the face of the Civil Service. More important perhaps is the fact that the very process of the painstaking scrutinies and

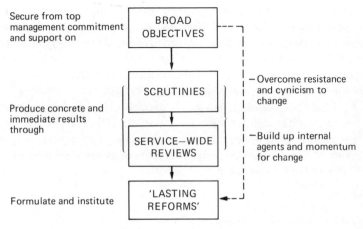

Figure 26    The Rayner effort: 1979 through 1982

reviews has brought into being a crop of young, energetic and dedicated officials who have now received their first training in concerted self-examination of government work. They might very well be the central core of the managerial vanguard in the Civil Service of tomorrow. Whilst these results are no doubt extremely encouraging, Sir Derek was well aware that by themselves they are no guarantee to long-lasting reforms. What he has been actively involved in since the third year of his assignment was the formulation and implementation of what have been referred to as 'lasting reforms', the elements of which were outlined in the Cabinet paper prepared by Sir Derek in 1979.

In retrospect, this sequence of events is a distinctive feature of Sir Derek's effort and can be represented as shown in Figure 26. As could be expected, most of the reforms proposed are 'radical' in nature—at least to the Whitehall mandarins, and as such, many of them are still the subjects of intense debate. A small number of them, however, have already had the blessing of the Ministers and are being implemented; for example, the payment for common services by user departments. Following Sir Derek's formulation, it is possible to think of these reforms in terms of two broad categories—namely, the work on 'people' on the one hand and the work on 'institutional arrangements' on the other.

As far as the work on people is concerned, the objective is to produce desirable changes and development in the managerial culture of the service to ensure that talented men and women are brought on to senior managerial positions as soon as possible. This includes, among other changes, the following:

(1) Ensuring that the staff who control and manage resources are fully aware of the management responsibilities and have the necessary training and experience for the job, while efforts are to be made to cut out unnecessarily detailed supervision and checking, and to increase delegation from headquarters to local offices, and from higher to lower grades.

(2) Changes in promotion and reward policies so that:

    (a) it would be possible to advance individuals by two or more grades in recognition of their track record, potential and the needs of the Service;

    (b) success in post where no further hierarchical progression is possible should be rewarded by bonus payments or by personal promotion (as opposed to the upgrading of the post);

    (c) individuals should no longer be entitled to automatic annual increments regardless of merit.

(3) A 'model succession policy' for the Civil Service, especially for senior appointments, through defining the managerial requirements of key posts, identifying in advance suitably qualified successors to the existing holders, and ensuring the key candidates acquire the experience and expertise that fits them to fill such posts.

(4) Requiring official heads of departments to give a regular, personal account of what they have simplified, streamlined or saved, and departments to publish an annual statement of their achievement in this respect.

As for the work on institutional arrangements the objective is to 'create the right conditions for managers to manage', to ensure the continuous exercise of good management practice, cost-consciousness and cost-responsiveness throughout the management chain. To this end, new initiatives include:

(1) A sharpening of responsibilities—clarifying the management responsibilities of Ministers and officials, both at the centre and in departments. This means emphasizing the Minister's ultimate responsibility for managing his department as well as its policies, and at the same time the central departments (such as the Treasury and the newly established Management and Personnel Office) must see that each department has a proper system for controlling resources and promoting efficiency, and that these are working well.

(2) Better management information. If Ministers and officials are to manage effectively the goods and services in their charge, they need first to know and then to question their costs. They must have adequate management accounts enabling them and the central departments to assess trends and to identify areas requiring closer examination and control. Action is now being taken in individual departments and across government to improve the standards of management information. For example, the Secretary of State for the Environment has set up a management information system (MINIS) which sets out the objectives, priorities, costs and results of each of his department's activities. On the basis of this information each

Director (generally an Under-Secretary) reviews the activities for which he is responsible under the direction of the Secretary of State. Similar systems are now being introduced in a number of other departments.

A further attempt is to break costs down between the different units in the department, to help create local cost centres and develop budgets for local managers. Local budgets are already operating in some places for particular running cost items: this is being widened and extended.

(3) Paying for common services. Previously, a number of services have been provided free to departments by central agencies, for example stationery and printing (HMSO), accommodation (Property Services Agency). Largely as a result of Sir Derek's persuasion, the government now believes that departments should be charged for such services, bearing the costs on their own expenditure accounts, as an incentive to efficiency and economy in their use. This will encourage them to define need with an eye to cost. From April 1980, departments have paid for supplies and services provided by HMSO and the Central Computer and Telecommunications Agency. The government has now decided to make departments pay for services hitherto provided free by the Property Services Agency and the Central Office of Information.

Reading through these proposals, it might strike the readers as being more revealing of Marks & Spencer's approach rather than mirroring the future of the Civil Service. Indeed, the basic principles underlying these measures are the same ones which Marks & Spencer have pursued with outstanding success for decades. Few people have envisaged that they could be applied to the Civil Service, and even today it is not at all clear that they will be embraced by this largest, change-resistant employer in the country without substantial adaptation. Only time can tell whether the lasting reforms are there to stay.

## Concluding Remarks

In the foregoing I have tried to analyse Sir Derek's advisory role to the Prime Minister on improving Civil Service efficiency. My emphases have been on the strategic approach of the exercise, the distinctive ways by which scrutinies and reviews are carried out, and the potential contribution the whole attempt can bring about. I have also tried to underline the fact despite the very encouraging results so far, final success—at least as far as 'lasting reforms' are concerned—is by no means guaranteed. Not only will it be necessary for the reforms to stand the test of time; the nature of the task also calls for sustained political will and impetus from the top. Nor is it apparent today that much, if any, of the reforms will be able to survive a change of political wind—for example, of a new government in power.

More significant still is the balance of internal forces at work. In the same period of time as the reforms were being introduced, the Civil Service was hit by the most serious industrial dispute since the war, resulting in unprecedented loss in labour days and accompanying depression in morale. Coupled with the high unemployment in the country and the continuous pay disputes across the Service, the prospect of an early return to normalcy is not particularly great. Developments such as these may not only impede the progress of reforms already under way, but may even negate some of the achievements thus far attained. In the meantime, whether or not the internal agents and momentum Sir Derek have brought into motion could constitute a self-generating force is still very much an open question. Finally, as the inevitable phasing out of Sir Derek's personal involvement sets in, this may yet be another factor bearing on the final outcome of the whole exercise. (Sir Derek has been Vice-Chairman of Marks & Spencer since April 1982, and may henceforth be devoting more time to the business after 3 years of active service in Whitehall.)

All this, however, can hardly detract from Sir Derek's immense contribution. His exemplary work has shown how much a business excelling in management can make a valuable contribution to the larger society it operates in. Consistent with the company's policy of sending the best men and women to community projects, M&S has made available one of their top-calibre executives to serve a national cause. The Rayner effort will no doubt occupy an important chapter in the contemporary history of the British Civil Service. If a man can give and *be* more, so may a business.

## Notes

1. Peter Kellner, 'How Whitehall is learning the lessons of Marks and Spencer', *Sunday Times*, 24 August 1980.
2. Sir Derek was the notable exception. He became the First Chief Executive of the Defence Procurement Organization which was set up as the result of a White Paper of which Sir Derek was the principal author. He remained in that post 6 months longer than he had originally committed himself to full-time government work. On cessation of his full-time involvement Sir Derek became a member of the Management Board of the Procurement Executive. He was asked to continue in that post when Labour were returned to power in 1974. Under Labour administration he also became a member of the Management Review Team of the Department of Health and Social Security and of the Ministry of Defence as well as Deputy Chairman of the Civil Service Pay Board and a member of the Permanent Security Commission. Sir Derek resigned from the latter two posts only on assuming his present role as advisor to the Prime Minister.
3. 'Rayner reforms face crucial test', *The Times*, 8 September 1981.
4. 'Efficiency in central government: Raynerisms reviewed', RIPA Report, Royal Institute of Public Administration, vol. 3, no. 2, 1982.
5. 'Raynerism: strengthening Civil Service management', RIPA Report, Royal Institute of Public Administration, vol. 2, no. 4, 1981.
6. London: HMSO, 1981, p. 2–3.
7. 18 February 1982.
8. Cf. Whitehall Brief, *The Times*, 8 September 1981.
9. Quoted in Peter Hennessy, 'Whitehall's waste elimination unit asks Civil Servants to gauge the true necessity of their tasks', *The Times*, 30 November 1979.
10. Quoted in Peter Hennessy, *op. cit.*

11. Peter Kellner, 'How Whitehall is learning the lessons of Marks and Spencer', *Sunday Times*, 24 August 1980.
12. The detailed findings of the review are included in the reports to the Ministers and to Sir Derek, and are summarized in Sir Derek's report to the Prime Minister and in the *White Paper on Administrative Forms*, HMSO, 1982. A useful discussion of the results of the review can be found in T. L. Lonsdale, 'Government forms', *Management in Government*, 1982, No. 2, pp. 107–112. Mr Lonsdale is a member of the central team which coordinated the review and reported on the arrangements for controlling forms Service-wide.
13. Lonsdale, *op. cit.*, p. 109.
14. 'The good form of plain words', *The Times*, 18 February 1982.

CONCLUSION

# WHAT CAN WE LEARN
# FROM MARKS & SPENCER?

CHAPTER 14

# For the Developed Countries—
# Second Thoughts on Learning
# from the Japanese

The seventies was a curious page in the world history of management. In that decade the industrial nations in the West ushered in an international wave of learning from the Japanese. This is particularly bewildering in the eyes of someone from the developing world. The latter, with few exceptions, have been so accustomed to regard the West as their 'reference society' that it has struck them as almost unbelievable that the West should bow to the East in an area in which it has long been the acknowledged leader.

## The Unexpected Challenge

It has been a painful process for the West to come to terms with the superiority and relevance of the Japanese management system. At least three major phases are recognizable. In the first phase, from roughly the end of the sixties to the early seventies, when industry in the West began to feel the pinch of the Japanese challenge, the characteristic response at that time was two-fold: a tendency to attribute the strength of Japanese industry to such factors as cheap labour costs, dumping strategy and disproportional government assistance and the like on the one hand and an attempt to explain—or mystify, which may be more precise—the Japanese management approach by referring to sociocultural characteristics unique to the Japanese. Whatever the achievements of Japanese industry, so the argument went, they are of little relevance for the managers in the West.

This, however, soon gave way to another phase in which there was a more objective and realistic assessment of the secrets of success underlying Japanese industry. This was the age of the great admiration. Scores of monographs, hundreds of articles, dozens of documentaries, an untold number of conferences and seminars, streams of study tours, all suddenly found one common subject-matter: the Japanese management approach and its relevance and lessons for the West. The most 'revealing' finding of this era was the belief that many of the basic Japanese management principles were not culturally specific after all and could be understood, appreciated and possibly adapted to practical employment in other cultures as diversified as the American and Scandinavian societies as well. The 'Learn from Japan in Management' movement had begun in earnest and such topics as 'If Japan can, why can't we?' became the international talk of the town.

There was, however, also a strong, uneasy undercurrent in the middle of this great wave of learning from the land of the rising sun. Scepticism, cynicism, and sometimes outright hostility were not unnoticed in many quarters among the 'silent majority' of the industrial work force in Western countries. While 'seeing is believing' has converted many a Western executive and consultant, how many of the middle-level managers and rank-and-file workers have seen Japanese management at work? Japan is, after all, a remote, exotic country. It is simply too much to expect that the 'Learning from Japan' movement could acquire a mass base in the Western nations if only because of the huge cultural gap.

At the same time, not unexpectedly, this undercurrent finds powerful expressions in learned circles. A typical example is B. Bruce-Briggs who has commented eloquently about 'The dangerous folly called Theory Z' in the pages of *Fortune*:

> America should learn from Japanese management, claim a recent spate of books and articles, including even some in *Fortune*. According to this outpouring of facile advice, Japan's economic success is founded on a superior concept of 'human resources' management that is direly needed here. One writer, William Ouchi, has called this approach Theory Z and claims it is already the practice in some highly successful U.S. companies. As the Japanese might say in their understated way, the idea is not quite so good as it seems. In plain American, Theory Z is downright silly. It is also dangerous. . . .
>
> To the Westerner, Japan may seem bizarre, even inhuman. But calling the Japanese 'robots' is unjust. The system was not adopted as policy by Japanese management nor willingly elected by Japanese workers. It has been imposed upon them all. . . . Do you think they like to work hard? Do you think they enjoy singing company songs? Do you think the Kamikaze pilots wanted to splatter their guts on the decks of American ships?
>
> Learned commentaries on Japanese culture emphasize dominant values of *on* (obligation) and *giri* (duty) and so forth—the values promoted from above. From below, however, the most relevant value is *gaman*—patience, endurance, putting up with it. . . .
>
> In short, to imitate the Japanese we would need a labour force disciplined by a social hierarchy controlled by an oligarchy. The danger of Theory Z and allied nostrums is that they may strip us of what little competitive advantage we now have. Americans . . . cannot match the Japanese at corporatism. We can, however, innovate and invent. We can also move faster than the Japanese, unless hobbled by

pseudo-consensus. It is appalling to observe how much time and effort is expended by business cajoling people into doing what obviously must be done. We may have too much Theory Z already, and inflating it may push us down to a position in the Japanese world hierarchy somewhere between the Philippines and Tanzania. . . .

Perhaps we'd better unlearn some bad lessons from false American teachers.[1]

These passages may sound outrageous to many informed observers. But they reflect in large measure the sentiment, if not the logic, of much popular opinion. The 'Learn from Japan' movement is not, and is unlikely to be, taking root in a Western society, as it is at the middle and grass-root levels that the message is not getting across.

## Second Thoughts

The early eighties saw the beginnings of a new phase. The 'Learn from Japan' movement not so much subsided but underwent a subtle transformation. The exhortation of Japanese management began to give way to a sober reassessment of the 'excellently managed companies in the West'. The upshot was that these companies have in fact a lot in common with the typical companies in Japan. To the apparent amazement of many, the very principles underlying much of the management practice of these Western companies are strikingly similar to those previously considered to be unique in the Japanese management culture. A whole array of best-selling volumes like *Theory Z: How American Business Can Meet the Japanese Challenge*,[2] *Corporate Cultures: the Rites and Rituals of Corporate Life*,[3] *In Search of Excellence: Lessons from America's Best-run Companies*,[4] was hammering the point that the best of American management is not inferior to the Japanese after all. The reception was overwhelmingly positive. The message caught on. A new item on the agenda emerges: Learn from the best-run companies in the West.

Thomas J. Peters and Robert H. Waterman Jr's *In Search of Excellence: Lessons from America's Best-run Companies*[4] provides perhaps the most powerful expression of the new wave. (In a significant sense the present volume is also an attempt in this direction.) Summarizing the findings of the book, Thomas J. Peters has written,

> What makes for excellence in the management of a company? Is it the use of sophisticated management techniques such as zero-based budgeting, management by objectives, matrix organisation and sector, group or portfolio management? Is it greater use of computers to control companies that continue to grow even larger in size and more diverse in activities? Is it a battalion of specialized MBA's, well-versed in the techniques of strategic planning?
>
> Probably not. Although most well-run companies use a fair sampling of all these, they do not use them as substitutes for the basics of good management.
>
> Indeed, McKinsey & Company, a management consultant concern, has studied management practices at 37 companies that are often used as examples of well-run organisations and has found that they have eight common attributes.
>
> None of these attributes depends on 'modern' management tools or gimmicks. None of them requires high technology and none of them cost a cent to implement.

224 Marks & Spencer

All that is needed is time, energy and willingness on the part of management to think rather than to make use of management formulas.

The outstanding performers work hard to keep things simple. They rely on simple organisation structures, simple strategies, simple goals and simple communications. The eight attributes that characterize their management are:

A bias towards action;
Simple form and lean staff;
Continued contact with customers;
Productivity improvement via people;
Operational autonomy to encourage entrepreneurship;
Simultaneous loose–tight controls;
Stress on one key business value;
Emphasis on doing what they know best.[5]

It might or might not surprise the readers that almost every statement in this quotation can be applied to Marks & Spencer.

The moral is a simple one. However advanced or progressive the experience from a foreign country may be, its greatest value is not so much to serve as a model for imitation but primarily to provide insights and stimuli to reflect on one's own experience and practice. For the developed countries in particular, there is a wealth of very progressive philosophies and approaches among the better-run companies. The experience from abroad may sharpen one's awareness of the major strengths in one's system as well as its inadequacies, but the reference point should always be local practice and achievements.

In any event, it is the better-run companies which are in a more privileged position to be enriched by management innovations from overseas, and for the average firms it is far more authentic and effective for them to learn from the well-run companies from the same culture and society. For instance, it makes more sense for an American company to draw ideas and lessons from, say, IBM, Procter & Gamble, MacDonald, than from Toyota, Sony, Mitsubishi. The situation is the same in Britain. If someone has described the operating principles of Marks & Spencer without mentioning its name, the guess would be that it is a Japanese company. Indeed, many of these principles may appear 'foreign' to many British firms, or most Western firms for that matter, and they would not hesitate to brand it as unique or Japanese-like. But Marks & Spencer is 100% British, 100% Western, right in the midst of a Western culture. It strips at a stroke all cultural counter-arguments from the 'Learn from Japan' debate. 'If M&S can, why can't we?' may appear a more authentic challenge than 'If Japan can, why can't we?'

### Notes

1. *Fortune*, 17 May 1982.
2. Reading, Massachusetts: Addison-Wesley, 1981.
3. Reading, Massachusetts: Addison-Wesley, 1982.
4. New York: Harper & Row, 1982.
5. 'Putting excellence into management', *McKinsey Quarterly*, Autumn 1980.

# CHAPTER 15

# For the Developing Countries— Capitalizing on the 'Late Development Effect' in Management

A silent revolution is currently under way in most of the developing societies as far as management is concerned. In a sense it is a 'modernizing' process. But the term modernization is now so much used and abused that its precise meaning is difficult to capture. Hitherto, modernization has often meant nothing more than 'Westernization' as implied in Daniel Lerner's definition: 'Modernization is the process of social change whereby less developed societies acquire characteristics common to more developed societies.'[1] But when the West began to talk about learning from the Japanese in management, one is not sure which of them, the East or the West, is the more modern of the two. In any case, from the developing societies' point of view, the West is no longer the only model. But what to choose from, or what combinations of the two models one should draw insights from, remains an intriguing question.

This chapter will not dwell on the modernization debate. What it attempts to do is to borrow a concept formulated by the British economic historian Ronald Dore in his explanation of the impressive success of contemporary Japanese industry and to apply it to an analysis of the management transformation problem confronted by most developing societies today.

## The Concept of 'Late Development Effect'

Ronald Dore, in his book *British Factories, Japanese Factories: The Origins of National Diversity in Industrial Relations*,[2] attempts to explain the relative ease and accelerated tempo of Japanese industrial development in terms of what he called 'late development effect'. Essentially he is arguing that as a 'late

225

developer', the Japanese benefited from the painful experience that the earlier industrial nations have gone through and acquired; they are thus in a position to avoid some obvious pitfalls in their own industrialization effort. Some of the examples furnished by Dore are:

(1) *Trade unions*—In early industrial Britain, free market principles of employment were upheld as they had a natural appeal to employers in a world where no unions existed or where they were prohibited by law. They became less attractive to employers when trade unions won their right to exist and so severely limit the employers' bargaining superiority. But by the time this happened in Britain the existing market principles were so firmly entrenched that change was difficult. Japanese employers, on the other hand, could see more clearly the writing on the wall. They knew that they had to live with unions at an early stage; they were able to adjust to that future prospect by *institutional innovations* before the unions became so strong that their options were foreclosed. Life-time employment and enterprise-based rather than craft-based unions are notable examples of such innovations, both of which defuse to a large extent the working of free market principles of employment.

(2) *Universal schooling and industrial training*—Universal education was a very late development in the history of British industrialization. Japan, by contrast, had 90% of its school population attending standardized and reasonably efficient primary schools at the beginning of this century, at a time when there were still fewer than 80 factories employing more than 500 workers. Preferential employment of young school-leavers was an option open to early Japanese industrialists more clearly than to their English counterparts. At the same time the Japanese employers were more keen to train up their work force than the British employers at a comparable stage. The reason is that late-developing Japan imported the latest nineteenth- and twentieth-century technology into a society where traditional artisan skills resembled those of sixteenth- or seventeenth-century Europe. Japan had to make a technological leap—whereas Britain made a shuffling technological advance. At a time when the British were holding on to an antiquated apprenticeship system, the Japanese were innovating a whole range of company-based industrial training schemes.

(3) *Labour cost structure*—A major factor underlying the Japanese willingness to pay seniority premiums and lavish welfare benefits has to do with the labour cost structure of Japanese industry. The Japanese engineering industry started late, with more advanced capital-intensive technology than the British industry, using expensive imported machines. Labour costs represented a far smaller proportion of total costs for the average Japanese manufacturer than for the average British manufacturer at a comparable stage of development. A 5–10% increase in labour costs would therefore have less serious implications for the health of the business.

(4) *Organizational technology*—The late developer begins with advanced production technology. He is also likely to start with advanced organizational technology. Another important difference was that whereas the owner-managed firm predominated in the British economy until an advanced stage, Japan was dominated by corporate organizations from the very beginning. Relative to the owner-managed firms, corporate organizations provide greater job security, better advancement prospects, and hence are more conducive to longer-term calculations of the costs and benefits of employment policies.

These are some of the features indicated by Ronald Dore as demonstration of the late development effect. Whether or not Dore's analysis constitutes a satisfactory explanation of Japan's industrial evolution is not our concern here, but it seems that the concept of late development effect can be applied to the question of management transformation in the developing societies as well.

## Late Development Effect in Management

In a sense the developing societies are a late developer in management. The following features are also apparent in most developing societies:

(1) *Management cost structure*—Unlike the advanced industrial nations at an earlier stage of industrialization, the management component in the cost structure of industrial enterprises in today's developing societies is significantly larger. In nineteenth-century Britain, or pre-war Japan, management costs took up but a fraction of an enterprise's total payroll. In an average manufacturer in today's developing societies the managerial payroll may take up a significant part of total labour cost.

(2) *International competition*—Unlike most early industrial nations the commercial organizations of developing societies face more pervasive international competition. This constitutes a more formidable challenge in management. The indigenous organizations in most cases have to compete with foreign business with more superior form of management.

(3) *More educated managers*—In a way analogous to the Japanese universal education at an early stage of industrial development, the managerial staff in developing societies tend to be more highly educated than their counterparts in other industrial nations at a comparable stage of development. Moreover, many of them are Western-educated or at least have received a Western-type education.

(4) *Availability of advanced management experience*—Just as the Japanese were able to borrow from the West advanced production technology and organizational technology, the developing nations of today are also in a privileged position to study and learn from the advanced management experience both in the West and in Japan.

(5) *National effort pays off*—The Japanese experience, among others, has demonstrated that in order to capitalize on the late development effect, national effort usually pays off. That is to say, where circumstances permit, a concerted effort on a nation-wide scale with the backing of government or semi-government bodies is often more effective than the exertion of individual organizations.

All these suggest that there may be a potential late development effect in management for the developing nations. The question remains whether it can be capitalized upon. From my limited experience in the southeast Asian region, it seems that the developing world cannot afford *not* to capitalize on this late development effect. The crucial issue is *how*.

## The Key Steps

At the risk of over-simplification, it is possible to envisage the following steps:

*Step 1    Systematically reflect on the most progressive management practices in one's country/area.*

Consistent with our discussion in the previous chapter the starting point should be the most advanced experience in the local scene. Special attention should be given to those cultural and socio-historical factors bearing on the evolution of such management systems.

*Step 2    Study the most progressive management practices both in the West and the East.*

This is primarily for the purpose of obtaining insights into the principles underlying excellently managed companies. It may become apparent that many of these principles are similar across cultures, or at least can be adapted to different sociocultural conditions.

*Step 3    Attempt institutional innovations based on the preceding.*

To capitalize on the late development effect in management, the developing societies must endeavour to *supersede* the early starters by innovating institutional forms *in anticipation of* changes in the global competitive environment. It is not enough to learn from the advanced models; the name of the game is to supersede the teacher. Japanese industry, for example, has not borrowed anything from the West intact; it adapts and modifies it in a superior form.

The challenge is conspicuous to all. This book represents a modest attempt to fill part of the gaps in Step 2. To what extent any of the developing societies today is able to capitalize on the late development effect in management is yet to be seen.

## Special Relevance for Hong Kong

It is believed that most businesses in Hong Kong—not only retailers—can learn a lot from Marks & Spencer. But in particular, the author feels that there is much relevance for the economic relationship between Hong Kong and China, especially in the long run.

In a sense, Hong Kong as a whole is a retailer or wholesaler of Chinese-made merchandise. Hong Kong importers buy very substantially from China, notably in light manufacturing products. The bulk of these are sold in Hong Kong while the rest are re-exported overseas. The importers are in a privileged position to know, study and assess the needs and tastes of the consumers here and abroad. If they are ready to take a similar approach to Marks & Spencer in acting as an interpreter of the customers' requirements to the manufacturers inside China, they could be providing a valuable service to the latter and would most likely be able to gear the suppliers' facilities and resources more directly to the needs of the outside market.

The importers or the buyers here have of course been doing this to a certain degree. But on the whole, they have not played a sufficiently active part. To be really effective, it must be done with great resolve and in a thorough and aggressive manner—as Marks & Spencer's experience has demonstrated. It appears that most importers here have not considered this important function to be part of their business and have not been investing sufficient resources for the purpose.

Taking this a step further, if these importers adopt a technological approach to procurement similar to that of Marks & Spencer, it would mean that they would have to invest substantially in technical support services. For example, they would have to employ a certain number of technical personnel who are knowledgeable about the technology and production process required for the production of the merchandise concerned. These personnel would be visiting—on a regular basis—the manufacturing facilities inside China, advising on technical and production matters. Ideally, they should be a technical consultant-plus, possessing the technical and consulting skills necessary for enabling the suppliers to upgrade continuously product quality, reduce production costs and improve on production techniques.

All these are, of course, long term endeavours and it calls for exceptional foresight and conviction on the part of the importers to attempt anything like this. But in the author's view, this is both feasible and desirable. We can say that this is feasible on at least two grounds. First, there are already some buyers of Chinese merchandise who are doing precisely this. But unfortunately, it is mostly done in a very unsystematic fashion, and very often, it is conceived as a favour for the Chinese manufacturers rather than a business strategy. Second, the Marks & Spencer experience demonstrates that such a collaborative relationship, albeit difficult to establish and sustain, can work to the great advantage of both parties. Without their experience, the above proposal may be seen as too idealistic or sheer wishful thinking. But with a careful study of Marks & Spencer practice, we can at least be confidently optimistic.

Such a relationship between the Chinese suppliers and outside buyers is desirable for a number of obvious reasons. In the first place, as China is attempting to modernise its industry, a close technical relationship with the customer could enable it to familiarise itself more directly with production techniques and management knowhow from outside. Hopefully, this may contribute to accelerating the process of modernisation.

Secondly, such an approach could enable the economic relationship between Hong Kong and China to become more organic, that is to say, transforming the existing 'trading' relationship between the two parties into a 'partnership' based on intimate technical collaboration in matters ranging from raw materials selection right through the entire production process. Similar to Marks & Spencer, the local importers should cease to be passive recipients of whatever products being manufactured inside China but could act as a catalyst for change.

Marks & Spencer's ultimate secret of success lies in its revolutionary role of linking together mass manufacturing and mass retailing. In the long run, Hong Kong's greatest worth to China may also be its pivotal position in effectively linking the vast manufacturing hinterland in China with the outside world.

There is little doubt that the economic relationship between Hong Kong and China will undergo a momentous transformation in the years to some. Whether or not it will take a shape similar to what has been argued above is too early to tell. A critical study of Marks & Spencer's experience could perhaps provide us with some insights in our effort to search for new directions in transforming Hong Kong's role in this part of the world.

## Notes

1. 'Modernization', *International Encylopaedia of Social Sciences* (New York: Macmillan, 1968), p. 386.
2. Berkeley and Los Angeles: University of California Press, 1973.

# Further Reading

There is probably more in-depth commentary on Marks & Spencer's management than on that of any other British companies. At the same time, senior executives of Marks & Spencer are also more ready to talk about the company's philosophy and practice than their counterparts in other firms. The following is a selected list of printed sources.

(1) There are two full-length books on Marks & Spencer:

Goronwy Rees, *St. Michael: A History of Marks & Spencer* (London: Weidenfeld & Nicolson, 1969). A revised paperback edition was published by Pan Books, London, in 1973.

Israel Sieff, *Memoirs* (London: Weidenfeld & Nicolson, 1970). An insightful autobiography by the ex-chairman of the company.

(2) In-depth studies in scholarly and trade journals:

Peter Drucker, 'The power and purpose of objectives: the Marks & Spencer story and its lessons', Chapter 8 of his *Management: Tasks, Responsibilities, Practices* (London: Heinemann, 1974).

J. H. Davidson, 'Offensive marketing in action: the Marks & Spencer story', in his *Offensive Marketing—How to Make Your Competitors Followers* (Penguin, 1979).

M. E. Dimock, 'Marks & Spencer', Chapter 11 of his *Administrative Vitality* (London: Routledge & Kegan Paul, 1960).

Christine Harris, 'Marks & Spencer Ltd.', a Harvard Business School case study, 1975.

P. A. Raveh, *Managerial Behaviour in Retailing* (a study of Marks & Spencer), unpublished Ph.D. thesis, 1977, London Business School.

Sandra Salmans, 'Mixed fortunes at Marks & Spencer', *Management Today*, November 1980.

Robert Heller, 'The inimitable magic of Marks', *Management Today*, September 1966.

'Marks & Spencer: be it ever so humble, there's no place like home', special survey, *Clothes* magazine (Australia), January 1978.

Michael Chamberlain, 'Marcus Sieff: reflections on higher values in retailing', *Marketing Week*, March 1982.

Sheila Black, 'Marks & Spencer's private welfare state', *The Director*, February 1973.

Gwen Nuttall and Lucy Halford, 'How Marks & Spencer brings its shoppers the best', *Design*, December 1979.

Eileen Mackenzie, 'Marksist approach to staff relations', *International Management*, June 1972.

Jules R. Arbose, 'A fresh approach to food distribution', *International Management*, July 1981.

Anthony Moreton, 'Marks & Spencer suppliers: how close links pay off', *The Financial Times*, 28 May 1982.

William Kay, 'How they sold their soul to St. Michael', *The Sunday Times*, 19 June 1983.

National Economic Development Office, *Changing Needs and Relationships in the U.K. Apparel Fabric Market* (London: NEDO, 1982).

Ministry of Public Building and Works, *The Building Process: A Case Study from Marks & Spencer Limited* (London: HMSO, 1970).

(3) For readers interested in Lord Rayner's role in streamlining the British Civil Service, the following are recommended:

House of Commons Treasury and Civil Service Committee, Session 1981–82, *Report on the Efficiency and Effectiveness in the Civil Service*, 3 volumes, HMSO, 1982.

David Howells, 'Marks & Spencer and the Civil Service: a comparison of culture and methods', *Public Administration*, Autumn 1981.

David Allen, 'Raynerism: strengthening Civil Service management', *RIPA Report*, Royal Institute of Public Administration, Winter 1981.

Andrew Likierman, 'Efficiency in central government: Raynerism revisited', *RIPA Report*, Royal Institute of Public Administration, Summer 1982.

Philip Nash, 'We tried before, but without the clout', *Management Service in Government*, August 1981.

Peter Kellner, 'How Whitehall is learning the lessons of Marks & Spencer', *The Sunday Times*, 24 August 1980.

Richard Norton-Taylor, 'St. Michael in Whitehall', *Guardian*, 18 September 1982.

(4) The following represents a partial list of public addresses by senior Marks & Spencer executives on various aspects of the company. (Copies of them may be obtained from the Publicity Group, Marks & Spencer p.l.c., Baker Street, London.)

Lord Sieff, 'Management's need to communicate', speech delivered at the Conference of the European Federation of Industrial Editors' Association and the British Association of Industrial Editors, Scarborough, April 1982.

Lord Sieff, 'It's people who matter', *The Sunday Times*, 13 December 1981.

Lord Sieff, 'Social responsibility and wealth creation', speech delivered at the Headmasters' Conference, Edinburgh, September 1980.

Lord Sieff, 'How Marks & Spencer co-operates with its suppliers: a joint effort for a common purpose', speech delivered to the Australian Retailers' Association, 25 September 1978.

Lord Sieff, 'Co-operation or confrontation', The Royal Institute Discourse, October 1975.

Sir Derek Rayner, 'The war on paper bureaucracy', Occasional Paper, Institute of Administrative Management, No. 4, 1975.

Sir Derek Rayner, 'A battle won in the war on paper bureaucracy', *Harvard Business Review*, January 1975.

W. B. Howard, 'Marks & Spencer's involvement in Europe', speech delivered to the Parliamentary Westminster in Europe Group, March 1981.

Jan de Somogyi, 'A simple approach: Marks & Spencer's human philosophy', speech delivered at the Retail Research Society, City University of New York, February 1982.

Jan de Somogyi, 'St. Michael—a marketing philosophy', *British Journal of Marketing*, Autumn 1967.

John Salisse, 'Bonds stronger than contracts', *Chelwood Review*, January 1981.

David Susman, 'Ethos of excellence: Marks & Spencer's most durable export', 1981.

Lewis R. Goodman, 'Better human relations for better quality', *EOQC Quality*, European Organization for Quality Control, part 3, 1978.

# Index